MW00789669

HOW TO GET
ALONG WITH
ANYONE

The Playbook for Predicting
and Preventing Conflict
at Work and at Home

JOHN ELIOT AND JIM GUINN

Simon & Schuster

New York   Amsterdam/Antwerp   London
Toronto   Sydney   New Delhi

Simon & Schuster
1230 Avenue of the Americas
New York, NY 10020

Copyright © 2025 by John Eliot and James Guinn

First Simon & Schuster hardcover edition February 2025

SIMON & SCHUSTER and colophon are registered trademarks of Simon & Schuster, LLC

For information about special discounts for bulk purchases, please contact Simon & Schuster Special Sales at 1-866-506-1949 or business@simonandschuster.com.

The Simon & Schuster Speakers Bureau can bring authors to your live event. For more information or to book an event, contact the Simon & Schuster Speakers Bureau at 1-866-248-3049 or visit our website at www.simonspeakers.com.

Interior design by Carly Loman

Manufactured in the United States of America

10   9   8   7   6   5   4   3   2   1

Library of Congress Cataloging-in-Publication Data has been applied for.

ISBN 978-1-6680-3307-4
ISBN 978-1-6680-3309-8 (ebook)

For Mom and Dad, the most precious souls ever.

—Doc E

For John Duncum, the man who taught me everything I know about conflict resolution, and even more about how to be a leader, a father, and a husband.

—Doc G

Contents

Introduction

You know those days: Flight delay after flight delay transforms a trip into an exhaustive test of patience. The airline reps assure everyone that boarding will commence in ten minutes despite no aircraft at the gate. Ten minutes morph into thirty. Sixty. The gate TV monitor reads *On Time*. Why do carriers refuse to post accurate status reports? That alone makes your ears steam, compounding the fret you have over not getting a good night's rest before the potentially career-changing interview you have in the morning. You manage to subdue the frustration—then customer service announces that your original 5:05 p.m. departure has been pushed back once again, with a new departure time of 10:59 p.m. You glance at your watch. Seven o'clock. What do you do?

Or envision an office scenario: Your company's CEO has hired and assigned their nephew—an inexperienced, recent college grad—to your team. You're tasked with a new product launch, the success of which is critical for your company to rebound from recent declines. With quarterly numbers due in short order, your direct reports need to be on their A game. Except that Mr. Neo Nephew regularly arrives late, doesn't complete paperwork, is constantly on his phone, and rolls his eyes when you give him instructions. Confounding the situation, your other team members are kissing up to him to garner favor with the CEO. What do you do?

There's no shortage of potentially exasperating interpersonal clashes thrust upon us. Some, admittedly, may be ripple effects of our own doing. Or we may be innocent bystanders roped into a mess. No matter the origin, these conflicts can elicit confusion, ire, and, often, a sense that we lack control over certain areas of our life.

An old college acquaintance hounds you to make more time to get together, right when you're slammed both at work and at home.

Commuting to work for a critical all-hands-on-deck meeting, you stop to pick up coffee and breakfast treats for everyone. What was an impromptu act of kindness becomes a stressful hustle as the line takes forever. Just when you think you're going to get to the counter with seconds left to spare, another customer cuts in front of you.

You're asked to sign a petition at work, and even though you can see how a divide between you and your colleagues will cause you difficulty down the road, you don't believe in the cause.

Your teenager has started running with a bad crowd and huffs out of the room the second you bring it up.

Your spouse disapproves of one of your favorite, but expensive, hobbies, and the two of you have gotten sideways on discretionary spending.

What do you do?

What if there were an efficient way to reliably turn the tables in your favor? From professional to personal, inconsequential to monumental, the conflicts you bump into can be vastly diverse, just like the individuals involved. No singular methodology will solve every problem. A strategy that succeeds in one case could backfire in another.

Ah, but there is a pattern. And patterns can be reprogrammed.

Human beings are capable of incredibly complex calculation and dynamic creation—if and when our environment allows. The evolved part of the brain, our cerebral cortex, houses the mechanics for reason, analysis, logic, thoughtfulness, and talents such as patience, listening, foresight, and altruism. We tap into our cortex on routine days, when life is proceeding as normal and we have time and energy. When we're stressed, it's a different story. Feeling overtaxed, overworked, frightened, cornered—these conditions push us substantially outside our comfort zone and can induce an involuntary suspension of cortical functions. In the face of pressure, the brain is designed to flip off information processing "luxuries," like memory and problem-solving, in favor of using subcortical structures (such as the thalamus, which regulates alertness, and the basal ganglia, which controls conditioned habits) that operate faster and with less consumption of resources. This protective mechanism and quick-response neural shift has served the survival of our species well.

For an oversimplified analogy, what do you do when you inadvertently rest your hand on a scalding surface? Do you weigh your options, assess the merits of rotating your shoulder left versus right, take a minute to ballpark your skin temperature? Of course not! You yank back your digits before a conscious thought can be formed. Humans react to conflict in a not-so-dissimilar way. When we're faced with external pressure, our deep-rooted habits, desires, and behaviors launch into action.

The good news: through three decades of building and facilitating team chemistry for Fortune 500 companies, professional sports franchises, schools, government agencies, medical centers, nonprofit organizations, and families (including marriage counseling and mediation), we've discovered that people all respond to conflict in one of five core, hand-on-the-stove ways. We've witnessed some truly wild $#!% and jaw-dropping relationship cacophony (some of which we'll share in the pages to come), but we've realized that no matter how unexpected or appalling the conflict, each person's approach to it can be distilled into one of five styles.

When riled by one another, humans will instinctively (1) avoid, (2) compete, (3) analyze, (4) collaborate, or (5) accommodate. Because these are ingrained by-products of the subcortex in action, they are predictable. If you can predict how someone might behave in a circumstance, you can formulate a game plan. All you need to know is which of the five patterns someone is wired to use when smacked in the nose by a stressor.

Enter *How to Get Along with Anyone*.

Intensive study of human performance and organizational psychology combined with careers full of trial and error have taught us that the escalation of disagreements is rarely a result of content. Blowups *appear* to be substance driven, and oft dressed up as such, but they're actually people driven. No, we don't mean bad-actor caused, though that certainly does happen. We mean that when people don't fully attend to one another, they miss cues, considerations, and opportunities to keep differences from mushrooming—or better still, to benefit from those same differences. The first step toward preventing and resolving conflict is to focus on figuring out the people participating in it, not the underlying "problem."

Section I of this book will arm you with tools to better understand your own style and the styles of the people around you. Central to this process, we'll supply you with a formula for identifying your coworkers' and loved ones' Conflict Personality Styles—whether they are Avoiders, Competitors, Analyzers, Collaborators, or Accommodators (or whether they are multi-styled, as is someone who's an Accommodator around their boss but an Avoider in family situations). You'll then learn how to use this knowledge to foster great communication and great relationships, designing a bulletproof conflict vest for yourself.

In Section II we'll point a microscope at the five Conflict Personality Styles, uncovering the inner workings of each. Once you have a leg up on knowing how a friend or foe responds when their buttons are pushed—to avoid, compete, analyze, collaborate, or accommodate—what's your next move? What should you do next to guide an otherwise sour interaction down a productive path? Leaning on real-world work and family illustrations, the second half of this book will walk you through the blueprints for thriving in your interactions with each Conflict Personality Style.

One word of warning: as in every Marvel Studios blockbuster, there are villains lurking. There are people out there seeking to bring others down by tapping into conflict sensitivities and weaknesses, intentionally pushing hot buttons, fearmongering, and worse. Today, an increasing percentage of the population struggles to have civil discussion over points of disagreement. There are those who fan these flames for their own personal gains. There are bad actors—"hackers" wishing to leverage human psychology to do harm.

We put hackers in quotation marks purposefully. Modern emergence of the term in the 1960s was meant to describe, according to the history of computing's *Jargon File*, "the intellectual challenge of creatively overcoming and circumventing limitations of systems to extend their capabilities." Advocates of true hacker culture frown on their terminology being misused to label nefarious or illegal activity. Hacking in its pure form is about meaningful, value-add expositions of aptitude. Respected hacks expand a body of knowledge, reveal openings for design improvement, and elucidate how to overcome obstacles. Life hacks are for the purpose of increasing productivity and happiness. What's more, revered hackers are passionately community minded. They favor working collectively—very anti-conflict.

In our polarized world, interpersonal interaction and empathy have taken nosedives to all-time lows. More than ever, we need to channel the original spirit of hacking: bringing out the very best of human psychology to heal divides, restore teamwork, and build a better future together. We need conflict heroes. We need *you*. Which is why we've written this book: to put in your paws the ingredients for immunity to conflict kryptonite. In addition to aiding you in becoming more impervious to ne'er-do-wells seeking to exploit your conflict blind spots, we aim to make conflict resolution *fun*. Rhetorically speaking, who adores relationship strife? The unpleasant and exhausting nature of interpersonal dissonance is why so many people try to steer clear of it or brush it under the rug. Visceral feelings about conflict are why we can struggle to see the forest for the trees. The trees are the hullabaloo swirling in and around a disagreement. There is a clear, productive path through the forest, if you realize the trees are useful navigational beacons rather than Halloween-inspired encroachments on your well-being.

We're here to give you the tools to see a conflict for what it is. We'll show you how to use it as a vehicle to shepherd organizational, family, and team unity. Junctures at which people are not exhibiting the best versions of themselves are turning points—portals for superheroes to save the day and flip the switch from interpersonal tensions to low-stress environments, and even opportunities to find humor in them, too. While our fingers are crossed that you'll prevent a horde of altercations altogether, we want you to have fun playing the superhero as well. We've therefore polished the tips of *How to Get Along with Anyone* to be as enjoyable as they are empowering.

Lastly, we'd be remiss if we didn't mention that we're also excited about the economic and positive impact you can make. Digest, if you don't mind, a few statistics regarding the volume of time and money sunk into inter-collegial conflict in professional settings:

156 The number of hours a salaried employee in the United States annually spends, on average, engaged in moderate to intense workplace conflict that is reported to adversely impact job performance. That adds up to essentially one month of work per year per person.

385 The *millions* of employee days, nationally, lost each year to conflict and conflict mediation. For frame of reference, if this figure were to be solely concentrated at Amazon (which today employs 1 out of every 153 American workers), the result would be a 100 percent shutdown of the company 350 days per year.

26% The proportion of supervisors' and managers' average time spent on addressing and resolving conflicts that disrupt workflow— essentially more than one full workday each week.

$395 The estimated *billions* of dollars in annual cost of conflict for corporate America.

To boot, these data points don't incorporate the residual fallout from conflict—for example, cooling off, coworker venting, stress reduction efforts, or taking sick days. Nor do the above numbers factor in the costs of litigation from grievance filings, insurance premium increases, sabotage to projects and equipment, brand reputation hits, and employment roster instability.

If left unresolved, workplace conflict leads to shifts in employee attitudes, behaviors, and interactions that spawn ripple effects to the culture and decreased motivation. As productivity declines, so does job satisfaction. Commitment wanes and morale suffers. Absenteeism increases, eventually resulting in higher turnover, increased hiring and training expenditures, and more frequent, disruptive restructuring.

To say that conflict takes a bite out of the bottom line is possibly the understatement of the year. Yet, alarmingly, *fewer than 40 percent* of full-time employees in the United States have received any form of conflict resolution training. We are struck by this gap every time we conduct a seminar and hear audience reflections, such as "Holy cow, why isn't this a required course in school?" and "Gosh, if I'd known about Conflict Personality Styles all these years, I wouldn't have been so obsessive about ducking issues with my colleagues!"

Whether you're consuming *How to Get Along with Anyone* to climb the ladder, break through a glass ceiling, succeed as a leader, or simply get along better with your office compadres; whether you seek to unwrap a riddle or two about quirky associates or friends, or make cocktail parties more interesting, or generally reduce friction in your daily interactions; whether you'd like to improve your win rate in disagreements with your partner or moody sixteen-year-old, or further cement bonds with those you love, or just be a grand master of human behavior—we hope that you find this book equal parts useful *and* entertaining. We hope, after reading, "difficult" people no longer seem so difficult.

So, without further ado, buckle up your rocket suit for a relationship-enhancing exploration of the bold frontier of conflict psychology!

Section I

Identify the Trigger

Think about a friend or relative of yours suffering from a malady or medical condition.

Though we might wish that the list of debilitating conditions was much shorter, or that our loved ones could be immune from illness, sickness is a fact of life. Crohn's disease, epilepsy, diabetes, depression, back pain, anxiety, chronic migraines, and on and on . . . mental and physical anguish is no joking matter, life-threatening or not. It breaks our hearts to see a loved one in pain.

Now, imagine, for a second, your loved one being ridiculed for their ailment. It's bad enough to encounter ignorance . . . the boss of a loved one with colitis not allowing bathroom breaks during a meeting, your family member with depression being "advised" to snap out of it, a perfectly healthy stranger pulling their car into a handicapped parking space. It's a whole other level of frustration to witness someone intentionally poking fun at your loved one for a struggle of theirs that is no fault of their own. Frustration is much too mild of a descriptor.

Cue Will Smith.

By now you've probably heard about "The Slap." In 2022, Will Smith won his very first Oscar—best actor in a leading role for *King Richard*— *thirty-seven* years into a legendary career. To say it was an emotional night for him would be an equally legendary understatement. Full of nerves, anticipation, hope, joy, pride, and more, Will sat front row while Chris Rock, albeit innocently enough, sought a few laughs at the expense of Will's wife, Jada, who suffers from alopecia areata. Smith's cauldron of emotion boiled over. He marched up on stage and gave Chris the business.

In the language of *our* business: Will got Triggered.

Emotions can get the best of us, the most reserved of us. We can suddenly flip from rational, thoughtful, mild-mannered Bruce Banner into some crazed compilation of Lou Ferrigno and Edward Norton. This is in no way because we're bad people, or even unskilled at emotional regulation. It's because a button gets pushed. Something to which we have a pronounced sensitivity gets called out excessively, or uncomfortably or inappropriately. At such a juncture, we are vulnerable to doing or saying things that we otherwise wouldn't condone. We are vulnerable to being Triggered. Just like Will.

"Whatever is emotional is opposed to that true cold reason which I place above all things."

—Sir Arthur Conan Doyle (as Sherlock Holmes)

Interestingly, not all stressors are created equal. A conversation that Triggers you might not Trigger your spouse. A situation that doesn't bother you in the least bit (one you might not even notice) could regularly upset your neighbor. We each have particular peccadillos. Awareness of others' hyperacuities is paramount to great relationships, teamwork, and fostering positively collegial environments. But how in the world are we to know everyone's particulars in the vast sea of pet peeves?

It turns out that disagreements, friction, strife, discord, arguments, clashes, and the like—interpersonal instances when someone loses or feels a lack of control, when they can't pull the puppet strings the way they want—can be grouped into three core categories, called Conflict Types. The good news: successfully navigating interpersonal tension— more productively stated, maintaining harmony—doesn't require the depth of friendship or trust that would be needed to understand all the nuances of someone's disposition. Complete strangers can overcome obstacles to collaborating. Having history is helpful, but, elegantly, half the battle of preventing dustups is being cognizant of which distinct *type* of conflict is most apt to Trigger you and which type is most apt to Trigger the people in your personal and professional circles.

The three Conflict Types are as follows:

- **Task Conflict.** Task Conflict centers on getting things *done*—done by their deadlines and in their required quantities . . . no matter how. You might hear, "The ends justify the means." Task Conflict flares up when due dates or target goals are unmet.

- **Process Conflict.** Process Conflict centers on the *way* things get done. Someone experiencing Process Conflict is not concerned with specific end goals or their delivery dates; they care, instead, about the methods, systems, or policies being employed. A "my way or the highway" attitude may come into play.

- **Relational Conflict.** Relational Conflict centers on the people involved in a disagreement and their individual habits, quirks, preferences, and tastes. In Relational Conflict, the parties will fight over anything . . . simply because they just don't like one another. When there seems to be no functional, objective rhyme or reason for a dispute, you probably have Relational Conflict on your hands.

A word of warning: we tend to have a blind spot for our own Triggers. That's part and parcel of how we get Triggered in the first place. When approaching pressure-packed interactions, people frequently make the mistake of not self-assessing, not taking a thirty-second time-out to ask themselves whether they are, or might become, Triggered by the circumstances. Before entering the ring, ask yourself: Is the subject of the presenting pressure a task, a process, or a relationship?

Admittedly, for this pregnant pause to be effective, you must know which of the three Conflict Types is your hamartia—your gateway to potential irrationality. To aid you, let's play a little game. We'll present you with three scenarios. Take your time and, as vividly as you can, envision being in the middle of each one. What does it feel like? What emotions might be bubbling below the surface?

In striving to visualize (really, *feelize*) each scenario, try to pinpoint which would most make you want to slam your head into the nearest wall. Read through each script, dwelling after each to mentally put yourself into the moment. Then, after enacting them all in your mind, pick the one that would generate, for you personally, the greatest amount of frustration, anger, annoyance, anxiety, or exhaustion.

Ready? *Go!*

SCENARIO 1

A decade ago, you took a giant leap of faith, quit your job, took out a small business loan (which, honestly, you couldn't afford), and launched your own business. It was scary but exciting. With failure not an option, you poured in your proverbial blood, sweat, and tears—every available waking hour. Over the ten years that have ensued, you've taken only one vacation, but your commitment to this longshot is beginning to pay off. Your start-up just hit midsize business status, last month reaching the one-hundred-employee mark.

To celebrate, you decided to take a ten-day beach-lounging excursion to Hawaii with your significant other, to whom you *promised* that you wouldn't check e-mail for the entire duration. For the recent company expansion, you brought on a hot-shot prodigy in your profession named Jasmine from Texas A&M University (whoop) to oversee the operations of the business. While you think highly of Jazz, it took everything you had to relinquish day-to-day control. Before departing, you hand Jazz a priority list with seventeen items you deem essential for her to complete before you return.

She of course agrees and says she's "on it," but not exactly in a confidence-exuding tone. You board your flight on Monday, switching on your e-mail's vacation settings, and prepare to kick back. Tuesday is wonderfully restful. Wednesday features a nice waterfall hike and drinks seaside in the evening. An unplanned Thursday starts out in a beach hammock, flipping pages of a spy novel you bought at the airport . . . but your mind begins to wander. You find yourself wondering, *How is Jazz doing with the tasks I assigned her? Is she running into any hiccups? Might she need my advice on anything?*

You sneak a peek at your phone while your significant other is nodding off. Logging into e-mail you see a screen-scrolling litany of unread messages. Clicking over to your company's customer relationship management platform, you find that *no* progress has been reported on any of the seventeen priorities you tasked to Jasmine. Two of them have yellow blinking caution symbols, which indicate that a customer has reported an error or complaint.

SCENARIO 2

Jump back to the beginning of scenario 1 but tweak the narrative. You're still the sole owner of a start-up into which you've devoted ten years of copious time and personal resources, all at the expense of your family, arduously growing the business to one hundred employees and, at long last, profitability. You've accomplished this by singlehandedly developing a systematic process that just won a J. D. Power award in your industry sector for systems efficiency.

You are *so* proud of the accomplishment. It has provided for your recent, confident workforce expansion (of course, taking out a substantially larger line of credit to fund). You relied on the process to guide job descriptions, interviews, and hires. The process has even permitted you to finally step back from day-to-day managerial activities and take the trip to the Aloha State that you and your significant other have always dreamed about.

Of course, this wasn't without hiccups. You tried hiring a COO— Steve, who turned out to be a jerk. In addition to ruining numerous previous vacation plans of yours, Steve had to be fired amid much hullabaloo for his complete lack of delivery in performance. That debacle set you back at least two years. So, before nailing down your plans for Hawaii, you made sure to methodically work through the decision to hire Margaret, a Stanford MBA grad with an incredible résumé, impeccable references, and a task-master reputation. With a feeling of relief that Margaret is a 180-degree pivot from Steve, you welcome her to the company, turn over the keys, and smile when she very soothingly and assuredly tells you, "There's nothing to worry about; I'm on top of it."

You sense you are in such a good place that you don't even take your phone on vacation with you. Ten days of bliss and a nice, deep tan ensue. When your plane touches down upon returning, you call Margaret to thank her for accommodating your unplugging and to let her know you look forward to seeing her tomorrow morning.

Margaret doesn't answer. You get her secretary, who can hardly talk straight: "It's a *disaster* here! Margaret scrapped the process you built! We've been frantically trying to reach you, but you forgot to leave a copy of your itinerary and we didn't know which resort you booked. We started cold-calling all the hotels on Oahu, Maui, Kauai. The seventeen-point priority list . . . it's like 170 items long now. I think we're going to go bankrupt!"

The line cuts out as your plane stops taxiing. What the #$@&?! The only words of advice you left with Margaret when you departed were *follow the process*!

SCENARIO 3

Erase the previous two simulations from your mind. Now, conjure up a pressure-packed Fortune 500 environment. You're a midlevel manager at a behemoth, publicly traded company that practices Jack Welch–style "rank and yank" employment policies. You are overworked. Exhausted. You want more than anything to finish out this quarter and escape to a leisurely two-week New Year's holiday with your family.

It's December 1. Your production numbers are wavering around the lower threshold that your boss typically uses to trim staff and cut budgetary inefficiencies each January. But at no fault of your own, you feel, given recent market declines in your industry. When you get into the office on Monday, you are greeted by a red exclamation-point-tagged e-mail from your boss titled "URGENT." The body of the message merely says, "See attachment." You click it. Up pops a litany of seventeen things that must be finished before the company shuts down at noon on Christmas Eve.

Ugh. How many hours are there between now and then if you work fifteen-hour days and don't take off any weekends? Is it even possible? You crack open the lid of your triple espresso caramel macchiato, close the blinds, lock your door, and prepare to grind.

A mere ten minutes into your first report, you hear *knock, knock, knock*. You ignore it. *Knock, knock, knock. Knock, knock, knock.* Reluctantly, you open the door. Your colleague, Bob, who might also be on the chopping block come January, barges in, plops down on your couch, and proceeds to elaborate (in no short words) on every detail of office drama, his family drama, his girlfriend drama, and especially every imagined slight from your coworker Clare, who, by the way, you are counting on to close one of your biggest yet most failure-teetering projects.

By the time Bob leaves your office, you're almost *happy* to dive into your boss's task list—cake compared to listening to Bob!

SCENARIO 3B

Just for fun, let's give scenario 3 an alternate-ending twist. The backstory is the same. But instead of it being Q4 with a month-long grind ahead of you, it's the last week of June. Your Mr. Spacely–esque boss has been breathing fire up and down the halls of your office building, threatening to rescind bonuses, cull the weak from the herd, and do a massive reorg if your team doesn't hit its quarterly numbers. You'd lose outstanding staff, people who'd become dear friends, whose families you care deeply about supporting. Production has been teetering, looking like it might fall into the red.

When you click on the URGENT e-mail, you roll your eyes at seeing yet another mismanagement effort. You get those kinds of messages from your boss on a regular basis. "Your precious 'rank and yank' is going to get *you* one of these days" you mutter under your breath. You know that a laundry list of to-dos would only derail your people, inciting nervousness, shifting concentration away from what's really important. DELETE.

You call an impromptu team meeting, give your best "win one for the Gipper" speech, pat everyone on the back, and get down to business. While you make sure your people get home for their family dinners every night, you stay late. You hit it as hard as you've ever worked. Your team is inspired. They step up, you find a new reserve of energy (and buy stock in Rauch Fruchtsäfte GmbH & Co. OG—Red Bull's manufacturer), and, together, *crush* it.

It's now Friday, June 30. What a helluva week! At noon, you stroll into your boss's suite and plop a printout of your Q2 final report on his desk. Thirty percent above target revenue. Ten percent under budget. "Thank you for the motivational push," you say. The figures are so sexy, you doubt he hears your sarcasm. You don't care; it feels great to stick it to him. Grinning ear to ear, you walk out. One by one, you hug each of your employees as you tell them to get out of there and take the whole week of July 4 off.

What a sense of satisfaction. You jump in your car and hit the road. It's as hot as . . . well, it's *hot*, and you run into early weekend traffic. You don't mind. Cold margaritas and a weekend of just-you indulgence awaits. You've got the windows down and your XM radio cranked up. Your favorite song is playing. Nothing could spoil your mood. Until . . .

Your cell phone buzzes. You answer without looking at the caller ID (you're a conscientious, hands-free driver, of course). It's the one family member you hate getting cornered by—the ultimate *drama* queen (or king). Extended family politics being as complicated as they are, you can't easily excuse yourself and hang up. Your relative launches into a tirade about a family disagreement that's been brewing. The family member calling you has been making it worse than it should be. *Way* worse, it turns out. An intervention has been scheduled for tomorrow. You feel your blood begin to boil. Your hard-earned, carefree weekend just got snatched away from you . . . glorious R&R suddenly supplanted by two days full of dealing with he said, she said BS.

So which scenario would be likely to cause you the most discomfort? All three can toggle your switches. But for most people, one is more apt to hit home than the others. If scenario 1 makes your pulse race to the point where the little vein in your forehead starts popping out, you are Task Triggered. If scenario 2 causes your left eye to begin twitching such that your family members duck for cover, you are Process Triggered. If scenario 3 or 3B makes you wish you were instead listening, on repeat, to the sound of someone's nails screeching down a chalkboard, you are Relationship Triggered. If all three situations give you an identically stark "Emotional EKG" spike . . . stop reading; put this book down and go to your nearest emergency room!

All kidding aside, sometimes more than one Conflict Type can Trigger a person. It's not common though. Usually, one of the three scenarios is distinctively more pronounced than the others in the angst elicited. For instance, when contemplating time, you might pose to yourself, "Does it bother me when someone misses a due date?" You might think, *Yes, of course.* But how would you respond to that someone explaining, as to why they didn't get their work done in a timely fashion, "I wanted to make sure to get the job done right"? Do you admit, "Well, yeah, that *is* more important in most cases"? If so, while you may prefer it when people adhere to deadlines, you are Process Triggered rather than Task Triggered.

Alternatively, your posture may be, "I don't like it when people are late. And I don't like it when people don't pay attention to details. What *really* bugs me, though, is when my boss does those things!" You look at tasks and processes as valuable commodities. But they don't launch you over a cliff. In this instance, you are Relationship Triggered.

Of course, it's possible that the scenarios we presented didn't have much of an effect on you (assuming you gave it the good ole college try in terms of genuinely internalizing the scenes). That's not a reflection on your Triggers; it's a factor of our choice of illustrations. You might, for example, find scenario 1 to be entirely unrealistic; if you were in Hawaii with your partner, you'd have zero desire to check your phone. Or you'd never hand over the reins of a company or project or assignment to someone else, thus making both scenarios 1 and 2 nonstarters. (Granted, an inability to delegate, or having an underlying compulsion to be in control of tasks or processes, suggests that there is a Trigger in there somewhere, but we digress.) Perhaps you dismiss scenarios 3 and 3B because, when you're in the zone (for either work or fun), door-knocks and phone ringtones don't exist. What ringtone? You pop on your Bose high-def, noise-canceling headphones or turn off your phone when it's go-time—or me-time. You're agile at doing do-si-dos when it comes to family members, or, in your family, drama tends to be overblown and fizzles out if you let it. All these situations might be a pain in the buttocks to deal with, but they don't cause, for you, a highly visceral reaction. If so, it's probably the case that we didn't pick examples particularly germane to your life. Try to think of alternate narratives that you know would give you the psychological version of hives or heebie-jeebies. Remember the last time you felt X. What were the factors? Is the crux of the conflict hitting to-do or time targets (a Task Trigger), process or policy adherence (a Process Trigger), or a basic dislike of someone or someone's personality (a Relational Trigger)? By putting your mental imagery talents to work, you can explore what sorts of things truly drive you batty and, thus, discover which Conflict Type will Trigger you.

It's also possible that no matter how authentically you try to mentally simulate them, none of the core Conflict Types get a rouse out of you. If this is the case, we're sorry but, no, it doesn't mean you are a superhero. (Well, you could be a superhero; superheroes have Triggers too!) It merely means that your Trigger is likely to, instead, be out on a more extended branch of the Conflict Type tree. There are a few relatives:

~ **Emotion.** A specific emotion displayed by another person, or a specific emotion elicited in you, causes your brain to go haywire. Maybe you can't stand intolerant people, or jealousy drives you bonkers, for example. This is a cousin of Relational Conflict, but a certain emotion (or emotions) in general rather than the emotional dynamics of a particular relationship or a particular person is your Relational Trigger.

~ **Events.** You find yourself, from time to time, getting nutty over a specific action taken by another person, or a specific phrase someone might say, or a stance they might take. For instance, you get pissed when you're interrupted, or your skin crawls when someone refers to himself in the third person. This is an interpersonal stepsibling of Process Conflict. Note, however, it's the action, the phrase, or the event that is your Process Trigger since the Triggering can occur regardless of who is involved—that is, it's not about certain individuals.

~ **Time.** Time pressure, such as feeling like the face of a clock on the wall is staring over your shoulder, or a volume of work with a limited window in which to juggle it all, causes you to short-circuit. This is Task Conflict's fraternal twin.

~ **Conditions.** You might be thrown off your game by overall environmental conditions. These Triggers can be internal, such as being out of homeostasis (being too hot or too cold, being overtired, being dehydrated, having a headache or low blood sugar, or having to go to the bathroom). Or these Triggers can be external, such as being in a place full of chaotic visual or auditory distractions, or the general malaise of a gray, rainy day. Yes, Conditional Triggers might make you snap, but they aren't really Conflict Types. They are highly transitory; they persist only until the condition dissipates and thus, though equally as powerful as other Triggers, control over them can be restored more easily, regardless of the tasks, processes, or relational variables involved.

In contemplating this matter, you might realize that you have a combination of Triggers, or situationally specific ones, or multiple Triggers spanning from your work life to your home life. That's perfectly normal. Just keep in mind, please, that figuring out your (and then your colleagues', friends', and family members') Triggers is not a point-scoring exercise. This is crucial to understand: you are not a better person or a more skilled professional if you have fewer Triggers or more concrete ones. One kind of Trigger is not healthier or superior to another. There is no one "Trigger Profile" that predicts future job performance or things like marital bliss. Nor does having fewer or less frequent Triggers correlate with happiness. And finally, no one is "Trigger free." Acknowledgment is the first step toward growth; how we handle our Triggers is a fundamental determinant of our character.

The key to all this is awareness—knowing what Conflict Type Triggers you, needles at you distractingly, brings out a bad habit or two, causes you to lose perspective. When we get Triggered, we tend to skip self-care and bypass conflict prevention steps. But when we maintain awareness of our Triggers, our emotion is less apt to escalate or, if it does start to escalate, we're more apt to remember the tactics we have at our disposal. We stay levelheaded. We're better equipped to solve problems. And we're better able to move through conflict rather than getting mired in it.

~~~~~

How about detecting others' Triggers? Do a Trigger Analysis. Pick a relative, friend, or coworker. Reflect on the last time they got sideways with you or were perturbed by something you said or did. Take your time; fully reimagine the situation or circumstance so that you have a vivid, realistic *feeling* for the moment. Then, ask a round of questions:

1. Was the focus of the disagreement or tension primarily on what was or wasn't done (or a quantity of honey-dos not accomplished), the time it took to complete, or a deadline that was missed or moved? Yes? Your loved one or colleague is likely Task Triggered. No? Move on to question number two.

2. Was the matter of contention about how something was done, a course of action that was taken (or wasn't taken, but your relative, friend, or coworker felt it should have been)? Was there a problem with some kind of policy, procedure, system, or stance? If a blinking neon "yes" sign pops to mind, the person you are imagining is probably Process Triggered. None of these? Go to question number three.

3. Did your family member or work associate make nontopical personal attacks? Was a wide or patternless range of justifications offered for their ruffled feathers rather than something consistently connected to Task Conflict or Process Conflict? Did they harp on your relationship with them? Did they express an emotion seemingly out of context or non sequitur in scale? Did they pick a fight? Just when the friction between you two began to subside, did they make an intentional effort to stoke the fire? Does this person, in general, not get along well with you (especially across a spectrum of issues)? In contemplating these questions, if you are thinking, "Oh yeah, and then some," the person you are doing a Trigger Analysis of is almost certainly, you guessed it, Relationship Triggered.

Unsure? If you answer "no" or "I don't know" to all three questions, perhaps there was a Conditional Trigger involved in the episode you envisioned. Did the problem occur when your relative, friend, or coworker was sleep-deprived or hungover? Had they not eaten breakfast or lunch? Were they late for another appointment? When a Conditional Trigger is at play, there may not be an actual conflict or, at least, you can't make a Trigger determination. You'll need to start again. Think of another clash and run through the Trigger Analysis anew. Here's a flowchart to provide you with an assist:

Trigger Analysis

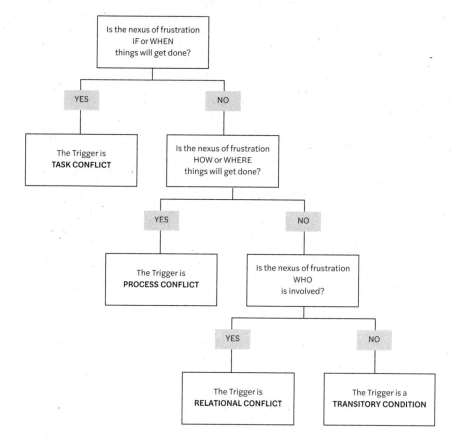

If you get to the bottom right-hand corner of the tree yet there doesn't appear to be a Conditional or Transitory Trigger you can put your finger on, you may not know the person in question well enough to figure out their Trigger(s) from a single episode. Or they are adept at hiding their Triggers; some folks are self-conscious of their Triggers, actively working to deflect or downplay them. A redo is required. To confidently predict which Conflict Type is apt to Trigger someone, it helps to consider multiple data points. Run a variety of skirmishes, scuffles, and squabbles through the Trigger Analysis, including ones that don't involve you. Try to ascertain the common denominator: Does it tend to be tasks or processes or relationships at the center of things that upset a special someone?

The more pain points of the people around you that you can assess via a Trigger Analysis, the more inoculated you'll be against conflict; you'll have the intel to ward off fights and fracases, to turn the tables when others' communication starts heading in an unproductive direction. Knowing people's Triggers gives you armor against two prevalent mistakes—two mistakes opposite of each other but both critical to preventing conflict.

One: treating all debates or differences of opinion as cauldrons of conflict. When you jump to a conclusion that someone is going to react poorly, subconsciously you treat them differently. You put up your guard, unnaturally overemphasize or deemphasize subjects, don your kid gloves. Subconsciously they, in turn, pick up on your changed behavior, posture, or language. They change their own behavior, posture, or language as a reflex. The interaction becomes clunky, contrived, uncomfortable. A problem has been created where there wasn't or needn't have been one. The self-fulfilling prophecy is in high gear. The error made here is treating a non-Triggered interaction as more problematic than it is. There are plenty of occasions when disagreements are of a Conflict Type that is not the dominant Trigger for anyone involved. If you know the parties' Triggers, you'll recognize when no one is going to lose their head. Your work is already done. All you must do is stay out of the way and be patient. Issues between people who are not Triggered almost always resolve themselves amicably, on their own, through the normal course of communication and "business as usual." This is because untriggered people do not experience a disruptive emotion spike; their temperature remains moderate enough to allow for rational conversation and problem-solving. They can see the issues fundamentally for what they are and make logical adjustments effortlessly. In fact, we tend to eschew use of the word *conflict* with these kinds of situations. We recommend you do the same.

Two: failing to spot when someone's cheese is about to slide off their cracker. In other words, you are working on a problem that isn't a Trigger for you, but you haven't stopped to realize that it *is* a Trigger for another person in the equation. You assume everything is hunky-dory. You overlook their budding frustration. You accidently push their buttons. The problem escalates unnecessarily. When confronting a challenge that is "no biggie" for you, don't presume that it won't annoy, worry, or fluster someone else. You'll be way ahead of the game if you query, *Will someone be Triggered by this challenge?*

And when the answer is yes, remember that in the face of significant stressors, people by and large skip over things such as assessment and planning; they can only see the situation as one big mess of conflict or unilaterally become fixated on one small detail. Under pressure, the tendency, for even the most pensive and talented of us, is to try to tackle "conflict" itself rather than the type of conflict. When pushed, pulled, or stretched, resist labeling the problem in general terms such as people not getting along, not seeing eye to eye, not trying to work together. That is a doomed recipe, dismissing the nuances of people's individual sensitivities. Each Conflict Type has a distinct methodology for achieving a positive outcome, each based on a set of variables. The key variables are as follows:

∿ Level and type of emotion.

∿ Timing of when issues should be addressed.

∿ Setting where issues are best addressed.

Let's learn the techniques for each of the three Conflict Types.

TACKLING TASK CONFLICT

People Triggered by Task Conflict like to work quickly; they get in, get the job done, and get out. They are to-do list makers and *love* to cross things off their lists. Many despise having those dots next to e-mail messages, indicating "unread." Task Conflict Triggerees are appointment keepers. They hate it when meetings get postponed (a Trigger in itself). Having to wait for someone who is tardy drives them up a wall. And they can be clock-watchers who tend to rush later in the day or when a deadline is approaching. They can even seem like they are always in a hurry. As a result, they may be perceived as sloppy, whether they actually are or not. They don't concern themselves with how things are getting done, nor the person or people doing them. They only care that things *are* getting done. Task-Triggered people may be viewed as high strung or impatient. This is not because of any lack of concern for people around them; it's that their focus is on completing work, checking checkboxes. Interestingly, this type of Triggeree is typically a good employee or entrepreneur but struggles with managerial duties, particularly delegating.

Folks who are Task Triggered often attempt to avoid Task Conflict altogether by completing all the tasks on their horizon themselves. Group work tends to stress them out, especially when a group member works slowly or meticulously; they'd rather do an entire project solo than worry about someone else not doing a part on time. Those sensitive to Task Conflict may have an aversion to outsourcing or delegating jobs. Upon jobs with soft deadlines, they will generally want to impose firmer delivery dates.

It's important to clarify here: deadlines, in and of themselves, are not the problem for people who are Task Triggered. Fundamentally, they *like* deadlines and the order that comes with them; they are usually quite uncomfortable with projects that don't have any time parameters. What causes feelings of conflict for Task Triggered people is working with others who don't hold the same appreciation for, who don't prioritize, the completion of tasks.

Those who are Task Triggered try to take care of everything sans assistance, and it can work . . . until it doesn't. Keep in mind that Task Triggered people may be in conflict because they're already deep in a hole; maybe they've been juggling a mountainous load and find themselves forced to do a handoff, or they predicted the mountain climb ahead, asked for help, but the help isn't keeping up with them. In either case, they are already on edge when outsourcing the completion of a task so they will get Triggered much faster than those who are impacted by Process Conflict or Relational Conflict.

It's important to also keep in mind that every Trigger type has substantial strengths. Someone who is Task Triggered can be counted on under time pressure. They excel at juggling multiple balls without dropping them or burning out. They get the job done. Task Triggerees require little oversight and take constructive criticism well.

Since Task Conflicts center around trust and responsibility and are escalated by a worry that to-do items are not going to be completed (or won't be completed on time), the longer it takes to settle the problem (and the less proactive people are in settling the problem), the more anxiety will rise in Task Triggered folks.

Task Conflict is best tackled by doing the following:

1. Focus on the type of emotion involved. You might think that frustration or anger would dominate the interpersonal friction in Task Conflict. The emotions displayed often look that way, but those are typically only surface manifestations. Beneath them, the true emotion elicited by Task Conflict is stress, a sense of pressure, and high anxiety. So strive to help Task Triggered people feel as if their issue is being handled quickly and efficiently. Tone is important: lower your voice in both amplitude and tempo. Communicate that the situation is being handled, and affirm that you care about completing the task as much as they do.

2. Attend to timing. Task Conflict is inextricably intertwined with a sense of urgency to get to-do items resolved. Not surprisingly, therefore, Task Conflict resolution hinges on moving expediently. The when outranks the how. Task Conflicts must be addressed *now*. Not soon, not quickly. Immediately. The acronym ASAP may be tossed around loosely for a range of office assignments, but when Task Conflict arises, "as soon as pos-

sible" is vital. The longer the conflict festers, the more upset Task Trig-gerees will become and the more the trouble will escalate. Not because these folks are bad actors, selfishly stomping their feet. Rather, because of their desire to quash problems. Addressing task-oriented challenges early, before someone gets Triggered, will prevent them from bubbling over with blinding, counterproductive emotions.

3. Realize, and give hearing to, the fact that people Triggered by Task Con-flict have a need to feel that action is being taken. The best way to as-sure them that their concerns are being headed is to engage with them directly, personally. Avoid bogging things down by incorporating lots of people. Definitely steer clear of any kind of e-mailing (or other digital) back-and-forth that inserts a pseudo barrier between the parties. This leads to inefficient communication, adds yet another entry on their "To-day's Agenda" calendar (responding to your message), creates another step in arranging meetings, and can seem like you're attempting to stall or minimize the immediacy of the situation. Pick up the phone and get on it! Or better yet, if it's an internal issue, get your fanny over to their office.

PROPITIATING PROCESS CONFLICT

People Triggered by Process Conflict are "quality over quantity" souls. They care more about the journey than the destination. They are the opposite of Task Conflict Triggerees regarding the pace of their efforts. Process Conflict Triggerees prefer to methodically pursue ideal results or what they deem is "right." But it's more nuanced than just arriving at a correct outcome. They aren't satisfied with a company or team win if inadvisable shortcuts were taken, or if the win was more luck than it was well-crafted performance. Achievements that aren't polished, and sustainably so, aren't acceptable. Take the basketball analogy of "moving the rock." It's a euphemism that refers to the offensive merits of making enough passes—and crisp, accurate passes—to create openings that lead to high percentage shots. A Process Triggered player who believes in moving the rock is likely to rip a teammate a new one (be it on the spot or in the locker room away from cameras), even when that teammate puts up thirty points or hits a game-winner, if that teammate failed to pass the ball per the game plan.

Process Conflict Triggerees are often accused of being too rigid, if not downright perfectionistic. Their comfort zone lies within the rubric of rules, guidelines, recipes, and procedures. They like to follow directions to a tee. When someone predisposed to Process Conflict gets a piece of furniture from IKEA, for example, they methodically lay out all the pieces and assemble the product, step by step, with the instruction booklet front and center. If a family member or coworker were to throw out the instruction booklet or just start winging it . . . yep, major sirens would go off. Watch out! If you are cooking with a Process Conflict Triggeree, don't creatively throw in a dash of this or that!

Interesting, these folks also get Triggered when a process or policy is too strictly adhered to—if it's not *their* process or policy. If they have a strategy they feel is valuable or effective and they are met by opposition from a boss (or vendor or host or other) who says, "Sorry, but that's not the way we do things here," or they are denied a request in the form of "Sorry, that's our policy," they may very well go Richter. Process Conflict can be Triggered by a lack of process as well as by a poorly conceived or disliked process.

For illustrative entertainment, put yourself in the mindset of a parent with a toddler. Maybe you are in this stage of life currently, or you can recall a time when your kids were that age. If you don't have children, think back to when your mom or dad (or guardian) told you to do something because "I told you so!" Have you heard that phrase or used it at some point yourself? The blood boiling feeling that wells up inside a parent, resulting in thought hijacking and the blurting out of that statement, is the same feeling someone has when they are Triggered by Process Conflict. At that moment, they fall back to insistence, because they know categorically that what they are asking or proposing is right. Others refusing to understand, or refusing to go along, drives them bananas.

In parallel, the sentiment of "why am I being questioned when I know what I'm doing" is incredibly powerful. It can cause a Process Conflict Triggeree to feel slighted and can lead to resentment, fury, and even hatred. At their core, they want people to trust them. Be it a colleague or loved one questioning their approach, giving pushback on a policy of theirs, or deviating from an agreed-upon plan, Process Conflict Triggerees take it as an insult to their abilities. This is key: process conflicts involve respect, or the perceived lack thereof. The emotions experienced in response to this perceived disrespect are often frustration and anger.

To propitiate Process Conflict, do the following:

1. Zero in on the frustration or anger expressed. Directly validate those emotions because of the concerns spurring them. Don't dance around the subject. Authentically communicate that you are keenly interested in the opinions and perspectives of a Process Conflict Triggeree. No matter how absurd or overblown an espoused idea may come across, give it a hearing.

2. Be swift. The timing for responding to a disconnect, problem, strife, and so on in Process Conflict—or at least demonstrating a genuine desire to respond—is identical to Task Conflict timing. If you use a "slow burn" strategy—that is, taking your time working through the conflict or waiting to get into it because you want to "do a little extra homework"—Process Conflict Triggerees' frustration and anger will fester. Thus, jump to it!

3. But be significantly deliberate in *how* you quickly act. Emphasize, as we just did, the word *how*; Process Conflict is all about prioritizing the way we are doing things over getting them done as expediently as possible. Process Triggered people want to feel as if they are in control of the situation. Process Conflict Triggerees' angst is about their ideals being adhered to. So use thorough communication and thoughtful planning. Often, a conference or team-style gathering works best—one in which the input of those Triggered is clearly valued and affirmed. Certainly, that can be done one-on-one, but for sticky conflict, a group setting can be an effective way to show that their opinion is valued.

REGULATING RELATIONAL CONFLICT

Relational Conflict is a beast of entirely different stripes. People Triggered by Relational Conflict go through or manifest a far wider spectrum of emotions, from fury to sadness to apprehension to hysteria. Why? Because there isn't a central issue as there is with Task Conflict and Process Conflict. Relational Conflict "participants" push and pull each other in unpredictable directions for unpredictable reasons, often in highly reactive manners. As we'll harp on throughout this book: when emotion is high, reason is low. In Relational Conflict, emotions tend to broil hotter, and there is less grounding the conflict, making it harder to infuse reason back into the equation. The most effective way to address Relational Conflict, therefore, is substantially divergent from the other Conflict Types. A specific subset of emotions is not the focus. Nor are particular goals surrounding work or project elements. And unlike for Task Conflict and Process Conflict, setting (one-on-one versus group) is relatively immaterial. So what do you do?

1. Put on the brakes. No, that's not to say quit attending to the problem. Rather, lean on the *Old Farmer's Almanac* advice: "Don't plant your seeds too early; don't pick your flowers too late." Applying this wisdom to conflict means knowing that Task Conflict and Process Conflict are rapidly blooming flowers; they'll wilt in a hurry if you don't tend to them soon enough. Relational Conflict, however, must germinate. If you spring to action, heavy-handedly, attempting to defuse Relational Conflict like a line cook trying to satiate a crowd during a breakfast rush, emotion will be too amplified to help people get where they need to go; you'll end up pouring gasoline on the fire (or in keeping with the simile, too much grease on the griddle). Indeed, when someone is riled, it's incredibly hard to stay patient, to refrain from fast-forwarding to the "fixing" part. With Relational Conflict, patience itself is a central objective. There is far more raw emotion in Relational Conflict, which, since lacking a basis in a task or a process, necessitates a peeling back of the layers. That takes time and thoughtfulness. Participants will likely need a breather. Perspective must be regained.

2. Devote time to reframing, away from all the swirling reactiveness, insulting, and manipulative behavior. The pilot light for the excessive emotion in Relational Conflict is primarily lit by a lack of communication, lack of listening (or, maybe better said, lack of hearing), lack of empathy, and selfishness. With these interpersonal deficiencies comes a strong, reflexive need to vent. Most people in Relational Conflict have unwittingly become bottled-up. A substantial part of your job, therefore, is to be a conduit for healthy, productive venting so a Relational Conflict Triggeree can get a little relief, while allowing you to foster communication, empathy, and unselfishness. The most effective strategies for positive venting and redirecting hinge on furthering your understanding of others. The rest of this book will lay out customized blueprints. Short of using those, let the other person know you hear them; let them know their feelings are not misplaced and they're not alone in a wish to work through them.

3. If the previous two steps initially prove impossible, separate the parties. Putting on the brakes and reframing communication as constructive sharing, listening, and empathizing sometimes requires people in Relational Conflict to discontinue their interaction temporarily. You may have to do double duty here, walking through steps one and two, individually, with each Relational Conflict "side" before working on unification. The goal is to defuse the amplitude of emotion caused by the interaction, itself having become toxic. Then the parties can reset, opening the door to reengaging.

"Once you replace negative thoughts with positive ones, you'll start having positive results."

—Willie Nelson

It is crucial to avoid making the mistake of assuming conflict is "personal"—that is, assuming that because a colleague or relative is angry with you, ignoring you, or flustered with something you did, it's an issue with the relationship. One of the most common errors we encounter—which substantially exacerbates conflict and feelings of ill will, preventing proper solutions from being revealed—is people labeling Task Conflict and Process Conflict as Relational Conflict. This is particularly pervasive in corporate America where people (alas, often women) can get mistagged as "overly emotional." An emotional spike when two people are interacting is not by default either or both having a problem with the other. Be a hawk in determining if the problem is a task or a process before jumping to relationship regulation.

KABOOM!

Years ago, our firm was hired by a Fortune 100 oil and gas company to "fix" a problem it was struggling with in its Permian Basin operations. In the span of six months, *half* of the company's drilling crew had left for employment with competitors. A 50 percent turnover rate is off the charts for this industry. What made it remarkably worse was that while the company was forking out an average of $36,000 per trainee to bring in replacements, the exiting employees were taking jobs paying an average of $0.25 *less* per hour. It was embarrassingly apparent that employees *really* didn't want to work for the company anymore. The crazy twist: we weren't recruited for the purpose of increasing the retention rate. We were hired, we were told, because a "team had a little quarrel the other day that we hope you can help us keep from recurring." Quarrel . . . that's one way of putting it, as we'd soon discover.

Blind as we were, we began with an investigation into the Conflict Type. The HR department told us, "There are clearly personality problems; the rig guys and the supervisors, they don't get along. We've been trying to weed out the bad apples. Getting people who are a better fit is slow-going, what with all the safety regulations and training requirements." Senior decision-makers were assuming that it was a relationship problem, Relational Conflict. They were making the all-too-common mistake of thinking that interpersonal conflict, because it is interpersonal, must be about the people, must be an issue of the individuals involved disliking one another, not getting along, or being unwilling to collaborate.

"What leads you to this conclusion?" we asked.

"Stupid little fights. Mid-level managers incessantly poking and prodding. Drillers talking back, not respecting authority. It winds everyone up," the SVP of Personnel offered.

"Like the quarrel you mentioned on our pre-engagement call?" we inquired, referencing the original request.

"That was just the tipping point for bringing you guys in, but yeah."

Sensing there might be valuable information hiding in plain sight, we asked to hear the full story.

Corporate headquarters had flown in one of the company's top quality control specialists to do a procedural accounting and ensure that all safety measures were being followed to the letter. He was appalled at the lack of compliance he found. Making rounds, he noticed one of the workers blatantly ignoring a placard above a bright red button reading:

DANGER!
High Pressure Buildup Risk
Wait 5 Minutes Between Pushes

"What the #@!! do you think you're doing?" the QC rep yelled, rushing over.

"My damn job. Who are you?" retorted the worker.

Aghast, the QC rep fired back, emphatically pointing at the sign, "Can't you read?"

"Sure can, dumba$$, but can you read this?" the worker said, flipping him the bird . . . then pressing the button again.

"STOP!" the QC manager screamed. "Don't you realize what you are doing could kill us all?"

"Just because you have a fancy degree and fly around on the company's fancy helicopter doesn't mean you know how things work around here. We do this all the time." And with that, the worker started repeatedly pressing the button as fast as he could.

PRESS, PRESS, PRESS, PRESS . . . **KABOOM!!!**

A reserve fuel tank in the adjoining room exploded. Thank heavens, there were no casualties, but the worker, quality control specialist, and two floor staffers sustained injuries. Obviously, more than childish spats were going on when the results were this combustible.

We ratcheted up our assessment. We posed the questions we've shared with you in this chapter to the managers and their employees (separately, of course, via a neutral "intake" technique). We interviewed the execs at HQ. We reached out to many of the former employees who'd recently quit.

The drillers, almost all of them, pointed their fingers at a new safety check procedure the company had implemented in the field without asking for their input. Completing the check each day required interrupting work flow, adding an arduous recalibration, and filling out a lot of paperwork. "We're in the business because we like working with our hands, not filling out forms. We're not desk jockeys," they said.

The bosses talked about the vital importance of safety above all else. "Minimizing the possibility of disasters and preventing our drillers from getting hurt is our number one priority. Taking all available precautions, no matter how it may impact oil production or bottom-line revenue, is paramount. We can't compromise on this."

Are you seeing the root of the conflict? There was no actual bad blood between the people involved, no real personality clashes. The colorfully worded exchanges on the floor weren't about who was doing the swearing. The problem wasn't relational. Nor was it about driller productivity; it had nothing to do with their drilling or oil barrel volumes or quotas or anything like that. Leadership wasn't concerned about the recent financial losses of the division. The workers were getting paid handsomely; there were no wage docking threats or anything like that. The workers' outsized desire to quit? It was based on a difference of opinion regarding a procedure and based, in part, on principle—the drillers not being consulted in a major decision that changed their work requirements. Process Conflict at its finest!

Discovering that the turnover was a result of Process Conflict made the rest of our consultation easy. We had the drillers elect one representative. The midlevel managers did the same. We then brought those individuals together, one-on-one, to hammer out a procedure that would accomplish leadership's safety standard while doing so in a way that recognized the valuable experience and input of the workers on the line—and in a way that wouldn't make them feel like pencil pushers on a day-to-day basis.

The new process didn't get rolled out overnight; it took careful development, but what mattered was that workers who were Triggered could see that positive action was in the works. And they felt respected.

Conflict resolved.

SHE DIDN'T UNCOCK THE TRIGGER

When in doubt about Conflict Type, look for clues in the feelings being generated. What is *causing* an emotional escalation? Is it a task, a process, or a person? Remember, though, the latter is often a smoke screen; a person is being blamed, obscuring a task or process problem.

For example, take a divorce mediation we conducted recently. As we do with all marital disputes, we required the husband and wife to each fill out a confidential disclosure form, documenting such things as court jurisdiction (family or civil); whether a suit has been filed and, if so, the status; the reach of the parties implicated; and any evidence of prior or existing abuse in the relationship or with elders or minors. This last entry is critical in determining if the couple can be in the same room during mediation or if precautions should be taken to keep them apart.

In the abuse box, the wife and husband both checked "No."

So we thought nothing of it and scheduled a face-to-face meeting. The day of the mediation arrived and in strolled the husband . . . wearing a giant surgical bandage on his neck. We asked him what had happened. With a slight shrug and in the calmest of voices, he replied, "Eh, I made a suggestion about our business and she shot me in the throat."

"She shot you? She pulled out a gun and *shot* you?"

"Well, yeah, but it was a .22. That doesn't count," the husband explained.

Just when we thought we'd heard it all. Despite having to rush to the ER, the husband didn't think it was a big deal. He had no worries about sitting right back down with his wife to talk through the divorce. That was the first hint that this probably wasn't Relational Conflict.

We got the mediation rolling. We had to go through assets, retirement savings, and what to do about their jointly run business. Each item prompted the wife to spin into an arm-waving rant about all the horrible things her husband had done—and how all those horrible things were tied to meth use. Each time, the husband either happily agreed to her accusations or said, "Well I was high at the time; I don't really remember, but I probably deserve what she's saying." The repetitive smorgasbord of emotion present in the wife's complaints were red herring hallmarks of intense Relational Conflict. Clearly, the wife was Triggered (literally too). Amazingly, the husband wasn't. Hint number two that this wasn't Relational Conflict. In true relationship-centered disputes, both sides are fond of tossing insult grenades.

As we explored further, a pattern in the wife's yelling became evident. Recurrently, meth smoking resulted in the husband leaving work undone, missing deadlines, and forgetting appointments. They both wanted to keep the business. She was okay with that, if he'd do his job—and on the condition that he agreed to get drug tested every week. He pushed back, offering to submit to blood draws every three months. The gap in their proposals continued to wind her up. She'd fly off the handle; he'd inquire softly, "Do I get any points for taking a bullet?"

We bet you have a darn good guess as to the Conflict Type in this proceeding: Task Conflict. As soon as we shifted the goal of the meeting to implementing milestone-based ownership vesting for their business, complete with task completion bonuses, the wife relaxed. Her frustrations were being heard, obvious movement was happening, and concrete measures were being put into place to guard against future noncompliance with task execution.

When it came to sorting out the timing of a drug-testing program, the husband pulled us aside. "I lit up yesterday. Can we not have the testing, like, tomorrow? I'm willing to do weekly . . . if I get into rehab. I'm just gonna need some help getting there. Any chance she'll pay for it?"

We presented the solution to the wife.

"Oh, honey, yes! I'm so proud of you," she gushed.

She was happily willing to compromise on the other matters because those were not her Triggers. Yes, the other matters were still issues, but not the core issue causing her grief: the Task Conflict jumbling her brain.

While this is a highly dramatic example, the lesson is to stop spending so much time and energy trying to solve all the problems in front of you. If you instead isolate the Trigger (as emotionally camouflaged as it may be), you stand a marvelous chance of having the remaining, more minor issues, fall away or, essentially, self-resolve.

~~~~~

Each Conflict Type has its own handling strategy. Relational Conflict, for instance, requires a significantly longer ramp during the assessment and communication stage. Process Conflict necessitates refocusing from the "what" and "who" onto the "how." Task Conflict demands signs of progress immediately. But armed with the knowledge you've gained in reading this chapter, if you can help people understand and respect one another's Triggers, you can prevent a plethora of divisive confrontations and resolve the rest. Yes, even the incredibly charged "attempted murder" conflict!

A frequent misconception is that for conflict to be resolved, for people to work well together, everyone needs to be friends or share the same values. Denzel Washington, courtesy of Coach Boone in *Remember the Titans*, said it best:

"You don't have to like each other, but you WILL respect each other."

Overarchingly, the core principles in this chapter are about engendering that respect and about building stronger relationships through recognition and awareness. It's about recognizing that there are distinctly different types of conflict. It's about being aware of others' Triggers. When you are cognizant of the Triggers of those around you, it's like having a crystal ball; you can see a lot of conflict coming and prevent it. And when you encounter someone who has been Triggered, you'll be able to apply the tools in chapter 2 to predict their behavior.

2

Predict Behavior

Undoubtably, you are familiar with personality typographies—Myers-Briggs, 16 Personalities, the DISC profile, Enneagram, True Colors, Gallup's StrengthsFinder, and so forth. They're popular in corporate retreats and leadership development programs. They're useful to complete alongside coworkers, helping us better understand one another. They're even a blast to fill out with family or friends. Typology quizzes are as entertaining as they are insightful. They have a substantial drawback, however: they assess *normalized* attributes—that is, how people comport themselves on average, on routine days, when everything is peaches and cream. When people are Triggered, though, they rarely think or act normally; they might lose touch with themselves altogether. The valuable information provided by behavioral inventories can go *whoosh*, right out the window.

Consider former football quarterback Tim Tebow. Tebow was a collegiate megastar for the University of Florida Gators—a two-time national champion, a Heisman Trophy winner, an All-American both on and off the field. Closing out his NCAA tenure as a record holder in both passing efficiency and rushing touchdowns, Tebow was sure to continue his career at the highest level, the NFL. There was just one problem: most professional football talent evaluators were concerned with his elongated throwing motion. When he dropped back to pass, he would wind up similarly to a baseball player before throwing. Historical data shows that "baseball throwers" generate too many interceptions. QBs can get away with this in college. But in the NFL, defensive backs are too fast; a long arm windup allows DBs to get a jump on passes. So when Tebow announced he would enter the NFL Draft in 2010, revered draft pundits recommended that he not be selected until the third round or later.

For those who don't know much about football, there was, at that time, a roughly *$20 million* difference in guaranteed money and endorsement deals between first- and third-round picks. Talk about motivation to get out of your comfort zone, to change an old habit. If only $20 million incentives were around in mid-January when your effort to adhere to your New Year's resolution begins waning, when you are pining for the lost friendship of a pint of ice cream to soothe a hard day. But we digress . . .

Tebow worked diligently with a professional coach in the offseason to shorten his throwing motion. Out of view of the paparazzi, day after day, he trained a new arm action to show off at the NFL Scouting Combine, where all the top prospects gather to showcase their talents. It wasn't natural for Tebow, but boy did he toil to execute the skill. Three months later, when the Combine rolled around, Tebow wowed the scouts. He was drafted in the first round!

In the ensuing football campaign, throughout the preseason, when no one cares about the score of games, Tebow continued to throw with his new, short motion. In practice, when team rules forbid players from hitting or tackling their QBs, he threw with the short throwing motion. Then the regular season got underway. In the NFL's blink-of-an-eye sixteen-game schedule, every contest counts, every play has the potential to determine whether a team makes or misses the playoffs. The 325-pound defensive linemen bring everything they've got to every down, endeavoring to disintegrate opposing quarterbacks. Scud missile DBs fly across the field in no-holds-barred fashion. Tebow stepped onto *that* gridiron . . . and threw with his long arm motion.

Truth be told, we are all like Tim Tebow. We may not have giant men barreling down on us, about to squash us into a Wile E. Coyote–style accordion if we don't execute our plan in under three seconds, but we all have a lifetime's grooved manner in which we respond to pressure. We're pretty good at trying new things, learning different skills, adapting to our environment—when there's nothing on the line. When the going gets rough, however, we are likely to revert to our most deeply ingrained behavior patterns. You might, for instance, be committed to cutting out caffeine. It's robbing you of essential REM sleep; the three-times-a-day Starbucks run is picking your pocket to an annual tune of nearly $5,000; your favorite venti caramel macchiato with extra whipped cream is certainly not kind to your waistline. Though challenging to resist the urge, you stick with your newfound discipline. Until you get hit with an emergency project at work that brings your job security into question. Or, already overloaded with your kids' math tutoring, music lessons, soccer games, essay contest entry, park cleanup volunteering, and planning for an epic international museum barnstorming summer trip, your spouse dumps a "I *really* need your help" honey-do on you as you're heading out the door to get to a twice-postponed parent-teacher conference. Mmm, the aroma of a fresh brew wafts to mind. Peet's is right around the corner.

Don't beat yourself up. No matter how well intentioned you are, Triggers are powerful. The greater the pressure you face, the greater the likelihood that basal thoughts and actions will surface. In athletics, like we saw for Tim Tebow, those thoughts and actions are generally familiar strategy choices and physical mechanics. In interpersonal interaction, they comprise what is known as a "Conflict Default"—a person's instinctive way of handling friction, arguments, disagreements, dissention, strife, or disharmony. Interestingly, a wide cross section of research on human conflict demonstrates that people are remarkably consistent in their defaults. So much so that we've been able to identify five core Conflict Personality Styles. Almost everyone, when pushed too hard or stretched too thin—in other words, when Triggered—goes to one of (or a slight variation to one of) these five personas. We call them Go-Tos, short for "Go-To Conflict Personality Styles." Go-Tos pick up where standard personality typographies like Myers-Briggs, Enneagram, and StrengthsFinder leave off.

Drumroll for the big reveal . . . keeping in mind as the drumsticks patter that the five Go-Tos are not shortcomings, liabilities, disabilities, or in any way negative. They are simply habits, predispositions, or comfort blankets that are summoned (often without a conscious pause) to address uncomfortable interpersonal situations—they are *not* genetically hardwired into your brain. They are merely by-products of a pattern you happen to have gotten strongly accustomed to using. You can retrain yourself or help your loved ones recondition their Go-Tos. Yes, it requires a significant commitment. And you must deliberately practice altering your Go-To Style *under pressure*. That's why Tebow ultimately fell short. It turns out that he logged scant reps simulating high-stress game conditions. It's also a lot harder to change biomechanics learned in childhood than it is to shift mindsets.

We hope you find these facts as exciting as we do; it's a major motivator in our work and in writing this book—arming you with the goods to be a Go-To Jedi master. We'll dig into the hows more in the chapters to come. For now, it's important to view the Conflict Personality Style Go-Tos tactically rather than judgmentally. They're actionable skill sets, ultimately at your disposal to drive teamwork and great relationships. Which is why we'll provide you with, in addition to formal psychological terminology, a range of alternate, entertainingly illustrative monikers for each Go-To. We've found that some folks prefer, for instance, sports or movie analogies in conceptualizing the application of each Go-To. Swap them in for the Go-To titles as you see fit. We're sports guys; we're of course biased. But athletics and teamwork do generally go hand in hand. With that said, down the field, together, we go . . .

In no particular hierarchy, the Go-To Conflict Personality Styles are as follows:

THE AVOIDER

We start the list with the Einstein of the group, the Avoider. No, not because one with this Go-To Conflict Style is smarter than others but rather because Albert Einstein makes for an excellent Avoider poster child: uninterested in minor details or incidentals, highly effective in (oft preferring, in fact) solitary work, capable of profound concentration, and a crackerjack problem-solver. Other famous Avoiders include Amelia Earhart, Barry Sanders, Ted Williams, Meryl Streep, Ayn Rand,

Mahatma Gandhi, Prince Harry, Warren Buffett, and The Roadrunner from Sunday morning cartoons.

When we plug in a sport theme into our talks and workshops (as well as our online resources; see **www.theconflictdocs.com**), we call this Go-To "The Golfer." In similar fashion to an LPGA or PGA professional lining up a putt to win a Major, this Go-To is geared to narrow in, with sharp focus on the immediate task at hand. Golf is an individual sport, and likewise, under pressure this Go-To performs best alone, with minimal distractions. The Avoider may consult trusted colleagues (a caddy parallel) when crucially difficult decisions must be made—as long as it doesn't involve back and forth; they look for quick, direct, actionable information. Regardless, they trust their own judgment implicitly.

Avoiders, hence their name, prefer to stay away from conflictual situations in the workplace, in group settings, and at home. As such, Avoiders are good at knowing when issues can be resolved without their interference. This Go-To Style is ideal for inconsequential disagreements or when a problem is better suited for the back burner. Don't misinterpret their avoidance though. It's not personal. One of the most important things to know about Avoiders is that they steer around conflict not because they are afraid of it but rather because they feel that dealing with small conflicts is distracting or a waste of their time or energy.

Avoiders usually sit back, waiting to see if a conflict will escalate. When they do decide to get involved, though, they get *fully* involved. Once Triggered, an Avoider will want to deal with a conflict forthwith, aiming to get it off their plate so they can get back to what they, personally, deem as more important pursuits.

While this Go-To lends itself to work efficiency, there are a few downsides to this conflict approach. An Avoider's preference to fly solo can reduce communication. Disagreements can arise over who is responsible for what since the Avoider would rather get a job done than delegate it. Their tendency to disregard or put off addressing complications can result in challenges intensifying until they become large-scale failures or too difficult to resolve economically. This Go-To can also be derailing when the process for completing a task must be followed robotically or according to someone else's explicit rubric. Avoiders bristle at the hint of excessive management oversight, ongoing process reviews, or nit-picking.

All five Conflict Personality Styles may be saddled (almost always inaccurately) with negative tags—stemming from a struggle the *perceiver* has when in conflict with the Go-To in question. Someone sideways with an Avoider, therefore, would be prone to viewing the strengths of this Go-To (e.g., ability to block out distractions in the quest for maximum productivity) as obstacles to dispute resolution. For example, Einstein at times could be mislabeled as aloof or unapproachable, just as people with this Go-To can be. Avoiders are not really aloof people. They are simply absorbed in whatever activity they've committed to doing.

To put a more personal face on this Conflict Personality Style, imagine your daughter is texting back and forth with her college roommate while home on break. Nonstop GIFs, emojis, laughter . . . until your daughter brings up the issue of rent. The bubble with three dots on her screen disappears and then silence. No reply for the rest of the week. The roomie is probably an Avoider.

Do you have a colleague who's always happy to "advise" or offer suggestions for how something should be done, but when you offer an idea for them to tweak their process, you get the stink eye? An Avoider on the job.

- ∿ **COMMON TRIGGERS:** Low-quality work; condescending tones; aggressive communicators or negotiators; people not being accountable

- ∿ **STRENGTHS:** Focus and efficiency; self-motivating; not getting bogged down in minutiae; using creativity to drive problem-solving elegance

- ∿ **WEAKNESSES:** Small talk and delegating; letting conflicts grow or fester; *appearing* as aloof or individualistic

- ∿ **IDEAL CONFLICT SCENARIO:** A narrow scoped or "routine" day-to-day type conflict

- ∿ **MAIN MOs:** Strategizing; trying to avoid conflict

∿ **NICKNAMES:** The Golfer; the Chess Master; the Artist; the Architect

∿ **BEST TEAMMATE:** The Accommodator

∿ **WORST TEAMMATE:** The Analyzer

THE COMPETITOR

To get a sense for the next Go-To Conflict Personality, put yourself in the shoes of legendary pilot Chuck Yeager breaking the sound barrier (the first in history to do so). One doesn't set records like that without a drive to push the envelope—characteristic of the Competitor Go-To Style. An ace of aces naval officer, Yeager never rested on his laurels, was willing to take risks in the interest of achievement, liked to one-up rivals, and didn't concern himself with others' criticisms. Yeager was a model Competitor. Fellow representatives of this Go-To include Steve Jobs, Ernest Hemingway, Danica Patrick, Ronda Rousey, Johnny McEnroe, Cleopatra, Bugs Bunny, Captain Georg von Trapp in *The Sound of Music*, and Mike Singletary.

We highlight Mike Singletary frequently in a profiling game that attendees of our seminars enjoy. The affable Singletary provides a shining demonstration that being a Competitor doesn't mean being a "jerk," as people with this Go-To can, unfortunately, be labeled when someone isn't receptive to their no-nonsense approach. Competitors are *not* bullies; they are aggressive for the positive intention of getting things accomplished. They are principled people who readily stand up for good causes and what they believe is right.

Singletary is a sweetheart of a man. He also happens to be an American football Hall of Fame linebacker—the position we use as the sports version of this Go-To. The Competitor Conflict Personality Style is like a linebacker blitzing a quarterback. NFL defenders don't wait around; they pounce the second the football is snapped. In similar fashion, the Competitor Go-To pounces on problems. Their approach to conflict—both real and perceived—is to (football reference in full effect) tackle it straightaway, going after solutions with unabridged force and effort. This Go-To is especially pronounced when there are clearly defined protocols for task completion. Competitors want to see action and results. They don't like to talk; they like to do. They thrive in tense situations and rely on competitive tactics, making this Go-To perfect for strict outcome-centric situations and for when people need motivating to meet lofty delivery expectations. Competitors like to delegate and trust others to work unsupervised . . . but expect follow-through and expect work to be done as they have defined.

Therefore, not surprisingly, people with this Go-To can be impatient. They are easily frustrated when tasks are not completed well (relative to their own high standards). They are generally quite intolerant of long or frequently scheduled meetings. And they are constantly pushing those around them to make progress or to improve on something, which can be a boon at making sure others are striving to be better at what they are doing but conversely can alienate people.

Micromanagement will almost always push a Competitor over the edge, as will supervision promoting constant change. Competitors are uncomfortable deviating from the playbook. This Go-To struggles when faced with demands requiring innovation or out-of-the-box thinking, as Competitors tend to be set in their ways. Competitors demand perfection; underperformance is one of their strongest Triggers.

We're guessing you've experienced sitting in bumper-to-bumper traffic. That driver behind you who sits on their horn . . . honking the second there is but a millimeter for you to roll forward? Surely a Competitor. The dear friend who calls when you're at work whenever something ruffles their feathers, yet, when you shoot them a quick message to let them know you're tied up, keeps calling and calling . . . and calling? Likely a Competitor too.

~ **COMMON TRIGGERS:** Back seat drivers; excessive opinions about how a task is or should be being performed; passiveness; inaction; excuses

~ **STRENGTHS:** Closing deals; calling the shots; competing

~ **WEAKNESSES:** Impatience and rushing in too quickly; lack of sensitivity; group work; *appearing* as too hard-nosed, aggressive, or inflexible

∿ **IDEAL CONFLICT SCENARIO:** A "bottom of the ninth" situation

∿ **MAIN MOs:** Leading; taking action

∿ **NICKNAMES:** The Linebacker; the Firefighter or First Responder; the Race Car Driver; the Gladiator

∿ **BEST TEAMMATE:** The Avoider

∿ **WORST TEAMMATES:** The Analyzer in the short term; the Accommodator in the long term

THE ANALYZER

Possessing a penchant for evidence-based decision-making, Dr. Phil, Judge Judy, Dr. Neil deGrasse Tyson, Dr. Marie Curie, Dr. Jane Goodall, Google founder Larry Page, George Soros, Billy Beane of *Moneyball* notoriety, and Owl from *Winnie-the-Pooh* are exemplars of the Analyzer Go-To Conflict Personality Style. When presented with a problem, Analyzers are methodical; they patiently gather information before acting.

Capitalizing on the trendiness of metrics in athletics, we find General Manager (GM) to be an effective nickname for the Analyzer. The GM of a pro sports franchise is the front office executive in charge of constructing the team's roster of players. In today's draft, free agency, and trade landscape, with contacts extending into the hundreds of millions of dollars, GMs are almost required to be hybrid data scientists/economists. But championships aren't won on a compilation of players' stats alone; GMs must incorporate clubhouse chemistry into their calculations. The winningest GMs pay fervent attention to information collection and study, while being adept at the art of balancing the needs of the business with the needs of the individuals involved—acutely apropos of the Analyzer Go-To.

Analyzers, as you therefore might deduce, are nimble at compromising. They are skilled listeners, willing to hear and consider all angles and concerns. They are markedly effective when those around them are also willing to compromise, making this Go-To ideal when cooperation is called for or when trade-offs are necessary to propagate conflict resolution. Humanizing complex problems is a strategy Analyzers typically use to reach their ends. This helps them to be viewed as genial and trustworthy.

The primary shortcoming of this Go-To is too much "meeting in the middle" for the sake of keeping people happy. Analyzers are beavers for fairness. They loathe someone being taken advantage of, which is positive, but they will concentrate their efforts on mitigating any potential relationship damage to an extent that they will favor easier-to-reach, partially satisfying outcomes over striving to reach optimal outcomes. This is apt to result in all sides giving up something instead of gaining win-wins. To boot, Analyzers have a vulnerability in blending business and personal relationships, leading them to bump into issues from the blurring of boundaries. Despite the voluminous effort of an Analyzer to gather data, their judgment can still be clouded by personal feelings or relationships.

A secondary shortcoming of this Go-To Style, when it comes to working under pressure, is that Analyzers are more comfortable when taking their time to explore all relevant facts and standpoints, so they don't respond well to imposed deadlines. Hounding them, trying to speed them up, or forcing premature conclusion-drawing will flip out an Analyzer.

The negative association that can get pinned on an Analyzer is being a control freak. The reality, though, is that people with this Go-To are dogged in their quest to be well-informed. Their thoroughness can inaccurately come across, early in the conflict resolution process, as an unwillingness to reach an agreement. But later in the process, Analyzers may genuinely become stubborn. Once they have exhaustively deliberated on what they consider to be an equitable plan, it's hard to convince them otherwise. Their level of effort and attention to detail can be self-fulfilling.

Think of a time, for instance, when you volunteered to spearhead a project, say a team-building retreat that your company had on the "unassigned" agenda board. You were excited; you wanted to go, go, go to make a great event happen. No matter how many proposals you put on your boss's desk, though, they shot them down . . . with no rationale offered. Accurate or not, something was missing or deemed insufficient by your boss—an Analyzer at work.

At home, were you a middle child who tried to always please everyone, tried to always keep the peace between your siblings? It wouldn't be a fluke if this instilled some Analyzer Go-To attributes in you.

- **COMMON TRIGGERS:** Haste or rushing; unrealistic offers or proposals; egotistical people; uncompromising people

- **STRENGTHS:** Defusing tension; listening; gathering data and intel; empirical decision-making; patience; compromising

- **WEAKNESSES:** Stubbornness; tight deadlines or time frames; trying to make everyone happy; *appearing* as controlling

- **IDEAL CONFLICT SCENARIOS:** Low-stakes situations or problems, or those hinging on "feel good" kinds of outcomes

- **MAIN MOs:** Investigating; thorough consideration

- **NICKNAMES:** The General Manager; the Detective; the Explorer; the Archaeologist

- **BEST TEAMMATE:** The Collaborator

- **WORST TEAMMATE:** The Accommodator

THE COLLABORATOR

Someone skilled at networking and relationship management who turns, first, to their propensity in these areas when handling challenging situations is a Collaborator. Think James Spader's character, Raymond Reddington, in the binge-worthy television series *The Blacklist*. An oration virtuoso, with great command of his reputation, and deeply caring— Triggered when someone he loves is in trouble—Reddington embodies the Collaborator Go-To Style. As does the character Belle in *Beauty and the Beast*, James Bond, Dr. Ruth, Dr. Don Shirley, JFK, Jamie Foxx, and Jason Sudeikis's title character in the hit show *Ted Lasso*.

To capture the multidimensional nature of the Collaborator Conflict Personality Style, we regularly lean on the metaphor of Agent (from sports to spies). Agents are pros at developing human assets. Collaborators, likewise, easily and quickly form bonds, and seek to maintain such alliances through adverse events. To do so, people with this Go-To arc both assertive and adaptable. They are effusive communicators with a preference for substantive debate over superficial interactions. They excel at engendering rapport. They are exceedingly attentive to relationship needs, as they have a seemingly innate desire to build, and be in, partnerships. Collaborators place premium value on their community and professional networks and their status with colleagues. Collaborators possess above-average empathy skills, devoting a considerable portion of their time to warding off personal discord. This Go-To Style comes in most handy when teamwork is required, when friendships are in jeopardy, or when integrative thinking is paramount.

As Collaborators idealize group membership, however, they may (often, inadvertently) isolate those outside of their group. They may also miss bigger issues by consuming themselves with all the minor hiccups that come along. Excessive use of this Go-To increases incidence of burnout due to the intensity with which Collaborators approach relationships. Collaborators rely on human interaction, so they don't cope well with people who avoid conflict, shut down under pressure, or are guarded with their feelings.

One interesting quirk to watch out for: rarely do Collaborators directly say what they mean. Underneath projecting as openly sharing, they play things close to the vest to keep interactions focused on others instead of themselves. They utilize every form of communication at their disposal to identify the interests and intentions of those around them, but if their motives are not pure, Collaborators can be supremely manipulative to attain their desires. Not shockingly, therefore, well-intentioned folks with this Go-To may find themselves misperceived as scheming or as "users."

To give this Go-To a little context, conjure up being at an office picnic. It's a pleasant day, save for a veteran member of your team who is disgruntled about your newest hire. Your old colleague corners you, peppering you with questions about the junior employee: "Why'd you pick them over the other candidates? What do you think of their performance so far? Will you let them work from home? How often will you do reviews?" You appreciate their interest, but whenever you ask a question, they ignore it or turn it right back on you. A classic Collaborator. Maybe you've experienced a similar dynamic in your family as well . . . a cousin, perhaps, always prying into your marriage whenever rumor surfaces that *they* are, yet again, coming out of a failed relationship. Their affairs are perpetually speculative; your cousin is the most close-lipped soul you know (or don't really know, come to think of it).

- **COMMON TRIGGERS:** Threats to status or group membership; avoidance; lack of communication

- **STRENGTHS:** Empathizing; communicating; making personal connections; partnering up; ability to act like a chameleon

- **WEAKNESSES:** Time management; burnout; diving in too deep or prying; trying to fix everything; *appearing* as manipulative

- **IDEAL CONFLICT SCENARIOS:** Lengthy negotiations; long-term planning

- **MAIN MO:** Collaborating

- **NICKNAMES:** The Agent; the Diplomat; the Hostage Negotiator

- **BEST TEAMMATE:** The Analyzer

- **WORST TEAMMATE:** The Avoider

THE ACCOMMODATOR

This Accommodator Conflict Personality Style prioritizes the achievements and well-being of those they care about over their own achievements and well-being. Atop the list of this Go-To's icons: Jimmy Stewart's character, George Bailey, in *It's a Wonderful Life*. He's joined on the list by Jackie Chan, Tom Hanks, Dr. Mae Jemison, Rosalynn and Jimmy Carter, Kenny Chesney, Pelé, Caitlin Clark, and Magic Johnson, to name a few. All remarkable team players. When put to the test: dedicated, selfless, resilient, having copious reserves of energy to offer those in their inner circle.

The matching sports figure that jumps off the page: a point guard in basketball. Point guards run their team's offense; their job is to see the whole court (the big picture), set up plays, and distribute the ball to facilitate success. Accommodators fit this mold seamlessly. They revel in their friends and loved ones shining and their organization or family winning. They are willing to make personal sacrifices to get to those wins. They don't want the limelight (many Accommodators intentionally duck headlines). And they thrive in high-responsibility, high-accountability environments.

The combination of the above makes Accommodators great at generating results. People with this Go-To are deliberate and relentless in their effort, though without an air of interpersonal competitiveness. They are inquisitive and creative—for the purpose of finding ways to help their team succeed as opposed to furthering their own agenda. This Go-To is perfect for problems with a transparent workload, tasks (and titles) that are clearly defined, or projects with a probability of dividend payout closely linked to determination level.

This Go-To is not ideal, on the other hand, when disagreement arises regarding the distribution of job assignments or uncertainty over who has final say. Nor is this Go-To effective when team members do not follow established protocols or project blueprints. This spurs Accommodators to arbitrarily take over; they would rather do all the work themselves than confront someone about a problem. Accommodators happily carry the lion's share of a group's burden, but when they are shouldering the load and a colleague or partner offers a new opinion about how to complete the work, or when someone questions an Accommodator's commitment, they usually snap. They do not abide freeloaders. And Accommodators *do* need to be appreciated (albeit away from the stage in most cases) for their contributions, lest they bottle up resentment. They tend to bottle and bottle . . . until they quit.

A soft underbelly of this Go-To is being in intrateam competitive environments. It's important to watch out for this clash. Self-assertive people who place low value on task completion can handily take advantage of an Accommodator.

It is also important to understand that while Accommodators will avoid conflict-laden situations, it is for different reasons than Avoiders. Avoiders are soloists; Accommodators are team centric. When Triggered, an Accommodator is apt to exhibit passive-aggressive behavior. Accommodators will dance around a subject. When they bring up an issue, it's rarely their true concern; their underlying interest usually pertains to one of a plethora of previous problems that they've buried 'til they can't stand it anymore.

Bringing this Go-To to life: no one enjoys dialing up a who-knows-where call center to dispute a mischarge or rectify a shipping error. Have you ever lost your cool talking to customer service (assuming you actually reached a live person)? Did the representative on the other end, initially pleasant and patient, abruptly change their tone . . . and hang up on you? While it *could* be their training, hanging up isn't exactly considered best-practice protocol. Chances are, they were an Accommodator. As an aside, it's worth chewing on: How often do customer service reps hear expressions of appreciation? How often do people spend the time to look up a company's 800 number so they can wait on hold . . . to give a compliment?

On the personal side of the coin, do you have a friend who likes to send thoughtful little notes, flowers, and so forth—nothing extravagant, and they never put their name on gifts, insisting that it isn't about them, that they don't want anyone to make a big deal out of their courtesies? Do they ever pull you aside to bemoan no one doing something nice for them? You guessed it, an Accommodator.

COMMON TRIGGERS: Selfishness or excessive individualism; lack of appreciation; slacking; low or limited effort

~ **STRENGTHS:** Sharing; teamwork; quarterbacking; accounting for diverse needs; humility; charisma

~ **WEAKNESS:** Dealing with ego-driven, competitive, or self-absorbed people; trying to do everything themselves; *appearing* as passive when pushed

~ **IDEAL CONFLICT SCENARIO:** A group project

~ **MAIN MOs:** Orchestrating; supporting; leading quietly

~ **NICKNAMES:** The Point Guard; the Concierge; the Conductor; the Sherpa

~ **BEST TEAMMATE:** The Avoider

~ **WORST TEAMMATE:** The Competitor

~~~~~~~

So which one are you? When someone or something completely tees you off, exasperates you, or overwhelms you, do you act like an Avoider or an Accommodator? A Competitor? An Analyzer or a Collaborator? As you read about the five Go-Tos, which resonated with you? Which hit a little too close to home? Which felt the most foreign? You can pinpoint your Go-To by examining your strengths and weaknesses under pressure. To reiterate, the goal is to figure out your default method for handling problems or sticky situations—what thoughts and actions you "go to" when you get Triggered.

Another way to get to your Go-To is to explore the "best teammate" and "worst teammate" matchups. In dealing with other people, which of the Go-To Styles would you be most comfortable hanging out with? Which would you least like to meet in a dark alley? Please allow us to reiterate: there are no right or wrong answers. There isn't a correlation between Conflict Personality Style and success (at work or at life). None of the five Go-Tos climbs the corporate ladder faster or makes more money than the others. There isn't a Go-To that has the lowest divorce rate. Each Style has both benefits and deficiencies. Each is best suited for a particular set of circumstances—a particular Conflict Type and the particular Go-Tos of the other people involved. Sorry, you don't get bragging rights for having a certain Go-To. You get bragging rights for, akin to Tim Tebow, being able to discern your Go-To, discern when it's an asset, and discern when a conflict calls for adopting a different Go-To. Better still, you get bragging rights for outperforming Tim by studying and practicing the application of all five Go-Tos to real-world discord.

> "It's not who I am underneath, but what I do that defines me."
> **—Batman (from *Batman Begins*)**

To that end, it can be helpful to look at Go-Tos through the lens of an ace pitcher in Major League Baseball (which, actually, is the etymology of our coining the "Go-To" abbreviation). All pitchers, starting when they are Little Leaguers, learn a go-to pitch—a pitch they throw when they *must* get an out, when bases are loaded, when the opposing team's leading home-run hitter strolls to the plate with confidence-exuding swagger. In this moment, the average pitcher's only real shot at preventing a grand slam is to throw their go-to pitch, and throw it with total trust. If they try to spin up a curveball that they haven't perfected, they're unlikely to deliver it assuredly. Undoubtedly, it'll be a hanger. It will go out faster than it came in. If their go-to is a poor selection for the batter at the plate at that juncture of the game, the coach should call a time-out and put in a pitcher whose go-to lines up well with the situation.

Ace pitchers, on the other hand, when they *must* get an out, have three or four different pitches that they can deliver with equal effectiveness. So which pitch do they throw (or more accurately, which pitch does their catcher signal)? You betcha: the pitch best suited for getting the particular hitter at the plate, at that particular time, to strike out (or pop up or ground into a double play). Their go-to is still the pitch they relied on when they were playing in sandlots or backyards. But they're an ace. Which means: (1) they recognize when they are in, as sports commentators like to say, high-leverage situations; (2) they don't automatically, without thinking, just throw their most instinctively comfortable pitch; (3) they (welcoming help from their catcher or manager or both) assess what go-to the moment calls for; and (4) they take a deep breath to defuse their emotion and then confidently fire away.

Aces aren't born with this range, of course. Through thousands of hours of training in the bullpen and watching scouting tape as they make their way through the Minor Leagues, they perfect pitch #2, then pitch #3, and so forth. They develop their skills so they have, effectively, a multitude of go-tos.

Similarly, being a champion at preventing and resolving conflict requires an awareness that, even if you have first-class interpersonal skills, when you're under pressure, it's not enough to bank on one finely tuned or "security blanket" Go-To. You must identify your potential blind spots—that is, which of the above five Conflict Personality Styles you might struggle with when you are Triggered. And you must be willing to practice those styles that aren't, at least initially, all that comfortable for you.

Thankfully, mitigating conflict is a cognitive exercise. Being good at it doesn't require the ten-thousand-hour volume of commitment that honing physical talents would; no mondo dumbbell hoisting, no gut-wrenching wind sprints, no choking down chalky protein shakes. The more practice you log using the various Go-To Styles, the better, of course, but you have a *huge* head start if you simply do two things:

1. A deep self-assessment dive to determine your core or favorite Go-To. Most people slip into their Go-To without realizing it, not dissimilar from holding one's breath at the onset of ominous music during a horror movie. Gaining an understanding of when and how your Go-To takes over puts you in the driver's seat to be proactive instead of just reactive to conflict. If your Go-To hasn't yet jumped off the page, not to worry; we've designed and validated an assessment instrument that will systematically help you uncover your Go-To. You can access the assessment online at **www.theconflictdocs.com**.

2. When a clash or crunch time hits, after you've used chapter 1's tools to identify the Conflict Type, read the people you're working with to as-

certain their Go-Tos. In chapters 6 through 10, we'll provide you with complete game plans for predicting, preventing, and resolving conflict with each Go-To. For now, the key is to know whether you should stick with your own Go-To or take a time-out so you can adjust your approach. Consider adapting your strategy when your Go-To isn't the "best teammate" for the Go-To of the person with whom you're upset or in disagreement.

HOW TO READ PEOPLE

Which Go-To is your boss? Which Go-To is your spouse? When their back is against the wall, how will they react? When you push their buttons, what will they say and do? What is their default manner when they disagree with someone or something? Perhaps you already know the Go-Tos of those in your innermost circle, or you immediately thought of them as you digested the descriptions of the five Conflict Personality Styles. If you aren't sure, or are itching to confirm a suspicion, or find yourself teamed up with a person with whom you don't have familiarity, or want to predict the behavior of an adversary to give you a negotiating advantage, how can you tell what their Go-To is? Run through the Big 4 Checklist.

While there is no surefire, singular way to exactly diagnose Go-Tos in an initial meeting or confrontation, the Big 4 Checklist arms you with the ingredients you need for accurate and relatively expedient classifications of how people handle conflict. Those ingredients: Mode, Timing, Tone, and Route.

Let's conduct a Big 4 Checklist for someone to whom you want or need to affix a Go-To Style. Pick a person. Then examine how they conduct themselves—*when they are presented with interpersonal stress*—with regard to the four ingredients as follows:

Mode
What mode of communication do they use? Do they prefer e-mailing, texting, social media posting, video chatting, phone calling, or meeting in person?

Competitors want direct confrontation, so if you share an office or dwelling with them, they'll opt for coming to you in person. If that's not feasible, they'll pick up the phone (calling if they are in an older demographic, texting if younger). They'll eschew communication mediums that can be stalled or require waiting for a response.

On the other hand, Avoiders and Analyzers (albeit for different reasons from each other) look to delay or circumvent conflictual interaction, so they tend to prefer e-mail: Avoiders so they can effectively ignore messages, Analyzers so they can use the medium to gather information before tackling a problem.

Accommodators and Collaborators are team and relationship-minded, so their communication will be effusive. Accommodators tiptoe about difficult matters, so they'll prefer the "digital shield" of social media and texting. Collaborators prefer the human contact of physical meetings or Zooms.

Timing

At what point in a conflict do they initiate communication? When an issue pops up, do they instantly reach out to you? Is there a brief pause prior to you hearing from them? Do weeks or months elapse?

Competitors and Collaborators will act immediately—Competitors because they are trying to prevent issues from boiling over, Collaborators because they want to get an early read on you.

Analyzers will take time to explore the situation from all angles. Accommodators will wait to see if they can solve the problem themselves. The response time of these two will thus, usually, be a few days (or weeks, depending on the complexity of a conflict).

If an issue festers on and on, if it seems like no confrontation is in sight, you're typically working with an Avoider. Unless forced to engage, Avoiders will be happy to let things drag out unresolved.

Tone

When pushed, how does their tone shift? Do they get louder or quieter? Does their body language become more demonstrative or more withdrawn? How do they structure their questions or comments?

Analyzers are data driven; they listen before they speak. At the start of interactions, they'll come across as quiet. So will Avoiders, by their nature of wishing they could stay out of it.

Competitors, of course, will be voluminous and loud.

Pinpointing tone is the quickest and easiest of the Big 4, but remember that there is more to it than merely amplitude. Sentence construction reveals a great deal about Tone. Does the person you're profiling probe, ask a lot of questions, get inquisitive? Likely they are an Analyzer. Are they chummy, more interested in the nature of the conversation than its substance? You're probably dealing with a Collaborator. Are they passive-aggressive? Surely an Accommodator. Blunt? Almost always a Competitor.

Route

If the person you picked was in conflict with you, what tack would they take? Would they come to you first and voluntarily? Would they go to others instead of you? Would they come to you *and* everyone else?

Competitors almost always start by attempting to meet people head on; they won't involve anyone else before speaking with you directly.

Analyzers will strive to get a sense of the whole picture, and Collaborators will try to identify underlying interests. They'll both engage with you but will also involve people around you in doing their "homework." At times, this may feel like they are going above your head or around your back—which they can and are willing to do (in their mind, well intending).

Conversely, before rolling up their sleeves with you, Accommodators are apt to seek support for their position elsewhere (or vent about responsibility, accountability, etc.).

And Avoiders will prefer to not engage with anyone.

It's critical to remember that the Big 4 Checklist pertains, specifically, to characteristic ways people react to being poked or prodded, needled, or put into compromised positions. Remember: evaluating Mode, Timing, Tone, and Route should only be done within the context of conflict.

When conducting a Big 4 Checklist, inquire not about how a person acts in general but rather how they react to weighty interpersonal friction.

Also remember that taken individually, each of the Big 4 Checklist ingredients provides only a partial picture of a person's Conflict Personality Style. Resist the urge to jump to a conclusion after examining just one of the four. Yes, sometimes Go-Tos will be obvious, such as a coworker who has been dodging staff meetings and never replies to messages about an annoying but relatively petty office policy. Without doubt, that's an Avoider. Or, take a case we were brought in to resolve about ten years ago—a case we affectionately call "The Great Post-it War of 2014."

A high-profile tech company hired us to resolve conflict between two of their top executives. From the outside, it looked like an idyllic culture to which college graduates flocked to recruiting luncheons in hopes of snagging a job. Armed with an alphabet of credentials after our names and a couple decades of battle-tested confidence, we were unfazed by power brokers. "Bring on the toughest you've got" was our reply to the company's request. Granted, we also knew that, when seriously Triggered, even the most restrained adults can behave like children. Sometimes, what is needed to resolve conflict is the "be nice to your neighbor, line up, raise your hand before you speak, say please and thank you" skill set championed by your old kindergarten teacher. (Shout-out to Mrs. Williams and Mrs. Harris, grandmasters of our educations.)

The two executives in the case—the CFO and the CMO—had corner offices (more like palaces) on opposites sides of the top floor of the corporation's headquarters. Breathtaking ceiling-to-floor windows lined both suites, overlooking a historic river. They had the latest exercise machines, overly fancy cappuccino makers, private baths . . . one could fantasize spending months on end in one of those spreads without any need or desire to leave. Taking into consideration the foreshadowing we dropped in the previous paragraph, does the label "spoiled brat" come to mind?

The dispute began almost literally over spilled milk. The CFO had decided to revamp the budget. In doing so, he made a switch to a new supplier, a start-up with a more efficient digital fulfillment platform, lowering costs. The first delivery was a container truck to restock the company cafeteria's nonperishable storeroom. It was late. By *three weeks*.

When this shipment finally arrived, the driver (who didn't appear to be old enough to have a license) backed into the loading dock safety barrier, scattering an impressive array of crates, cardboard boxes, and water cooler jugs. Packages of powdered milk and creamer burst open and blew all over the parking lot.

Upon watching the debacle unfold, the CMO grabbed a Post-it pad and a Sharpie and marched to the other side of the floor, scribbling a snarky comment about shortsighted, get-what-you-pay-for budgeting. She slapped the note on the CFO's door and returned to her office.

The next morning when the CMO arrived at work, she was greeted with a Post-it on her own door. "Marketing 101: ads should actually drive some revenue," it read.

She didn't enter her suite. Fishing into her shoulder bag, she turned around and headed directly to the CFO's office. No knock. No bursting in. *Smack!* Another note on the door.

By lunch, the CMO found a second return Post-it on her door. She Post-it noted right back.

For the next ten days, *slap* . . .

Smack . . .

Shwup.

The scrawlings on the Post-its, mostly in all caps, escalated. From commentary on job performance shortcomings and leadership foibles, the messages elevated to personal attacks.

"What kind of no-personal-life loser cuts employee vacation days?" the CMO wrote.

"Heaven forbid you actually have to do some work. Are you worried it will get in the way of the affair you're having?" wrote back the CFO across a whole row of Post-its.

"Is someone still mad at their mommy for giving them a pocket protector instead of a bicycle for their sixth birthday?"

"Insults are meaningless from someone who slept their way to every promotion they've ever had."

The company rumor mill went full tilt. Meetings that necessitated participation of both the CFO and CMO were canceled. Some employees were afraid to visit the top floor. Others started working from the conference room as a front-row seat, wondering what would happen when their execs bumped into each other in person. Within hours of the CEO returning from a spiritual retreat in Nepal, our phone was ringing.

We didn't need to conduct any interviews or give the CFO and CMO the Conflict Personality Style Assessment. A *major* conflict without screaming, furniture tossing, or lawsuit filing; passive-aggressiveness at every turn; the adult equivalent of teenage frenemies refusing to speak during a high school fight; conspicuously involving everyone around them by publicly displaying the Post-its—a classic illustration of dueling Triggered Accommodators.

You may have nailed this one easily; the drama lit a neon directional arrow to the Conflict Style. In less obvious cases, it's helpful to start with one fact about the conflict, and work from there. Start with the Big 4 Checklist, and notice the Mode, Timing, Tone, and Route of those in the dispute. Then layer on what you know about wider conflict—mainly, the Triggers of the colleague or family members involved. From there, their Go-Tos will emerge.

For example, imagine you are the sales and marketing director of a medium-sized regional agricultural equipment manufacturer. You oversee a sales staff of thirty. You feel you are well liked; your team even presented you, unexpectedly, with a considerably expensive year-end celebration gift last December. Recently, however, you've begun hearing rumblings through the company grapevine that your number two, Shonda, is upset with you. You strike up a casual conversation with Shonda in the breakroom. She is polite and her usual upbeat self, as if everything is fine. The next day you manufacture a one-on-one to give her an opportunity to share. Nothing. Just small talk. It's not until you corner your HR director to discuss corporate morale that you learn of Shonda's disapproval of the policy you initiated two months ago governing work-from-home accommodations. Ticking Route and Timing off the Big 4 Checklist, you can eliminate Competitor, Collaborator, and Analyzer. If Shonda was one of those, she would have approached you, and sooner. To figure out if she is an Avoider or Accommodator, you need to investigate Mode and Tone to get a sense for why Shonda isn't voicing her concern. Mode: In the past when warding off conflict, has

Shonda leaned on e-mail or social media? Tone: Is she more dismissive of problems or passive-aggressive toward them? Discerning that Shonda is an Avoider (the first of the two preceding questions' options) would clue you into her avoidance stemming from not wanting to deal with the new policy or feeling it's not worth her time. Alternatively, discovering that Shonda is an Accommodator would help you understand that her reticence to confront you concerns the impact it might have on the team's performance. Two very different sentiments. Accordingly, you'd take two different paths to discussing the matter with Shonda, because you'd know her priorities and steer clear of her Triggers. Knowing Shonda's Go-To could very well mean the difference between your unit's chemistry eroding until someone loses their job or making some tweaks that lead to record-setting numbers (with corresponding employee bonuses) and a spotlight in *Fast Company*.

We recognize that we've given you quite a density of ammo for reading people. There's a lot to process when you use the Big 4 Checklist. To aid your facility with the tool, here is an abridged "quick start" chart you can use as a cheat sheet:

Big 4 Checklist

	MODE	TIMING	TONE	ROUTE
THE AVOIDER	E-mail	As Late As Possible	Dismissive Then Blunt	Avoid Then Straight to the Source
THE COMPETITOR	Face-to-Face	NOW	Direct and Blunt	Straight to the Source
THE ANALYZER	E-mail	Immediate Communication; Slow Decision-Making	Inquisitive	Reach out to Everyone *Else* First
THE COLLABORATOR	Face-to-Face	NOW	Friendly and Inquisitive	Incorporate Everyone
THE ACCOMMODATOR	Social Media or Text Messages	Delayed	Passive-Aggressive	Avoid

THE WATER BOTTLE AND THE PEN

There are folks—those in your inner circle, for instance—whom you know intimately enough that you can reel off their Mode, Timing, Tone, and Route without a second's thought. We caution not to be too hasty in assessing these variables. Check your assumptions. Under duress, our closest of friends may think or act like an entirely different animal. We can't emphasize this enough: you're not assessing people's Mode, Timing, Tone, and Route in handling everyday, nonconflictual interactions. The goal is to enhance your relationships by better understanding colleagues' and loved ones' deviations from normal behavior. But what if you don't have the luxury of time to carefully work through a Big 4 Checklist? What if someone is already Triggered and you don't know why? What if you must read, on the fly, the variables we've been discussing? A simple water bottle or pen can make all the difference! Here are the steps to a useful, noninvasive technique:

1. Meet with the person you wish or need to assess. Ensure they have a drink in front of them for this meeting, preferably water due to our psychological (and socially reinforced) disposition toward hydration. A plastic water bottle is ideal (alas, not environmentally so) since people subconsciously play with, crinkle, and hold on to plastic bottles.

2. Start up a conversation on a benign subject—the weather, last night's box score . . . any small talk they are comfortable with. Over a couple-minute span, jot in your mind the number of drinks they take and their frequency of bottle fidgeting. This establishes a baseline.

3. Switch to the "main topic"—the reason why a need to assess their Go-To arose, the issue they are concerned about, why they're worked up, why they turned to you for help or are confiding in you. Work in references to Go-To Style differentiators, such as, "You know, my buddy Phil would charge that problem like a bull." Or, "I bet Sally in accounting would give the farm away to make everyone happy." Or, "Cousin Billie would run from that like the plague." Watch for drinking, bottle-squeezing, or

cap-turning occurrences to speed up or slow down. Rates noticeably greater than baseline are telltale signs that someone is anxious, thereby teaching you which Go-Tos you can eliminate or which Go-Tos may be the "worst teammate" of the person with whom you're conversing.

4. Continue, covering a range of issues or a range of Mode, Timing, Tone, and Route strategies, as needed, until you can narrow down the person's Go-To. If, at any point, they get uncomfortable, return to small talk or take a time-out before continuing to learn about their Go-To predilections.

We call this (shockingly) the Water Bottle Technique. A variation is the Pen Technique. Follow the same 1–4 steps above, incorporating a click-top pen instead of a water bottle. Either way, it's soothing to have something to occupy our hands with, and playing with a bottle or clicking a pen is nearly irresistible when we're not perfectly relaxed. If you'd like, include a pad of scratch paper. Many people doodle when discussing a unpleasant matter or one they'd rather keep at arm's length. When the setting allows, providing something to drink adds the benefit of a positive, health-conscious, generous gesture.

These techniques are effective first and foremost because they get people talking. The more people talk, the more clues they share regarding their preferences, peccadillos, and priorities. Thus, the easier it becomes to detect their Go-Tos—and their Triggers if those are not yet clear. Second, the Water Bottle and Pen Techniques give you a mechanism to explore sensitive items without having to directly call them out, without having to pry, without having to put someone on the spot. You can tangentially point to Mode, Timing, Tone, and Route or lean on other examples of them.

THE STARING CONTEST

What if you're dealing with an introvert who doesn't like talking? Or someone polished at workplace self-restraint? Or an Avoider? Avoiders long to avoid conflict. That means they'll want to avoid chatting about the kinds of things that Trigger them; they'll try to say as little as possible or try to change the topic when you're using the Water Bottle or Pen Technique. Good news: by definition, you're already homing in on their Go-To Style.

To tell the difference between Go-To-connected avoidance and either (a) simple introversion or self-restraint or (b) lack of interest in the narrative you posed, take a crack at the Staring Contest Technique. It works like this:

1. Ask a question about a hobby, recreation, or area of interest beloved by the person you are assessing—fly-fishing, foreign travel, art museums, biopic movies, you name it . . . or the ultimate: their kids. People let down their guard a bit when in one of their "happy places." Even the most reticent of folks will share when conversation is about their passion.

2. Casually and calmly inquire as to how they might handle an interruption to their happy place. For example, when they're bragging about their daughter's Little League stats, inquire, "What if another parent filed a complaint to nullify those stats on totally BS grounds?" *Very important*: Do not criticize, belittle, or insult them. You are not trying to get a rise out of them. You are exploring hypotheticals in a *positive*, conversational, understand-each-other-better manner.

3. Shut up and let them talk.

4. When they get to a stopping point, just sit back. Don't say a word. Smile and nod. Patience is the key here. Wait until they resume talking. Silence is a bit awkward for all of us; it prompts us to unveil more of our thoughts.

5. Keep this up until you feel you've gained adequate insight or until the other person is cuing that they're ready to stop (or until you, yourself, are tiring of the pregnant pauses).

The Staring Contest works thanks to human beings' innate desire for self-actualization. That basal need is tickled when Triggered, which prompts venting, wanting to get things off one's chest, and seeking validation for positions and opinions. The beauty of the Staring Contest is that it taps into this human nature without stirring up any actual conflict. To reiterate, you're conversing about hypotheticals. You're discussing them while sitting together, in friendly fashion. Staying quiet to allow the other person to ramble on gives them permission to open up. Nodding and encouraging demonstrates that you are supportive of whatever Go-To tendencies they divulge. Validation for them. Learning valuable insight for you. And a path for your relationship to strengthen via greater understanding.

Bear in mind, you should feel a decent sense of rapport (which we'll do a deep dive on in chapter 5) with someone before pulling out the Staring Contest. It can backfire with complete strangers; they'll likely excuse themselves from continuing the dialogue. "Oh, look at the time . . . gotta run." The Staring Contest requires a little faith, a level of comfort with each other, and your own willingness to settle for gaining just a snippet or two of wisdom if that's all the other person wishes to reveal.

WHO AM I?

Don't be surprised if the Go-To Style of someone you live with or work with is starkly different from their "usual self." It's no coincidence that Superman, Wonder Woman, Spider-Man, Batman, Iron Man, Invisible Woman, Wolverine, name your favorite superhero, all have alter egos. Steve Rogers transforms into Captain America, Orono Monroe turns into Storm, and so forth. Under what conditions does this change take place? When pushed or provoked, when humanity is threatened, when a wrong needs to be righted . . . when they get Triggered! Superheroes are their mild-mannered selves when there is no conflict at hand, just as your family members and colleagues are their mild-mannered selves on an ordinary, ho-hum day. The silver screen divergence from the real world is that superheroes transcend and defeat conflict thanks to military experiments gone awry, radioactive spider bites, and secret, physics-defying metallurgy. The rest of us are subject to human nature. We must wrestle conflict armed only with common sense, a little elbow grease . . . and a copy of *How to Get Along with Anyone*.

Because Go-Tos can snap someone completely out of character, it may take you a tad to get used to distinguishing Go-Tos from everyday personalities. To help you practice, here's a game:

Picture five friends or colleagues sitting, silhouetted, behind an opaque game show curtain. Their voices disguised, they each announce an abbreviated biography.

Person A. I like long walks on the beach and getting caught in the rain. I strongly prefer communicating through e-mail. When Triggered, I prefer to settle things right away. I always go directly to the source of conflicts, toward which or whom my tone is blunt. Friends have told me that I can get too impatient at times. Who am I?

Person B. I love big dogs, strong coffee, and red wine with Thai food. I don't love electronic communication, but I will settle for Zoom if I must. When there is bad news, I like to hear it directly from the horse's mouth and I'll go to the stables to get the news myself. When I'm bothered, you may couch my tone as aggressive. I'm unapologetic for that. Who am I?

Person C. I like cuddling and lazy Sunday mornings. I prefer sending e-mail to getting stuck chitchatting on the phone or at the watercooler. When I have to debate with someone, I make sure I'm prepared and I like to recruit allies before jumping in. While you know me as someone who takes weeks or months to deal with uncomfortable interpersonal situations, when I get geared up for them, I make strong, firm decisions. Who am I?

Person D. I like the outdoors, but if I can't be strolling through nature, I love cracking open a good adventure novel. In-person interaction is the best way to communicate. A phone call will do in a pinch. When conflict arises, I will make sure to talk with everyone involved, directly and indirectly. I prefer to keep the peace. Even in heated exchanges I do my best to maintain a friendly and engaging tone. If I'm not involved in a conflict, I'll still be happy to try to help. Tell me your secrets; I'm here to listen. Who am I?

Person E. I am not at all a cold-weather person. If I get stranded by a storm, give me some hot chocolate to sip alongside a fire in the fireplace. Company and warm chitchat is even better. I'm a calm person. While I rarely lose my cool, if something gets me out of my comfort zone, I'll lean on all the friends and family I have in my support system. I hope doing so makes issues go away on their own without me having to get my hands dirty. Who am I?

We like to play this "Who Am I?" game in our seminars and training programs. Attendees frequently comment on how the lightheartedness of the exercise helps take personal judgment and critique out of the equation. We often hear, as well, how people can't help but connect the dots to folks in their real-life networks. Did you find yourself doing the same? Whom do you know that is most like each of the game show participants?

How did you do on the Go-Tos themselves? Here are the answers:

A. AVOIDER

B. COMPETITOR

C. ANALYZER

D. COLLABORATOR

E. ACCOMMODATOR

Your understanding of how people behave, how they modify their behavior, when they're in conflict equips you to predict what they'll do—and equips you to see past a whole host of horse hockey, smoke screens, misdirection, manipulation, and worse, getting you out of the muck that traps people in conflict, getting you through to the goodies that are the nourishment of problem-solving. For tips on conquering this next step to conflict resolution, read on.

3

Get to the Underlying Interest

What feels like centuries ago, Doc E was blessed to enjoy a two-sport Academic All-American collegiate athletic career. He intended to parlay baseball exploits into a phone call during MLB's amateur draft. He ended up playing fullback for Dartmouth's top-ranked rugby program under the tutelage of legendary University of Cambridge and World Cup champion rugger Nigel Topping. Funny how unplanned twists of fate intertwine to teach us some of our most valuable life lessons.

Alex Mooney (now the first Hispanic US congressman from West Virginia) was a typical college kid. He studied hard, went to frat parties, volunteered for the Boys & Girls Club. He liked rap music. Typical, except for being a gifted athlete with incredible peripheral vision, able to discern patterns of an entire defense at a moment's glance. He grew up in the United States not having played high school or club rugby, but in short order he became a starting prop for a Dartmouth team loaded with overseas students from the sport's preeminent regions . . . Australia, New Zealand, South Africa, England, and France. Alex had a penchant for bull's-eye-hitting, no-look passes, making him an uncommon forward who could peel off the pack and play with the backs—a duality of play reflected in his current career in politics: being devotedly industrious at his core job (anchoring the front three of a scrum; fighting big government) while being able to quickly switch hats to serve those outside his purview (running the ball into open field; standing up for diversity on both sides of the aisle).

Alex's ability to see the big picture from multiple vantages allows him to identify opportunities most might overlook. So when the Big Green rugby team was a tick shy of the pace of play needed to contend for a national championship, he invited his speedster center fielder buddy, John Eliot (obviously not yet called "Doc E"), to come out to watch a game. It was a crisp autumn day in New Hampshire. Fall baseball was winding down and John, though he didn't express it to anyone and probably couldn't have put his finger on his torpor directly, was itching for competition. Alex picked up on it.

"I can't come to the game; I gotta hit," John told Alex as the two were wolfing down lunch, postclass.

"Aw, come on; you're in the cage all the time," Alex goaded. "Besides, the hitting in rugby is *way* better."

John chuckled. "Okay. I'll get in some swings at Leverone and then head over. You guys have your JV games before varsity, anyway, don't you?"

"They're called A-Side and B-Side in rugby, and we play 'matches.' And they're flipped today; we go first, so don't doddle around with all your 'routine' baseball perfectionism pine-tar-jock-scratching hokey-pokey. Get your butt over to the rugby pitch and see what real men do!"

"Yeah, yeah," John said. "Keep talkin'; that's what you're good at."

Three hours later, John was watching his first rugby contest. Truth be told, he'd been wanting to see a match for a long time. He'd been friends with Alex and a couple of the other players since they went on Dartmouth's famous First-Year Trips together. It was a sport he knew nothing about, and John loved learning about things completely foreign to him.

The final whistles blew. Dartmouth 54, UConn 0. A drubbing, highlighted by two Mooney tries, one an epic run from midfield, breaking tackle after tackle.

John hugged Alex in congratulations as he came off the pitch. "Man, that was *sweeeet!*"

"Thanks, bro. Your turn now," Alex replied as he cracked a giant Cheshire Cat grin and wrestled John to the ground.

Teammate and Scottish phenom Jon Eburne joined in, grabbing John's feet as Alex and another player held him down. Coach Topping yanked off John's sneakers, whipped on a pair of rugby cleats, and laced 'em up tight with John barely able to get out a "What the h@!&?" objection.

"The boys say you can run, mate," Nigel directed. "You got a bloody English bloke's name. An Eliot right oughta be able to play *this* game."

"Dude, get in there," Alex said, referring to the B-Side match about to start.

"You'll have a blast, man. *Do it!*" Eburne added.

"I don't know to play . . ." John fumbled. "I don't know any of the rules."

"You'll figure it out. Don't get caught up in the technical stuff. Just go out there and have fun," Alex said in a case-closed tone.

And with that, spawning an encouraging, beer-raising cheer from the A-Siders, Eliot haphazardly jogged onto the field. He didn't even know where to stand. Over the next ninety minutes he drew a record-setting number of penalty whistles. But he scored *four* tries! He was hooked.

Mooney watched from the sidelines, thrilled. His instincts for navigating conflict have served him well in his elected appointments, especially in today's increasingly divisive political arena. He works tirelessly to push people to remove blinders, temporarily set aside their biases, to try to understand how a seemingly parochial or unpopular opinion might be lain in a bedrock of basic freedoms, vital to protect, around which it's critical to find common ground. Granted, Alex has professionally polished his observation skills since his years as a coed. But even as a college rugger, Alex knew that people tend to get hung up on superficial exigencies, or use them as excuses, failing to get at what is really important. He understood that Eliot needed to unleash his competitive juices, be out on a ball field, and play with abandon. Those needs weren't being fulfilled in fall baseball practice. They would have continued going unfulfilled if John had remained focused on the issues of lacking experience, not knowing the rules, not having cleared it with his baseball coach, Mike Walsh (who, in all fairness, was a huge proponent of two-sport athletes), potentially risking injury, and so forth. Reasonable concerns, for sure. Any rational person can make a convincing argument against leaping into the middle of a sporting event without an iota of training or education, especially as one as "elegantly violent" as rugby. But there's a huge difference between what *sounds* fundamental to a problem and what *is*.

In conflict prevention and mediation seminars, we teach that in every skirmish or disagreement there is *position*, supported by *issues*, driven by an underlying *interest*. Together, these three components make up what is called the Conflict Agenda.

The *position* is what we see, or talk about, on the surface. (Not) playing rugby.

The *issues* are the problems associated with the position. In this case, messing up, looking foolish, costing the team a win, getting hurt. Very rarely will people offer only one issue to defend their position; people tend to bolster their stance (and quickly, to boot) with a veritable shopping list of issues. During Doc E's invitation to jump into his first rugby match, as you read about, he followed the script to the letter.

The *interest* is, ultimately, what matters in the end. Breaking free of an offseason rut that was causing a motivational drought—potentially on the way to physical conditioning loss and psychological malaise.

Interests get overlooked, disregarded, buried by the weight of issues. Often, it's unintentional. We develop positions quickly and forcefully, not stopping to consider what we want to accomplish. Thinking of the Conflict Agenda as an iceberg, one's position is the visible tip. Because it sticks out above the water, it's what garners focus. You can pull out a pair of binoculars and scan the horizon. It's still the only attention-catching item in the sea. When people engage in conflict, their positions therefore get the brunt of arguments. To try to "win," issues are layered on. It's common for tangential issues to be pulled into the fray (or fabricated altogether). But this is exactly why interpersonal friction can be so difficult to smooth. Positions and the myriad of issues swirling around them, disjointed or not, distract us from identifying each party's fundamental interest. Addressing interests is how conflicts get resolved.

THE ART OF ACTIVE LISTENING

Arguably, Alex Mooney's tactic for helping Doc E get past a counter-productive position, and the superfluous issues supporting that position, was, to be kind, cavalier. You might call a forced shoeing an archaic demonstration of camaraderie. We certainly won't claim that the ends justify the means. The takeaway of this story is that you can create more possibilities—open new doors . . . often, open others' eyes—when you get to underlying interests. Just get there wisely.

Active Listening is one of the wisest, most thoughtful strategies for identifying the interest triad of someone's Conflict Agenda. In our travels, we bump into many supremely smart, talented people. Despite their abilities, we find that many don't utilize Active Listening—the capitalized version, as there is a methodology to listening actively when in heated, uncomfortable, or pressure-packed situations. Typically, people either (a) don't realize there is an art to effective Active Listening, or (b) get caught up such that they lose perspective and neglect the processes that allow for successfully working through conflict—the very reason we've written *How to Get Along with Anyone*.

Chapters 1 and 2 have hopefully armed you to circumvent the pitfall of (b). If you know the answer to (a), congrats! For those wanting a refresher, take a second to reflect on the breakdown of communication components. Research has shown that between Homo sapiens (fascinatingly, between all primates, in fact), exchanges are comprised of three elements: verbal, vocal, and visual, with a disproportional amount of information transferred by each element. The distribution is as follows:

7%	VERBAL	What is said; the words themselves.
38%	VOCAL	How something is said; a speaker's projection, resonance, and tone.
55%	VISUAL	The way it's said; a speaker's facial expression and body language.

Less than one-tenth of a message proffered has to do with word choice. Have you ever been in the middle of an argument when the other person calls out, referencing a much earlier point in the conversation, "Well, you said _____." The blank is an oddly or surprisingly nuanced, decentral, or taken-out-of-context statement. It's a stark interruption. Likely, the person missed a substantial amount of what you've been trying to get across. How do we know? That statement illustrates a priority placed, rigidly so, on specific verbiage that isn't germane to present dialogue. When someone does this, they've clearly been holding on to a piece of minutia that Triggered them and they haven't let go, mulling on it while you've been talking. By definition, upside-down "listening."

Further, more than half of communication requires using your eyes instead of your ears. A tricky conundrum of neurobiology is that our five senses, to a degree, compete for a place in our consciousness. The more you try to narrowly hear with your ears, the less you are Active Listening with your eyes and intuitions. The key to Active Listening is observation. Which is one big reason why we're witnessing an escalation of hostility in society in general: the personal interaction pendulum has swung heavily in favor of digital mediums—e-mailing, texting, Twitter and Threads posting—using platforms that leave off, truncate, compromise, or discourage taking time for the vocal and visual components of communication. You may have to use such media. Do so with care; limit their incorporation as best you can when you need to implement Active Listening, particularly when seeking to identify and understand interests. And absolutely refrain from staring down at your phone while you're chatting with someone. If you want to be an elite communicator, don't even do a periodic glance to check notification pings.

Active Listening is, indeed, more time and energy consuming than "letting someone talk." You can't just "pay attention." You've got work to do. You must watch, encourage, empathize, wait, reflect, ask, clarify, and accept. Notice that we didn't list items like share, converse, explain, correct, banter, inform, or really any verb related to you running your trap. Active Listening is about the person in the other chair. It's their show, to which you are tuning in. Active Listening is not dialoguing. In a nutshell, you are trying to embolden someone to put their full monologue on display, with as much animation as they may wish to express. If you slide into dialogue, adding yourself on the stage, you fall prey to giving an appearance of listening without properly doing so. You can fool yourself into thinking that you've heard what's important to them.

> "None of us has a monopoly of wisdom and we must always be ready to listen and respect other points of view."
>
> **—Queen Elizabeth II**

Ask yourself, how often in conversations are you partially tuning someone out because you're contemplating the subject matter, reframing it in your mind, tending to how you feel about it, or planning your response? Be honest. You're not alone. We all do this; we all want to be prepared when the interaction baton is handed to us. Gathering your thoughts and crystalizing insightful comments are valuable, high-utility skills—just not at the juncture of discerning another person's Conflict Agenda.

Don't worry; there are a few rudimentary, easy-to-execute techniques that can help you foster functional, conflict-quashing communication. The next time you find yourself stuck on a position or its orbiting issues, flip on Active Listening turbo mode by doing the following:

- **Be Present; Be Centered.** When you want to hear someone, fully—and want them to know they are being heard—you need to be all in. You need to demonstrate that the other person, in that moment, is your entire world. Temporarily suspend any other concern you have beyond the goal of simply listening (actively). Remove distractions. Mute your cell phone *and* put it away. Close the lid of your laptop; turn off your desktop. Put down your pencil (or pen). Take a slow, relaxing breath. When the other person is talking, let what they are saying fill your consciousness. Make mental notes, yes, but don't be in processing mode. For the time being, don't be judgmental of what they are saying. Don't plan your response or "get ahead" in the interaction. By all means, never interrupt.

- **Make Eye Contact.** While people don't like the confrontational feeling of someone being "right in their face" (hence why we'll sit side by side in chapter 5), they very much want to be heard. When they are talking, look them in the eyes. That is a surefire way to establish that you are attending to them. Remember, though, take in the whole picture, their body language, expressions, mannerisms, and shifts in posture. Do your best to monitor them all without your eyes darting all over the place. Channel Alex Mooney's peripheral vision. Peripheral vision is about wanting to see the whole picture rather than picking out a singular target.

- **Stay Off the Stage.** You really do have to dial off your desire to participate, to add your take or thoughts. Elite Active Listening requires just that, listening—in spades. Observe, listen, observe, listen, observe, observe. We can't punctuate this enough. Spend the time entirely centered on what (and *how*) the other person is sharing. We mean 100 percent. Fight the urge to weave in your opinion, view, and so on. Fight the urge to oppose what is being expressed, even if you vehemently disagree or know a statement is false. There will be time for that later. Put the need in a little figurative lockbox.

- **Be Patient; Wait for It.** Heading into Active Listening, remind yourself that there will be ebb and flow; there will be natural pauses. Don't fill those pauses! Wait. Invite the other person to continue. Employ encouraging body language. Nod. Smile.

- **Use Volley Phrases.** When waiting for someone to continue doesn't work, exercise Volley Phrases—neutral phrases that merely return the conversation to the other party without changing topic or meaning, or without adding anything new. For example, when it feels like someone is stopping, say, "That's interesting. Can you tell me more?" And go back to patiently waiting. Words that relay you are *genuinely* engrossed stimulate further sharing. Other Volley Phrases include the following:

  "Hmm . . . " (with a correspondingly positive, interested facial expression)
  "Tell me more."
  "Tell me more about _____."

"That's a fascinating point."

"Huh, I hadn't thought about that." or "I haven't thought of it that way."

"You don't say!"

"Run that by me again."

"That's quite something."

"Please, go on."

～ **Use Reflexive Questioning.** If you grill someone or pepper them with inquiry, it will cannibalize your efforts at getting them to talk. There's a decent chance they'll become defensive, escalating conflict. Asking questions, though, is a golden Active Listening tool for learning about underlying interests. How do you effectively do the latter without treading into the former? Reflexive Questioning: feeding someone's words—and often, more importantly, feelings—back to them, in the form of a question, regarding topics on which you want to move past positions and interests. For instance, a business partner is annoyed about the number of client calls you're scheduling every week. She fumes, "You don't consult me. You micromanage my calendar. You rack up meeting after meeting when I'm already swamped." Using Reflexive Questioning, you ask, "You're super swamped, huh?" Although pissed, she dives deeper into her stress over feeling time strapped. It turns out that she has a *fantastic* brainstorm for a game-changing product . . . without enough unstructured time to develop the idea. By honoring her language choice, you give credence to her views, aiding in her feeling heard and valued, while permitting her to open the floodgates on a subject that's important to her. The result is her revealing her true interest—something of great interest to you as well. There are logistics to be ironed out in balancing biz dev with customer service, but you're off to the problem-solving races. Reflexive Questioning is a simple way to keep an exchange focused on searching for underlying interests. Make sure to ask this type of question in a respectful tone, authentically showing that you care.

～ **Use Open-Ended Questions.** When you're asking questions, don't let the other person off the hook by being able to supply a one-word or finite answer. If a mere yes or no will do, your prompt was Close-Ended. Use Open-Ended probing; use cues that necessitate elaboration.

〜 **Tap Your Inner Columbo (aka Clarify).** The late, brilliant thespian Peter Falk gave the world an incredible gift in his eccentrically genius television character, Lieutenant Frank Columbo. Winning four Emmys for the TV series, Falk deftly portrayed the craft of clarification for disarming others and engendering their divulgence. The basic principle is to periodically check in with someone about what you're hearing *and observing* instead of assuming you are correctly judging their words and expressions. You check in and allow them to correct you or tweak your interpretation. It's extremely empowering. Here are a few variations on this technique's phraseology:

"I heard you say _____. Did I hear that right?"

"It sounds like _____?"

"I'm picking up on _____. Am I in the ballpark?"

"If my takeaway was _____, what would I be missing?"

"Would it be reasonable to assume that you _____?"

"Tell me if I'm on track. What I'm hearing is _____."

"I sense that you _____?"

"I'm noticing _____. Would that be fair to say?"

"I'd guess _____. Hopefully that's not far off?"

〜 **Attend to the Total Meaning.** We'll wear you out with reminders that the verbal portion of communication contains a minuscule fraction of the information available. It is essential to figure out the emotional, attitudinal, and contextual lattice to what is being communicated. As a rule of thumb, when you respond (including via the strategies provided above), respond first to the feelings and attitudes displayed. Also, look for congruency: what is being said and how it is being said should match. When they don't, something's not right. The speaker is being disingenuous, hiding an interest, throwing up a smoke screen, afraid to open up, attempting to manipulate the discourse (or you), or not ready to address a topic.

ᔰ **Empathize.** Of all the Active Listening tools, perhaps the most crucial is empathy. To get at underlying interests, especially when someone is shielded, nervous, on edge, or wary of your intentions (the whole host of which, and then some, are bread-and-butter feelings in conflict), you must proverbially put yourself in their footwear. With positive regard. Unconditionally. A central objective of Active Listening is to decipher where a person is coming from and why. Don't guess—that is, don't look inside yourself for clues. Find out; look to them for answers. This means that you must be accepting. You may not like what you hear or see. You may not like the other person, period. You don't need to; you don't need to agree. But you do need to accept what they are communicating, from where they are communicating it. Otherwise, you'll never completely uncover their interests. If you find it hard to suspend your own perspective, play the Time Travel Game. Pretend you're an archaeologist. Pretend the person you're speaking with was just teleported back from the year 5000 AD. Who knows what life will entail then, what daily ups and downs will be like, what quagmires will be similar to today's, what will be vastly divergent. Your viewpoint doesn't apply. It's your job to put the picture puzzle together by having someone describe the pieces to you.

That fall afternoon in Hanover, John stayed on the rugby pitch long after the sun went down, showering Coach Topping with questions about every intricacy of the game. He joined the squad on the spot. Little did he know, his *real* education was about to take off. What he'd learn about working with people—seeking first to understand, relationships over results, and so much more—from his rugby mates and his world-class college roommate, John Goff, transcended the theoretical behavioral science he studied in the classroom.

Eight months later, Eliot found himself on the A-Side's annual international tour, that year barnstorming Canada, playing sevens against the top university programs and professional clubs. The tour concluded in Montreal. Dartmouth defeated McGill, Concordia, and the University of Montreal in a clean sweep, posting 164 points. John snagged 45 of them. Customary in rugby culture, the four sides joined together for a night on the town, teaching each other songs and cementing bonds of friendship still enjoyed to this day. With Hanover being an easy three-hour drive south, a few of the lads decided to make it an all-nighter and hit the road for home. Mooney, Eburne, and inside center Tim "Elvis" Dunning, with Eliot as the designated driver, piled into the team's support car, an old Isuzu Trooper, loaded with balls, medical supplies, training equipment, and uniforms. There wasn't enough room, so Dunning wedged his way into the back, burrowing into the gear.

The miles ticked by. In a short hour they were at the border, John barely holding his eyelids open, the others completely passed out. Eliot rolled the beat-up Isuzu to a cautious stop at the US Customs station, rolling down his window. The boys hadn't showered. No doubt there was an ample wafting of liquor. The overflowing duffle bags of mud-caked jerseys didn't scream out "diplomatic convoy." Imagine being a border guard and watching this Greek tragedy pull up at your gate.

It was three o'clock in the morning. The Customs agent raised his industrial-sized flashlight, shining it in John's eyes. He skipped right past the formality of asking citizenship, purpose of trip . . . "Anything to declare?" seemed laughably unnecessary.

"What's going on here?"

The picture they were projecting hadn't registered in John's mind. He was a swirling mixture of euphoric from victorious play and almost-coma exhausted. "We're Dartmouth students," he said, accidently infused with a wee bit too much John Belushi–esque confidence.

"Uh huh," the agent muttered without a nanosecond's consideration. "What do you have in the truck?"

Eliot roused a bit, thinking it was an invitation to brag on the team's conquests. "Oh, our rugby kits. We're on the way back from a Canadian Tour. We—"

The officer cut John off promptly, unimpressed. He scanned his flashlight beam across the back seat and into the cargo area. Alex woke up.

"Dude, why are we stopped? And who's the @$$ shining a light in my face?"

Then from under the ball bags Tim squawked, "I need a beer."

The border guard snapped his light into the rear as his other hand quickly slid to the holster on his belt. "Is there a *person* in the back?"

"Oh," Eliot chimed, "that's just Elvis."

"GET OUT OF THE VEHICLE. NOW."

That US Customs agent wasn't credited a gold star for Active Listening that morning. We don't blame him given the hour, the dangers of his profession (and the anxieties that go with them), or the fact that the day prior the US Border Patrol had distributed a warning about a recent uptick in drug trafficking. But he did restrict the verbal, vocal, and visual data at his disposal via curtailed questioning. He was too busy processing assumptions (and his safety plan) to gather valuable clues as to the innocuousness of the ragtag bunch in front of him. He misassessed. Quite uncharacteristically, actually. Law enforcement officers are usually well trained in Active Listening techniques. They are pros at using tools like Volley Phrases and Reflexive Questioning. The shrewdest detectives take empathy to a whole new level. Timmy, Jon, Alex, and John didn't get much empathy.

Contrast that to another, more recent experience of Doc E's. His mother needed to consult with an orthopod about knee pain that had been gradually worsening. He accompanied her to see Dr. Gregory Brick, a professor of orthopedic surgery at Harvard and a lower-extremity trauma and complex reconstruction specialist at the renowned Brigham and Women's Hospital. Dr. Brick's curriculum vitae is as impressive as it is lengthy. You might expect a scholarly ivory-tower champion of champions to be overly intellectual, so advanced as to struggle relating to the common care recipient. Not Greg. Far, far from it. Unreservedly, Doc E would rate Dr. Brick's patient interaction skills as *the* best he's ever beheld in a physician.

"Teach me about yourself," Greg led with as he sat down alongside Doc E's mom (not having her propped on an uncomfortable, sanitary paper–lined examination table, by the way). "What do you like to do? What are your daily hobbies and passions?"

He listened intently. He encouraged Doc E's mom to wax on about reading, tending to neighborhood wildlife, walking the beach on foggy days. He was *genuinely* interested. In an age of patient contact hour metrics, volume demanded by clinic CFOs and, more insidiously, by the insurance industry, Dr. Brick's words and actions instantly dismissed any sense of rush or time limit.

"That's really lovely; tell me more!" he commented. Textbook Volley Phrase usage.

Greg waited for Doc E's mom to signal that she'd shared all she wanted before he dove into knee mechanics and therapeutic options. And when he did, it wasn't a cold barking of instructions to move her leg in various directions while he recorded flexibility angles and pain ratings.

"How does it feel when you reach for a plate or glass on a shelf above your head?"

Greg was striving to understand the total meaning, the *feelings* that accompanied the biomechanical explanations. The beautiful art of Active Listening!

Eye contact and clarifying, honest, and deep empathy—Dr. Brick had the works. What's more, he didn't recommend a treatment. He thoroughly walked through every option, from doing nothing to a full knee reconstruction, providing every ounce of insight needed to make an informed decision, yet making it clear that the best choice was Doc E's *mom's* choice.

Doc E's mother departed her doctor's appointment knowing she'd been heard, understood, respected—confident that her surgeon had her back.

> "We have two ears and one mouth so that we can listen twice as much as we speak."
>
> —**Epictetus**

ANGRY MOMMA BEAR

An entirely different mother story exemplifies the importance of getting to underlying interests—and the implications for ignoring this step or remaining mired in positions or issues.

Doc G was hired to conduct a two-part conflict training program for school counselors at a large, urban academy. The backdrop was a lawsuit filed by the parent of an Ivy League–bound senior, who believed her child had been unfairly suspended. But tips for preventing parent meltdowns (maybe even, fingers crossed, for resolving the pressing legal battle) was what the administration hoped they might glean. Doc G wasn't ten minutes into the in-service when the principal, putting on an air as if he was starring in a *Law & Order* episode, piped up.

"So how do you resolve conflict with someone who is certifiable?"

Doc G immediately donned his Active Listening hat. As bad luck had it, a veteran English teacher, Mrs. Stevens, had fallen ill a few months prior. A junior substitute, Ms. Lane, was brought in to cover for her. On the substitute's last day before Mrs. Stevens was scheduled to return, the students finished with their busy work (which this substitute was prone to assigning in lieu of instruction) nearly as quickly as it was handed out. The students congregated in the back of the room, gathering around a ringleader, Logan. Shouting and whooping soon emanated from the congregation. The substitute rushed over, bursting into the huddle. Logan was showing a video on his phone. Snatching the device, the substitute was greeted with a clip of several girls, who attended the school, snorting cocaine off a bathroom vanity. Aghast, she fumbled to shut the phone off while ordering Logan to the front of the room.

"This use of technology in this manner is strictly prohibited. Your phone is being confiscated," Ms. Lane bellowed. "And worse, you're a cyberbully," her lambasting continued. "You have violated those poor girls' privacy. I will personally see to it that you are punished to the fullest extent. Get yourself to the principal's office *right now*."

The principal, Mr. Adams, was already watching the forwarded video link when Logan arrived. "This is unacceptable," he said. "Ms. Lane is exactly right. You are a cyberbully, Logan. I am suspending you from school this instant."

Logan was sent home at one o'clock. Afraid to call his mom, he hoofed it. The principal didn't call Logan's mom. Nor did Ms. Lane, or anyone else. A single caretaker working two jobs, Logan's mom didn't get to the house until after he was asleep. Logan conveniently neglected to share the suspension news with Mom at breakfast the following morning. He pretended it was a perfectly normal day, proceeding to show up at school like nothing had happened. His old English teacher would be there. Mrs. Stevens wasn't aware of yesterday's calamity, right?

Oh, was she. The substitute had posted the whole circus on Facebook—her slanted recount of the classroom episode, links to articles on "Criminal Child Psychology," the cocaine video clip, and, no less, a clip from another student's phone (which she also commandeered) showing the public humiliation of Logan in front of his peers.

The moment the start-of-class bell rang, Mrs. Stevens paraded Logan up to her desk. "You have the gall to show your face? After what you've done? Logan, bullying will *not* be tolerated."

Off to the principal's office Logan went. Again, he was lit into. Again, he was suspended. On this day, however, Logan's mother decided to swing home for a quick lunch siesta. Little did she know how restful the getaway wouldn't be!

Logan explained the whole confluence of events, emphasizing, of course, his incredulity over the "victim" labeling of girls, who were portraying substance abuse as socially sexy. They hadn't been yelled at, sent to the principal's office, suspended, or held accountable in any way. Logan's mom went *ballistic*. She blasted the school, the entire district, calling out teachers and administrators, on every social media channel at her disposal. She went to the local NBC news station. She recruited an attorney friend to file a seven-figure lawsuit. When the school's general counsel proposed mediation, she refused and demanded a sit-down with the superintendent, principal, teacher, and substitute teacher.

The meeting was reluctantly arranged. Logan's mother stormed in, intentionally a half hour late. She adamantly reeled off her positions:

∿ Revoke Mrs. Stevens's tenure and fire her.

∿ Ban Ms. Lane from ever again substituting in the district.

∿ Suspend Principal Adams for the rest of the year.

- Publish a formal School Board apology in every state newspaper.

- Allow her son to retake the English class with a different teacher, or allow him to take the equivalent class as a transfer at another school in the district because obviously there was a bias against him.

- Put $50,000 in unmarked bills in a duffel bag and leave it behind the gym at 2:23 a.m. next Tuesday night.

We kid you not. To this day we're still chuckling about the last request. But back to positions, issues, and interests. As you can probably reckon, Logan's mother brought a variety of issues to the table to support her positions. Her chief issues were as follows:

- **Protocol Breaches.** She was not notified when her son was suspended . . . *twice.*

- **Lack of Security.** Her son was left to walk home on his own . . . without his phone to protect him in case of emergency.

- **Lack of Due Process.** Her son was "convicted" by the principal—and by public opinion—without representation or a fair hearing, violating state law.

- **Double Jeopardy.** Her son was prosecuted a second time without a second action.

- **Discrimination.** Her son's gender was being held against him. Case in point: the substitute's Facebook message referencing the "crime" of "boys being boys" while the cocaine-snorting girls were let off scot-free.

- **Lack of Enforceability.** Her son had finished all assigned work, including the in-class busy work, and no further directives had been issued, thus giving him implied freedom. Watching and showing open source, unrated video is not illegal, unlike the drug use, which is a felony.

The meeting didn't progress to anything resembling a negotiation. It broke down minutes later. The school officials zeroed in on the issues they felt they could tackle. They tried to address them with a retraction and public apology by the teacher and substitute, along with a suspension of the girls and turning that case over to the police. The offer did nothing to quell Logan's mother's anger. She walked out. The conflict festered on.

During the in-service, Doc G took the opportunity to help the group debrief. The school's personnel were treating Logan's mother as if she was a Competitor. They were being as direct as they could—and presuming Momma Bear was doing the same, taking her at face value. Doc G assisted the group in walking her actions through a Big 4 Checklist.

"What Go-To are we dealing with here?" Doc G posed.

"*Competitor*!" blurted out most in the group.

"What behavioral data shows us that?" Doc G asked.

"She's being *so* aggressive," said one of the school counselors.

"And . . . ?" Doc G continued. Blank stares. He waited; no additional comments. "Keep in mind that you usually can't draw a straight line from one point on a graph."

"Whoa; hold up," another counselor interjected. "I've got it in my notes here. There's Mode, Timing, Tone, and Route, right?"

The group caught on immediately and started tossing in what they knew.

"She's all over social media."

"She didn't waste any time filing that ridiculous lawsuit."

"She's going to everyone and their cousins and their cousins' dogs." A chuckle from the crowd.

The second counselor then said, "Doesn't that mean she's a Collaborator?"

Bingo. The Competitor posturing was a smoke screen for pushing positions and issues. Collaborators tend to do that; they hide their core interest. Or they circumvent it to push an agenda for someone else. To keep from being upfront about what they are really after, Collaborators lean heavily on issues, a lot of issues, exaggerating them, creatively spinning them into *big* issues, making some up entirely. The bag of cash request was the tip-off that the mother was definitely a Collaborator—it had nothing to do with the situation at hand or the rest of her requests. Competitors don't muddy the water or complicate things; they go right after the elephant in the room.

Though the situation was drastically mishandled, stepping back to conduct a Big 4 Checklist saved the day. Thankfully, most conflict is like that. Regardless of how bad interpersonal interactions have become, despite any "botching," putting problems aside for a minute to properly assess and understand the people involved can completely turn the tables.

Once the school counselors finally got a grasp on the mother's Conflict Personality Style (her Trigger being obvious), the next piece of the equation was to dig in to *why* she put forth the positions she did. Without Momma Bear present, all Doc G could do at the time was simulate the strategies of this chapter. But with the pending lawsuit hanging over the school, every person in the room had skin in the game, and it turned out to be a stimulating conversation. The staff keyed in on how to identify an outlier, then how to use Active Listening to explore where it was coming from and why.

We realize you don't have the luxury of having participated in the initial meeting with Logan's mom and can't access any of the vocal or visual communication. Take a stab anyway. Look back at Logan's mother's list of positions. Remove judgment. Take your own emotion out of play. Reflect on being Logan's mom, someone who just wants the best for her child. Knowing that a Collaborator will flood the zone with issues to distract, knowing in the end they are looking for a collaborative solution that prioritizes their team rather than themselves, can you pinpoint which position is the outlier?

Retaking English. That's the sole position, underneath all the smoke-screening issues, that leans toward partnering (of sorts) and toward helping the "team" (in this scenario, Logan).

Doc G uplifted the counselors and their administrators; they had a new, substantially positive mission: understand the motivation behind the position of retaking English.

Since the training program was aligned with the school's fall/spring teacher in-service release days, Doc G was champing at the bit to return to conduct part two a few months later. Between the sessions, he'd gotten word that the suit had been dropped.

"What happened? Tell me everything," Doc G said as he rejoined the group.

"It was *so* great using the Active Listening tools," one of the participants narrated. "Logan's mother completely changed her tune. She admitted that Logan had been offered a bunch of scholarships . . . one by Yale worth nearly $300,000! The trouble was, that kind of award is contingent upon maintaining a top grade point average through graduation. It turns out, Logan was bombing a certain English class with a certain English instructor (you got it, Ms. Stevens) who he didn't like, and his GPA had dropped below the required threshold. His mom had thought it through. If she ranted on Twitter about how a teacher was out to get her poor baby and ruin his big Ivy League scholarship and had given him a B when he deserved an A, she wouldn't garner much sympathy. But the suspension dustup presented leverage. From her perspective, create a lot of big, sticky, hairy, embarrassing media flash-point issues and the low-hanging fruit would be a cinch."

All Momma Bear was after was a path to her baby bear walloping senior English. If the superintendent had fired everyone involved, published an exposé on *Hard Copy* blowing the whistle on high schools skirting constitutional rights, cast a bronze statue of Logan, and supplied that duffel bag stuffed with $150k for good measure, would that have succeeded? Heck, no. None of those positions satisfy the underlying interest: Logan receiving a full ride to Yale University.

"Way to go!" Doc G applauded. "Where do things stand?"

"We told our admin what she really wanted. No joke, *the* next day, Logan's mom was in our principal's office shaking hands to drop the case in exchange for allowing Logan to retake the English exam and finish the semester with a different teacher."

Hopefully you'll never have to deal with an Angry Momma Bear. If you do, or find yourself in some other iteration of conflict that involves a plethora (and then some) of positions and issues, from genuine to fabricated, Active Listening is an ace up your sleeve. Use it to shut off the spigot of time, money, and energy syphoned by conflict that drags on, stalled on the surface or bogged down in inconsequential details, smoke screens, and distractions.

And don't forget to listen to yourself. You, too, can get caught up in your positions and issues. Similar to what Doc E discovered with his rugby coaches and teammates, it's advisable to surround yourself with people good at Active Listening, who will watch out for you and help you stick close to your cherished, underlying interests. We're all human; we go down rabbit holes in our odd little existences. We make decisions for irrelevant reasons, then must live with those decisions. If you do nothing else before you flip to the next page, take a second to do an accounting of the all-pro Active Listeners in your inner circle. Ask them to Actively Listen the next time you're bound up in a conflict. Lean on them to help you refocus so you can get back to putting the goods of this book to work.

IT'S A TWO-WAY STREET

In the regular course of conversation, a misunderstanding arises. You cordially run through your thesis. The other person is dumbfounded: "How could you possibly _____?"

You explain it a second time. A third time. They *still* don't get it.

"What's the problem?" you ask. "I've laid it out perfectly clearly."

The chat abruptly turns personal. "No, it's *not* clear; you're obscuring the point. I think you're doing it intentionally to try to spin the argument because your stance is indefensible otherwise."

Yeeesh! What was a friendly debate is suddenly an attack. How did that happen?

By and large, this sort of conflict begins unintentionally. Either you were explaining your position (and leaning on issues to advocate for your position) absent the context of your underlying interest or the other person wasn't attending to your underlying interest. Neither of you did so of any ill will. But failing to mutually understand interests created discord that then escalated.

Regardless of whether an escalation is innocent or accidental, or a product of less than ethical behavior—regardless of whether the escalation originated in your camp or theirs—you've got to bring the rocket back down to Earth. You've got to get to a place where you can both clearly elucidate your underlying interests and turn the conversation down a path where *both* parties' interests can be satisfied.

Sometimes the tools we've covered thus far are all you need. Sometimes, as we'll see in the next chapter, you need a specialized gear kit to turn off the rocket boosters—to defuse the emotion of escalated conflict . . .

4

Defuse Emotion

hristian Bale has enjoyed a robust and diverse forty-year acting career. During one stretch of acclaim, *Forbes* pegged Bale as the highest-grossing male performer in the United States. He calls himself the luckiest guy in the world. Humble? You bet; Bale maintains one of Hollywood's most low-key, most private of profiles. Lucky? No, not a word we'd use to explain Bale's success. From serial killer (*American Psycho*) to superhero (Batman in *The Dark Knight* trilogy), from POW (Dieter Dengler in *Rescue Dawn*) to vice president (Dick Cheney in *Vice*), Christian has physically transformed himself to such a degree, repeatedly, that reviewers have lauded on him monikers such as "the most versatile actor in history." Consider the self-control required to add and subtract one hundred pounds of body weight at will between roles. He restricted himself to eating nothing more than one can of tuna and one apple a day—for four months, without a single cheat day, without a moment's lapse in willpower—to portray the sleep-deprived, emaciated Trevor Reznik in *The Machinist*. He bloated himself to the point of being almost unrecognizable to play Cheney. His track record for embedding himself in his characters is dotted by 76 film and television awards and 196 nominations. True tradecraft.

Bale's command over mind and body is impressive, highlighted by the remarkable personal anonymity he adheres to—dodging attention in a fishbowl business, with paparazzi around every corner, with even a quick trip to pick up a bottle of milk turning into a PR event (no matter how dark the shades he dons). So it came as quite a shock when an audio recording of Bale completely losing his cool surfaced on social media.

It was February 2009, three months before *Terminator Salvation* opened in theaters. It was supposed to be *the* summer blockbuster, and studio executives were hoping that it would jump-start the lagging *Terminator* franchise. But the film took far longer than anticipated to get off the ground. There were starts and stops. Creative disagreements among producers led to casting challenges; the script had trouble recruiting star power. Award-winning screenwriter Jonathan Nolan suddenly, without warning, left the project. And then the publicity nightmare hit.

> I want you off the %#@&ing set, you prick . . .
> Think for one %#@&ing second. What the %#@& are you doing?!

> For %#@&'s sake, man, you're amateur.
> It's the second time that he . . . he doesn't give a %#@& about what's going on in front of the camera. Do you understand my mind is not in the scene if you're doin' that? Stay off the %#@&ing set, man.
> You're unbelievable, man. You're UN-%#@&in' believable . . .
> I'm going to %#@&in' kick your %#@&in' @$$ if you don't shut up for a second, alright.

You could viscerally hear the steam coming out of Bale's ears, the hair on the back of his neck standing at full starch. He railed on and on . . . and on!

> You're trashin' my scene. You do it one more %#@&in' time and I ain't walkin' on this set if you're still hired.
> I'm %#@&ing serious!
> You and me, we're %#@&in' done professionally.

Right when positive promotional press was paramount, out comes twelve-plus minutes of Bale going absolutely Looney Tunes. The master of composure, caught on tape, having an epic meltdown.

During filming in New Mexico, the movie's director of photography, Shane Hurlbut, walked onto the set in the middle of a take—right through Bale's sightline. Apparently, it wasn't the first time Hurlbut had done that. Bale finally snapped.

Bale was in the process of channeling a seething, inner rage for a highly confrontational scene . . . for a role he was deeply passionate about, that he'd worked his fanny off to resuscitate through countless production hiccups. He'd just logged a multiweek string of eighteen-hour days on location. Filming was way over budget. The entire crew was anxious about getting the movie done, and done right.

Most people could understand how Bale was feeling at that moment, sympathize with him, and maybe even excuse his behavior altogether. We all have bad days at the office.

But it was Christian Bale.

The recording went viral. Bale's f-bomb tirade was taken wildly out of context by fans and critics alike. Despite his long-standing history of ducking the media, Bale, mortified by the episode, immediately booked airtime on Los Angeles radio station KROQ. He was unreservedly apologetic, taking full responsibility. "I was out of order beyond belief," he said. "I make no excuses for it. There is nobody who has heard that tape who has been hit harder than me. The one thing that disturbs me so much is that I've heard a lot of people saying that I seem to think I'm better than anybody else. Nothing could be farther from the truth. I'm a lucky man. I never forget that and that is why I put so much into what I do, and why I care so much about it and why sometimes that enthusiasm just goes awry." Bale went on to say that barely an hour after his rant, he and Hurlbut made amends.

The damage had already been done though. The flood of swirling negative commentary created a backlash that put a serious dent in *Terminator Salvation*'s box office earnings. The film was panned. Ironically, Bale's crack-up is probably the most memorable thing about the movie.

And remember it we should. If even the most measured, most collected of trained actors can't keep his emotions in check when he gets knocked off center one too many times, how can we expect it of the rest of the mere mortals that we are surrounded by daily—and of ourselves? Alas, without realizing it, we do tend to maintain this expectation. Research demonstrates that people subconsciously interpret others' behaviors through a "rational" lens. In other words, we assume that others' words and actions are guided by reason. We don't pause in the middle of an interaction with someone to contemplate, *Is there an emotion at play here which could be throwing this person off their game?* Colloquially, we expect them to use their head.

Even under pressure. Even when pushed, pulled, or stressed to the max.

At work, when your team is scrambling to meet a deadline, when the proverbial poop is hitting the fan, you still hold your teammates to the gold standard of making decisions as if no looming disaster exists, as if out for a smooth sail. You still presume they'll use rational thinking.

However, this is also when emotion is most likely to hijack the brain—theirs and yours. Christian Bale was responsible for weaving back together the fraying threads of $200 million of sunk investment. No pressure there. The world expected him to act, figuratively *and* literally, as if it was no big deal; that was the job he was entrusted to do. He expected the same from his cast and crew, that they would perform perfectly, even under intense pressure. All unreasonable expectations! When frazzled by things not going our way or as we anticipated or as desired, our cerebral cortex (the part of our squash that uses logic) gets into conflict with our amygdala (which controls functions like fear, excitement, anger, impatience, and frustration). Put simply: reason and emotion don't play nice.

It's the ultimate paradox of being human. When reason is most needed, we are least apt to use it—especially in communication. Meanwhile, we presume those around us are unaffected by this paradox. To be honest, we pretty much think we aren't affected by it. Therein lies the challenge. And the opportunity. If you identify occasions in which the assumption of rationality is, as the saying goes, "making an @$$ out of you and me" and turn your attention to soothing the underlying emotion, your problem-solving success rate will skyrocket. As much as we bask in the belief that we are a highly evolved species, capable of incredibly complex analysis, we are ultimately fallible, emotional creatures who, most of the time unwittingly, filter information through the prism of our feelings.

THE PROBLEM-SOLVING LYNCHPIN

We don't want you to conclude that emotion is an Achilles' heel. Far from it: Emotion is the lifeblood of creativity, connectivity, invention, resilience, and altruism. It's the birthplace of motivation. The key to solving interpersonal problems, rather, is understanding that reason and emotion tap into very different neural pathways. Trying to use both pathways simultaneously in the face of a stressful situation is like trying to drive out of Manhattan during rush hour on a Friday afternoon—everything gets jammed up. Problem-solving hinges on detangling the brain's two fundamental skills.

> "Emotion can be the enemy, if you give in to your emotion, you lose yourself. You must be at one with your emotions, because the body always follows the mind."
>
> **—Bruce Lee**

Visualize a toddler on a beautiful sunny summer's day, out in the backyard, playing in his sandbox to his heart's content. He's carefully arranged his matchbox cars in a neat line and is busy building a sandcastle as an imaginary parking garage for them. His engineering little mind is completely engrossed. He'd stay happily occupied like this well into the evening if left undisturbed. But dinnertime is approaching. You need to get him washed up, fed, and then off to bed. Uh-oh. You see where this is going. The nightly MMA main event. Kicking, screaming . . . outright wailing while those matchbox cars are hurled like Scud missiles.

Forcefully picking him up, carrying him into the house, and strapping him into his high chair certainly isn't the answer. There is zero chance of vegetables making it into his tummy via that route. Nor will you get far listing out carefully crafted talking points on the virtues of a good night's sleep. Nevertheless, these are the predominant types of approaches people use when dealing with difficult circumstances or difficult people: jumping right to a solution (e.g., just plopping the child down at the table) or jumping right into the issues (e.g., lecturing him). There is a third common course too: "If you don't get into the house *this* minute, your matchbox cars are going into the garbage can." Adults in conflict often default to threats when they find their situation going south.

The latter is flat-out poor behavior. The impulse to fling criticisms and ultimatums a bit Christian Bale. It can bite every one of us. It happens when the tension of a situation snowballs before we address that tension. It happens when someone else's irrationality pushes your buttons such that you parrot the irrationality. It happens when your efforts to reason and your desire to emote get jumbled together. It's at this point that we say a disagreement has escalated into a full-blown dispute. You need to separate yourself from the situation and do a full reset. Just as our kids do, on occasion we all need a good time-out.

While equally ineffective as an initial move, the other two predominant approaches to difficult circumstances or difficult people are usually rooted in good intention. For starters, almost no one *likes* the prospect of getting into conflict. We prefer to nip disputes in the bud. Further, conflicts are hiccups in the otherwise well-oiled machinery of your job, or team, or office. You no doubt have a routine that you like to follow, a plan for how you will complete the tasks of the day. An interruption to your preferred process is annoying at best, potentially catastrophic when it derails hard-earned momentum on a career-defining project. It's human nature to want to fix the issue immediately. The quicker we can get a dispute off our hands, the quicker we can return to our priorities (or the sooner we can call it quits for the day). Hence, we tend to skip ahead to devising solutions rather than taking a beat to assess what's actually going on with the people involved, ourselves included. It seems counterintuitive, but slowing down to lower emotion, evaluate, and be more deliberate will save you much more time in the long run by preventing conflict escalation and the resulting problem proliferation.

For more than a decade now, we've polled students on the first day of our undergraduate classes: "When should a problem be solved?" Overwhelmingly (at a rate of nearly 90%), they choose "As soon as possible."

When we reframe the question to ask about resolving arguments, the ASAP choice is selected at a rate of *more* than nine out of every ten. Countless surveys across diverse workforces and c-suites have formally replicated this finding, showing our inherent bias for speed over substance when it comes to dealing with uncomfortable situations.

The repercussion of this bias, in organizational psychology jargon, is "Artificial Harmony." Rushing to solutions causes only surface-level issues to be resolved. Resolution feels good. A trouble is doused. An item is crossed off a list. Everyone gets back to work, and all is copacetic, or so it seems. Yet almost certainly, the core issue has been missed. Emotions continue to smolder, undetected.

Have you been camping? Enjoyed sweet, gooey s'mores by the fire? Hopefully you heeded the wise words of Smokey Bear. The leading cause of forest fires is a campfire or cigarette not put out properly. Dirt is kicked over the woodpile and the flames go out. But hot embers continue to burn underneath and reignite the remaining logs or neighboring brush. Whoosh, up goes the timberland.

Haste to quash a disagreement is the enemy of good, long-term relationships. Similarly, so is leaping to the Xs and Os of a problem. Both fast-forward past the emotion involved. Thinking back to the parenting example can be helpful here: you wouldn't calm a toddler by launching into a stats-laden PowerPoint presentation. Dealing with difficult people is not unlike negotiating with a tantrum throwing two-year-old (and can certainly feel like it at times). No amount of logic, sensibility, or rational planning will work if you don't first defuse the emotion. In the backyard, your only hope is to find a way to quell your son's emotional spike. Or, if you're *really* talented, stave off that spike to begin with by strategically entering the sandbox.

> "If I were given one hour to save the planet, I would spend fifty-nine minutes defining the problem and one minute resolving it."
> **—Albert Einstein**

We can't emphasize enough that the first step in tackling personally challenging conditions is to open a release valve, let off some steam, and allow the pressure to dissipate for both you and for others. Remember a key takeaway from this chapter: reason and emotion don't function well together. You must help your emotionally charged peers modulate their emotions, so they can transition back into the realm of reason.

Fortunately, we have a "Temper Tool Kit"—four remarkably efficient techniques for lowering emotion and shifting cognitive processing from the exceedingly reactive, primitive amygdala to the mature, refined, thoughtful centers of the cortex.

THE VOICE TECHNIQUE

Shortly after Doc G was certified as a mediator, he was handed a divorce case. An ordinary couple . . . with one glaring detail. The husband was easily six foot five and weighed well north of three hundred pounds. He wasn't fat. He was Incredible Hulk ripped. In the right light, you'd swear his skin had a green tint. And boy did his eyes pierce right through you.

Per our family mediation policy, for this particular dynamic, the husband and wife were initially placed in separate rooms. Doc G started with the wife, as she was the one who'd filed for the divorce. Doc G asked her what she'd like have happen.

"I no longer have feelings for my husband. I'd like us to move on with our lives. I'd be happy to split everything down the middle but if that's not agreeable, I'd be happy to hear his ideas as well."

Very tranquil. Very fair. Doc G went into the next room and presented it to the husband. He went absolutely *bonkers*, screaming that it wasn't true: his wife still loved him and she didn't really want a divorce. Doc G turned on a southern drawl and asked the husband to write down the time line of events so he could better understand when the wife moved out and when the divorce was filed. This shifted the husband's focus and defused his emotion.

Returning to the wife, Doc G shared the husband's position.

"It's nothing personal," she explained. "I'm just not into men. I haven't been attracted to men for a while now. I've been dating another woman for the past two years and we're in love."

Doc G took this detail to the husband. He blew up again, this time at an even higher volume.

"*No way.* There's no way she's seeing someone else. You're lying!"

Again, Doc G leaned on the strategies in this chapter, calmed him down, then went back to the wife. Did her husband not know about the affair?

"Oh yes," she chuckled. "We've been openly dating. The three of us have even slept together multiple times." Then she casually mentioned that her husband liked to mix meth and steroids. In an innocent tone, she posited, "Maybe that has something to do with him not remembering or not thinking about this rationally?"

Ya think?

Off to the husband's room went Doc G.

He started to inquire about what the wife had shared. But before he could get out the words to ask for clarification, the husband grabbed the conference table, all eight feet of it, and in a blink slammed it into the wall. Ducking for cover, Doc G glanced over to where the table had been. Incredibly, there were remnants of bolts in the floor. Time for a new technique.

You don't have to have a deep or long-standing relationship with someone to connect with them and establish a modicum of trust. You merely have to encourage them to join you on the same playing field. That starts with tone of voice. Yelling is exhausting, both mentally and physically. People can't keep it up for long periods. Further, when people are in an emotional tailspin, they are grasping for some semblance of control. If you provide it, even in a tiny way, such as offering a chair or cup of coffee, or simply listening to their grievances, they'll eventually soften. Putting these two facts together, we've found that it's nearly impossible for someone to maintain a significantly higher tone of voice than you for longer than sixty seconds. People are conditioned to adopt congruent postures and patterns of speech. It's based on a survival mechanism. The human brain is wired, when we're in some form of opposition with another person, to pick up on and parrot their mannerisms. Therefore, if you're in a heated dispute and gradually take your tenor down a couple octaves, pretty soon your counterpart will echo the timbre. This is the essence of the Voice Technique.

The steps are quite straightforward:

1. Maintain calm body language. For example, use smooth, encouraging hand movements; nod your head positively (but not rapidly or vigorously). Take even, relaxing, deep breaths through your nose, into your belly.

2. Maintain solid eye contact. Looking down and away suggests you're untrustworthy. Looking up indicates that you are unsure or are fishing for answers. Looking someone in the eye communicates confidence and comfort with them. It promotes the perception that you are in control and are not intimidated.

3. Ask a valid question with a tone of voice that is markedly lower and slower than the other person is using. Most likely, if they're amped up, they will not be able to hear you and will have to ask you to repeat it. That's a good thing.

4. Continue these three things. Patiently wait for the other person's voice to start matching yours.

When you attenuate the level of someone's voice, you correspondingly attenuate their level of emotion. You can also use the Voice Technique to engender other positive speech patterns. For instance, if you demonstrate a pattern of pausing to carefully choose words, the other party you're dealing with is likely to take more time as well—another surefire way to bring greater reason into the equation.

One caveat: this won't succeed with someone who is supremely guarded. For such a person, you must validate their ego. Ask for their opinion. Remember: do so in a tone of voice that is low and slow. This won't succeed with someone under the influence of drugs or alcohol. Luckily, the husband was not high at the time; he was merely freakishly strong. When in doubt, push pause to assess whether foreign substances are at play.

Back in the mediation room, Doc G took a long, deep belly breath and said, "It's okay." He peacefully walked over to the table, now on its side, and tipped it back onto its feet. He slid a chair out and to the husband's side of the table and then eased into one himself. As he did, he smiled subtly and asked, again in a cool drawl, nodding positively, "All right. Now we can get down to business. Could you give me a little more info about your mortgage?"

It was a time-out combined with the Voice Technique. Doc G gradually transitioned back into discussing the divorce case, all while continuing with what is affectionately known around Texas courthouses as Doc G's Matthew McConaughey voice. Within the hour an amicable settlement was reached . . . and the husband was talking like Matt McConaughey too!

THE VALIDATION TECHNIQUE

When someone is having a tirade, by definition they are spewing out everything on their mind. It's easy to dismiss it all as verbal vomit. It's easy to call balderdash on statements that are self-serving, overly emotional, or unreasonable. Resist that urge. Why? Because people in an escalated state have a basic need to tell their story. If they didn't, they wouldn't be so adamant to talk. They're just doing so unproductively, letting their feelings muck up their points. The majority of what comes out of their mouth may be BS. But amid the BS, they will share what is genuinely impacting them. Here's how to use the Validation Technique to reverse the momentum:

1. Let them fuss and fume. Yes, you indeed heard correctly. Don't cut them off or try to deter the diatribe. As much as it may be unpleasant, awkward, painfully voluminous—as much as there may be a lot of falsehoods or criticisms that you want to shoot down—let 'em roll.

2. As they "share," be a data collector. Remain calm. Sift through what they are saying, making note of their core positions and listening for their underlying interests. Keep in mind that these items are apt to be buried in

the blather; they are unlikely to be neatly framed for you. Let all the rest of the rant go in one ear and out the other.

3. It may feel like people on a tirade are going to go on forever, but they'll reach a pause. Wait for it. When you hear it, whatever you do, don't use your turn on the floor to refute any statements or to interject your views. This is your big opening. Use it to repeat back to them what you heard—specifically, what you heard regarding the most important of their issues.

In keeping with our worked-up youngster analogy, it's no secret that one of the best methods for getting hyper kids down for the night is to let them run around. Tire them out! The Validation Technique is the grown-up version of this. Allow an irate person to go off. After they run (their mouth) for a bit, their gas tank will get to E. Their emotional tide will recede. At that point, you can then steer the conversation to rational strategizing.

Equally important, someone who is upset with you generally believes (whether accurate or not) that you are ignoring, dismissing, or acting counter to their well-being. One reason people start shouting is that it seems like no one paid attention when their decibel dial was on "indoor." By listening to them and clearly communicating that you are listening, you validate their concerns. Once they feel validated, once they feel that you will take their issues seriously, they are open to productive dialogue; they are open to listening to you in return. The power of empathy is now on the menu, and the table is set for a feast.

Note: While the Validation Technique incorporates Active Listening, the two instruments differ in primary objective. Active Listening serves to fill your bucket of intel. The Validation Technique serves to empty the bucket of ego, entitlement, and other such counterproductive emotions. It helps get someone off their heels. It's not agreeing with them or taking their side. Quite the contrary, the Validation Technique provides a mechanism for them to loosen their grip on their stance, which has become white-knuckled due to misperceptions regarding how they're being treated.

Likewise, the Validation Technique removes the tension of judgment from the equation. At the time we were writing this book, the Academy of Motion Picture Arts and Sciences held its ninety-fifth Oscar awards show. Host Jimmy Kimmel did us proud. He channeled this chapter in his monologue, defusing emotion.

"We know this is a special night for you. We want you to have fun. We want you to feel safe. And most importantly, we want *me* to feel safe," Jimmy opened, putting the audience, who was sensitive to the program's recent history à la Will Smith, at ease.

"So we have strict policies in place. If anyone in this theater commits an act of violence at any point during the show, you will be awarded the Oscar for Best Actor and permitted to give a 19-minute-long speech." Raucous laughter.

"Seriously, the Academy has a crisis team in place. If anything unpredictable or violent happens during the ceremony, just do what you did last year," he said. "Maybe even give the assailant a hug."

Thank you, Jimmy. Be on the lookout for a complimentary copy of *How to Get Along with Anyone* that's on its way to our local FedEx branch.

THE DETOUR TECHNIQUE

Have you ever been to a magic show? A magician shows you an empty black top hat, rotating it and shaking it to demonstrate that it's a regular hat with nothing in it. He sets it down on the table, in plain view, center stage. He then waves his colorful long wand in an arc of dramatic showmanship, bringing it down with a flare of finality to tap on the brim of the hat. Out jumps a rabbit! The audience oohs and aahs. Of course, we know there is a trick to it; the rabbit didn't really materialize out of thin air. The magician used an age-old technique: distraction. While your eyes were following the theatrics of the wand, the magician's other hand pressed a button on the side of the table that caused the hat's rigged top to open down into a hidden compartment in the table where a rabbit was awaiting its treat-trained cue. Because you didn't see the alteration to the hat, your mind perceives that the bunny had nowhere to come from. Magic.

The magic of the brain, actually. Sleight of hand, mirrors, elaborate props, simple verbal prompts—all of these are tools magicians use to leverage a neurological phenomenon called change blindness. The human sensory system is limited and cannot possibly focus on every little detail of the world around us. So our clever cortex fills in the gaps with past experience—in this case, what we knew about the hat from its earlier display. Perhaps the most famous scientific demonstration of change blindness was a study by Harvard psychologists Dan Simons and Chris Chabris in which subjects were shown a clip of a basketball game and asked to count the number of passes by the team wearing white jerseys. In the middle of the action, a person wearing a gorilla suit walks onto the court, pauses briefly to pound its chest, and walks off. Fascinatingly, in this experiment as well as a wide variety of replications since then, most subjects do not see the gorilla. They are dumbfounded when the video is played back and there, in plain sight, is a hairy ape. Subjects' brains are busy counting, cannot attend to the whole basketball court, and as a result "fill in" the picture in their mind with what should be happening during a basketball game. Change blindness at work. Even more fascinatingly, there is a strong positive correlation between counting accuracy and change blindness. The better subjects do at recording the number of passes, the more likely they are to miss the gorilla. Some even fail to see it when they are told ahead of time that an ape is going to enter the play.

You don't have to be a Vegas performer, nor a neurobiologist, to use the science of focus to improve your relationships. Simply implement the Detour Technique:

1. Make a mental list of three issues, at least tangentially related to the problem at hand, of significant importance to the person with whom you are dealing—but issues that either (a) have positive emotions attached to them or (b) are far less emotionally charged than is the topic of the current argument, disagreement, or debate. If you have difficulty making this list or need more context to assess which issues are less emotionally hyped, you can use the Validation Technique to gather more information.

2. When the conversation you're having with the person escalates such that they stop using reason, interrupt in a collected fashion, asking for clarification on one of the items you identified in step one. For example,

"You know, that reminds me of what you were saying a minute ago about
_____. That was a good idea; could you walk me through that
again?"

Your question takes a second for them to register and respond to. It's a mini time-out—without the formal or artificial feeling of calling a time-out. It's a detour in the conversation, and that pause is likely to lower high emotion. Then, because you've chosen a more rational topic, as the person begins talking about it, they shift to using reason.

You can wash, rinse, and repeat this as many times as it takes to modulate emotion so that when you return (if you even have to return) to the hot-button subject, everyone will be more levelheaded, more collaborative minded.

"Whoa, no way that works! People hate being interrupted," you might be saying to yourself.

A legitimate concern. Which is why, when you pull out the Detour Technique, you ask a question instead of interjecting your ideas, suggestions, or opinions. Questions allow the other person to still perceive being in control of the dialogue; it's still about them so "you" are not interrupting. Also make sure you go to a matter that's at least somewhat relevant. Magicians don't distract you by telling you to look offstage. It would be obvious that you were being intentionally manipulated. The best performers distract you in subtle ways, keeping you still directly engaged with them, thus not giving away what they're up to.

THE E-MAIL DRAFT TECHNIQUE

One might surmise that the reason-emotion clash in the brain doesn't affect written communication. Writing takes time. Writing takes substantial cerebral cortex processing. Participants aren't in direct, physical battle. Emotion shouldn't spike, should it?

Well, it turns out the opposite is true . . . *especially* with e-mail.

Writing brings about a sense of distance, a protective bubble of sorts, as you aren't in jeopardy of your recipient doing you immediate harm. Building on the classic Milgram experiments, in which participants doled out electric shocks to other people, psychologists have established that the less in-person contact humans have, the less polite, thoughtful, and cooperative they are. Road rage is a perfect example. Within the pseudo-anonymous confines of your car, barreling down the highway, you are more apt to say adverse, hurtful things that you wouldn't say to someone's face. Moral judgment and behavior decline as we become more isolated—as we move from sitting around a conference table, to logging into Zoom, to being on a voice-only call, to e-mailing from home.

Writing also removes tone and body language, giving you plausible deniability. "Oh, I didn't mean it that way." You can hide behind your computer screen. You can blame your typing on autocorrect (or Siri or Alexa or any number of convenient AI scapegoats).

Suffice it to say, when it comes to dealing with interpersonal friction, written communication—and e-mail in particular—is ripe with opportunity for suspending your better judgment and taking emotion in the wrong direction. Complicating matters: what you send by e-mail is *always* there. There is no absolute-delete button. Nothing in the digital world is truly confidential.

So make it a commitment to never send an e-mail in anger, fear, or even excitement. If you are amid a tense situation with someone that you must e-mail (or are just feeling a simmering urge to ping them), invoke the E-Mail Draft Technique:

1. Have at it . . . but type the message in your Draft folder and do *not* enter an address in the "To:" box.

2. When you're finished typing, *do not press send*. Save the draft and then close the message window (or shut your laptop's lid or flip off your desktop's power switch). For fun, if you want, you can make this step ceremonially cheeky; it can help you transition away from a less-than-profitable mindset.

3. Go get some form of exercise. Walk around the block, go for a hike, hit the gym, shoot some hoop. Any form of exercise will work great as long

as it's (a) at least thirty minutes and (b) vigorous enough to release some endorphins.

4. Return to your computer. Reread your e-mail, making edits to any instigating, passive-aggressive, or emotionally charged language. You may find it helpful, when feasible, to recruit someone else's impartial input.

5. At this step of the technique, you've lowered emotion. You know that you are not making any irrational decisions. Type in the recipient's address. Send!

Doc G and his wife have an ongoing contest to see whose work conflicts are crazier. The winner gets to pick the restaurant for date night. As a mediator, Jim is sent into a lot of environments full of pissed-off people. But his wife is a night shift ER nurse. You know what those waiting rooms are like—not typically a confetti-throwing party. Jim's wife has enjoyed a lot of steak dinners during their marriage, but one occasion when Doc G took the cake stands out.

He was hired to do a training with the upper-level staff of a small East Texas school district. This specific district had a long-standing reputation for intense, escalated conflict—a fancy way of saying a lot of calls to the cops and, more than once, the FBI. An in-service was scheduled for January 2, before the students returned from holiday break. The superintendent had sent out a scathing memo requiring all counselors, principals, administrative staff, and head coaches to attend the planned eight-hour training, threatening to garnish the wages of any no-shows.

Doc G arrived on New Year's Day, and booked at the local Holiday Inn Express (yes, you too can be a mediator). It was empty. The front desk clerk's nose was buried in a Stephen King novel; she slapped a keycard on the counter without a glance up. Brr. His room wasn't any warmer; the bed (unmade!) sagged terribly. No matter, Doc G's reception the next morning would be much more inviting, right? He set the alarm for bright and early.

At seven o'clock on the dot, he pulled into the high school parking lot. The building was padlocked. Yikes, had there been another incident?

Doc G walked around back, peering in a couple windows. All dark. It was twelve degrees outside. Back to his truck to blast the heater and wait.

The program was set for eight o'clock. No life stirred until a quarter after when the high school principal rolled up to take the chain off the front doors. Doc G told her he was here for the training and was looking forward to meeting everyone. She rolled her eyes. As she directed him to a stuffy, windowless auxiliary room, jury-rigged with plastic "temp" tables and chairs, Doc G asked if they had roll-in monitors and Wi-Fi.

She laughed at his question. Then silence. Upon reflection, it was the only laugh he got the entire day.

By nine thirty, all the participants were present except the head football coach. He didn't saunter in until after ten. And saunter he did, grabbing everyone's attention, plopping himself down in the farthest chair from the front that he could find. He crossed his arms. His pursed lips told you all you needed to know about his stance on this workshop.

To say the day was unproductive would be incredibly kind. Doc G's postmortem log had "DISASTER" written in bold letters across the top. Attendees were there against their will, crammed into a fire-hazard shoebox of a room. Doc G had no technology to help break up the monotony of lecturing, and the space was inadequate for audience participation exercises. All his jokes flopped. When people were listening to them, that is. Doc G had been denied his request to have all participants leave their phones in their vehicles. A record-setting number of text messages were sent in that eight-hour span. The football coach took frequent and oddly long bathroom breaks, if that's what they were. When he was present, he shook his head and grumbled in disapproval at each take-home point.

At the hint of the program beginning to wrap, the coach got up and left. The rest of the staff conga-lined behind him while Doc G scrambled to squeeze in his final remarks. No applause. A lone thank-you. As Doc G packed his materials back into his handbag, the superintendent walked in. He hadn't attended. He asked how the program went.

"Um, not too well, I'm afraid. No matter what I tried, they just wouldn't engage."

"That's okay. I'm requiring them to attend a follow-up in April. See you then."

The superintendent spun around and walked out.

Oh no!

January, February, and March zipped past. Doc G saddled up for round two. He was armed this time around. He commandeered the gymnasium, where he set up dual portable Bluetooth projection screens. He brought stadium seat cushions for everyone. He had in tow a collection of his most hilarious video clips as well as brightly colored printed handouts. And he brought snacks!

Once again, the folks dragged themselves in by nine thirty. Once again, the coach arrived after ten. This time, as his John Wayne entrance interrupted the group's attention, the coach asked if he could say something.

Nervously, Doc G told him, "Of course." He braced for whatever blistering commentary was about to hit him.

"I left that session back in January thinking it was the most useless waste of air I'd ever attended." Doc G winced as the coach continued. "The next Friday I get this bull$#!% e-mail from a parent claiming her daughter had been kicked off the team. It wasn't even to me. It was sent to all the admin. I was copied on it. The gal wasn't kicked off the team; she's our new *kicker*! The crap of it was that the message was full of other baloney, dragging every aspect of our school through the mud, and this angry mother demanding an immediate meeting with the school board, the superintendent, and me. I wanted to rip her a new one. I was on the way out of the office, but I sat right back down at my computer and hammered that keyboard. But, you know what? For some reason the E-Mail Draft Technique from that training in January popped into my mind. I thought, yeah, you know, a run would feel pretty good right about now. So I went home, went for a jog, and then had my wife read the e-mail I wrote, describing to me the tone of the mother's message and the tone of my message. It was so clear. I'm a Competitor and my e-mail was just like my style, but this mom, see, her best teammate would be an Analyzer. So I rewrote the message that way. Yeah, my wife helped." He smiled.

Then the coach put a stamp on it: "Thirty minutes later that mom writes back and wouldn't you know it, the whole darn thing was resolved. I'm tellin' ya; *thirty minutes*. This mediation stuff actually works."

The coach has since become a good friend of ours. He gave us the gift of demonstrating that keeping the principles in this book simple can make a big difference and can help get through to even the most reluctant of people. You don't need to catalog everything we teach; just find one or two techniques that you can put into practice. And, he's living proof that the Draft Technique is effective.

MAKING A RELATIONSHIP INVESTMENT

During our training programs, we routinely request of the audience, "Raise your hand if you've ever been in an argument with your spouse or a significant other." To date, we're batting 1.000. It's a rigged exercise, of course. Couples argue. It's universal. We pose the question to help the group feel a commonality with one another—and on the off chance that someday we'll meet a person who has genuinely never had an argument. That'd be a fascinating case study (though, a boring book . . . no attention-holding drama; but we digress).

Family members, who underneath any dust and debris of a scuffle love each other, already have the wherewithal they need to reach a resolution. The stumbling block is generally that the emotion of a situation has gotten out of kilter. It's an excellent arena for this chapter's Temper Tool Kit. Here's how to be the Muhammad Ali of your relationship (keeping in mind that one of the cardinal rules of a great marriage is to *never keep score*).

The next time you walk into the house only to be greeted by "the look," be prepared to pull out both the Validation Technique and the Detour Technique. Don't assume you know what's eating at your spouse; getting that wrong risks opening up a new, entirely different can of worms. Rather, your first move should be to validate, validate, validate! Ask them what's wrong—and mean it. Use a "low and slow" tone of voice, encouraging them to talk while maintaining eye contact the whole time. Do not, under any circumstances, defend yourself or make rebuttals. This combination demonstrates that you truly care about their response.

Once they feel a sense of validation, you'll be able to successfully "short circuit" the escalated emotion using the Detour Technique. But be patient. Don't rush to try to Detour. Authentically accept the venting and validate their emotions. Then, when your spouse's collar begins to steam a tad too much, calmly ask a reasonable question about a related but less emotional subject. If done correctly, this forces your significant other to pause and contemplate for a second. Psychologically, people cannot sustain a high level of fire when their brain is shifting topics.

Keep Detouring until the overall level of emotion between you two is significantly lower than it was at the launch of the conversation. At that point, you can start brainstorming solutions to the issue(s) at hand. Your bedrock sense of being a team will have returned. You will have averted the classic big blowup before bed.

Be aware though: switching subjects can be temptingly easy. If you Detour too quickly without first Validating or do it too abruptly (skipping to something completely unrelated), it will be obvious that you're intentionally interrupting. The effort will backfire. And whatever you do, don't take it personally; don't leverage your Temper Tool Kit to interject your own, alternate agenda. Bringing up your mother-in-law as a scapegoat is not an illustration of how to use the Detour Technique. If your spouse goes right for your underbelly, remind yourself that you're investing in the relationship. Investments sometimes dip before they soar; don't sell low.

Using your Temper Tool Kit is not, nor should it be used as, a quick fix. The tricks of the trade in this chapter all work best when approached with the mindset of committing time and energy (and humility) to gain substantial long-term reward. Think about the last time you went to a ski resort or a zoo or theme park. Did you notice anything odd about the ticket pricing? The Franklin Park Zoo in Boston, home to a family of incredibly charming lemurs, is a typical example. At the time of writing this book, a single adult admittance on a peak day with a special event was $35. A year membership was $60. You don't have to channel Archimedes to figure out that if you're going to stroll the zoo's grounds just twice, you might as well buy a pass for the whole year. Two or three individual tickets ringing the cash register for a larger sum than the equivalent of 365 tickets is standard pricing across America. (Disney is an outlier; go figure.)

We find this parallel resonates with people contemplating the best way to approach a difference of opinion with a friend, a policy clash at work, or getting cornered at family reunion by an obstinate relative. Making the bigger commitment upfront is typically cheaper in the long run than trying to "save money" with a one-off. For amusement parks, it's purchasing a membership instead of paying visit by visit. For conflict, it's investing the time to attend to emotions rather than rushing to solve an individual problem quickly. Quick fixes may temporarily feel satisfying but come at the expense of the relationship—making an ends-justify-the-means mistake, inadvertently brushing your partner's needs aside or failing to seize the opportunity to strengthen your understanding of your partner. The strategies provided to you in this chapter are fantastic for getting a disagreement sorted. Frankly, though, they're even better for building and nurturing friendships, from professional to romantic. We urge you to take a minute to brainstorm areas in your life where you can proactively put this chapter's skills into action.

Thank you, Christian Bale, for reminding us that we're all fallible. Pick your favorite saying. Your buttons will get pushed. Your feathers will get ruffled. Your cheese will slide off your cracker. Your emotions will get away from you on occasion. You now have a toolbelt to reach for the next time they do.

5

Play the Player

The 1998 film *Rounders*, starring Matt Damon, Ed Norton, and Gretchen Mol, is a window into the seedy, Mob-infested world of underground gambling. At the time, in the nascent days of the Internet, legal betting on cards in the United States was limited to casinos in a few states. There were no gaming apps yet. One could join a poker game online, for fun, but if you wanted to play for hard cash, you had to hoof it to Vegas or Atlantic City. Or try to get into a secluded-from-authority basement at your own peril. As Damon's voice-over discloses coldly before the opening credits roll, "Listen, here's the thing. If you can't spot the sucker in your first half hour at the table, then you *are* the sucker."

Rounders became a cult classic. In addition to providing a little history and offering a fascinating glimpse into an edgy microcosm of gambling, replete with the pastime's very real dangers of predators and addiction, *Rounders's* gift to its audience is showcasing the psychology of card playing—*high-stakes* card playing, which is all about making decisions during moments of tense interpersonal conflict. Damon distills it perfectly for us:

"The key to the game is playing the man, not the cards."

Oh how tempting it is, when you clash with someone, to try to bolster your position or better explain it. To try to solve the problem. To strategize which Xs and Os will make everything right. As well-intentioned as these efforts may be, they are ineffective starting points for resolving conflict. Worse, they can spark backlash, causing the other person to dig in. Have you ever experienced a loved one coming to you with a frustration, laying out their concerns, and then, when you respond with a suggested course of action, telling you, "I don't want you to fix it; I just want your support"?

All the above result from playing the cards—the hand you're dealt or another hand you're trying to beat—instead of Playing the Player. Playing the Player means figuring out your opponent and leveraging their personality and approach to achieve positive results. In poker, you can lose with a full house and you can win with nothing at all. Players' decisions to stay in, raise the pot, check, or fold are dictated by the human element. You'll sit at the table longer, and amass more chips, if you attend to the *way* the other participants are playing. If you use their style, mannerisms, tendencies, and routines as a guide to the tactics you should take rather than relying on your cards, your chances of success increase. The cards you draw are random, out of your control. People are not.

Conflict is the same, dictated by the human element. You don't have to have pocket aces (i.e., negotiating leverage) to emerge, victorious, from interpersonal turmoil. If you Play the Player—as long as you attend to how others are approaching difficult situations and adjust accordingly—you'll thrive in the face of conflict. We'll give you the blueprint, in Section II, for Playing the Player with each of the five Conflict Personality Styles. But first, it's important for you to understand how to tune three key fundamentals of relationships: rapport, leadership, and energy.

BUILDING RAPPORT

Rice University is affectionately called "The Ivy of the South." A tiny college in Houston, it's recognized for its uber-competitive academics; the administration has been known to boast that the school outscores Harvard in percentage of perfect SAT enrollees. Triple majors and all-nighters in the library are the norm. Suffice it to say, elite athletes (anyone, for that matter, valuing talent diversity) frequently struggle to fit in at Rice and can feel like their contributions are not appreciated. Coaches run into recruiting challenges accordingly. But though the Rice Owls rarely enjoyed appearances in NCAA postseason play across men's and women's sports, Wayne Graham, who played Major League Baseball under legendary manager Casey Stengel, was undeterred.

At age fifty-six, Coach Graham took the helm of Rice baseball, a program with a .339 winning percentage dating back seventy-eight years. It was 1992. He persuaded future MLB All-Stars Jose Cruz Jr. (now Rice's head coach) and Lance Berkman to attend the university. In 1995, the squad earned its first-ever NCAA Regional playoff bid. In 1997, the Owls punched a ticket to the College World Series in Omaha, Nebraska.

Graham wasn't satisfied. He was convinced that Ivy League–caliber kids, without compromising their scholarship, could compete at the highest levels of sport. (Wayne, himself, turned down an acceptance to Harvard.) But something was still impeding his players from reaching their potential. He put his intellect to work exploring avenues to improve the Rice program. *What about the intangibles?* he pondered. Locker room chemistry, rebounding from tough losses, fielding the pressure of the media's magnifying glass . . . the list of interpersonal skills contributing to the accomplishments of all-stars is substantial.

Through a friend of a friend, a call was lobbed to Doc E. He was intrigued by the challenge. He'd just assisted the University of Virginia in winning the Cavalier's first-ever ACC baseball championship. His experience roaming the outfield for the Big Green didn't hurt either, making it easy to agree with Coach Graham's theory. And Graham's vision for crossing old-fashioned mental toughness with a Ted Williams–esque student-of-the-game approach was provocative. Wayne clearly relished the value of teaching his players how to hack human behavior. The next day, Doc E was packing his bags for Houston.

In the NCAA recruiting arms race (pun intended; pitching is always a premium), there is no time to waste. Coach Graham and Doc E were aligned in thinking, "Jump in and go; we'll figure the rest out later." They were fired up to try some things that other top-twenty-five-ranked teams weren't yet contemplating. It hadn't dawned on them to advance a formal plan of attack to the players. Whoops. We all can be casualties of our own enthusiasms. So Doc E walked into a classroom, unintroduced, and greeted the leaders of the Owls' baseball team. The team had been told only that it was a required captains' meeting. At 9:00 p.m. It was the only meeting time available amid everyone's schedule of classes, exams, fall baseball practice, weights, and homework.

"Good evening, gentlemen," Doc E initiated.

Blank stares.

"I'm Doctor Eliot. Your coaches asked me to teach you the psychological skills that can give you an edge over your opponents."

More blank stares, dotted by a couple raised eyebrows. Not the "hmm, interesting" kind of raised eyebrows.

"Let's start by getting to know each other a little bit," Doc E continued. "Who wants to share a fun fact about themselves?"

Crickets.

"Uh, well, okay then," Doc E fumbled. "How about I share with you what we're going to be working on this offseason and then I can answer any questions you all have," Doc E posed as a pivot, albeit as more of a transition statement than a question. Perhaps an attempt at forming a "y'all" would've been wise. Body language suggested the players weren't too keen to hear what he had to say. Doc E pushed forward nonetheless.

Over the ensuing ten minutes, arms began to cross. A few eyes rolled. Doc E grew increasingly uneasy with the reception. It didn't help that Doc E was a northerner, new to spicy Tex-Mex, and who, a half hour before the meeting, had chowed down a mondo burrito he'd grabbed at a late-night food truck. It was an evening of poor choices, for sure.

When Doc E broke to ask if there were any questions, the team's ace semiraised his hand: "Yeah, why're we here?" He paused, looking around at the other guys. "We went to the College World Series last year. We know what we're doing."

"Yeah, man," the star first baseman chimed in. "What the #@!! do we need you for?"

The room was teetering on hostile. The beans in the burrito had made quick work of Doc E's digestive tract. Discomfort wouldn't come close to adequately characterizing the gas buildup, nor the mood in the air. Doc E knew what he had to do.

"You know what?" he responded. "You're totally right. This whole get together was ill-conceived, right from the get-go."

The inconsistency with what they expected to hear interrupted the players' trains of thought. Facial expressions shifted from skepticism to cautious curiosity. What might Doc E say next? The pilot light for listening was ignited.

"You wanna know what I *really* think of tonight?" Doc E threw out.

A receptive shift washed over the classroom. And then Doc E did it. He let 'er rip.

"PHRRRRRRRRRRRRRRRRRRBBBT!"

Quite possibly the loudest, most astonishing fart of Doc E's life. Instantaneous laughter took over. The kind of self-propelling hilarity that resurges right at the point of waning.

Unable to resist joining in the laughs himself, Doc E chortled, "Nooo . . ." Chuckle, chuckle. "I'm serious . . ." Guffaw. "Really."

And then an aftershock hit: "PHRRRRRRRRRBT."

Another raucous wave of howling. Doc E just grinned, pulling up a desk alongside the players and plopping himself down. Breaking wind meets breaking the ice.

The Owls' venerable catcher leaned over and patted Doc E on the shoulder. "You're good in my book, Doc. But let's get outta here while we can still breathe."

"HAHAHA." The laughter escalated . . . then rode on out the door with the guys as they ditched the meeting, inviting Doc E to join them for a beer. By 2:00 a.m., charioted by the swapping of dozens of baseball stories, a fast friendship had been cemented.

You may be thinking, *I'm not comfortable passing gas in public.* It's okay; you can leave that to the comedians (and uncouth professors). Building rapport doesn't require farting. But it does require, at its most basal level, people feeling comfortable with one another. Comfort leads to trust, to opening up (intentionally or unintentionally), to revealing the ingredients needed to Play the Player.

Many of us can be guarded around strangers or those we don't know well. We put up invisible shields when we're nervous, stressed, or uncertain of outcomes, such as the case is when we're in conflict. Guardedness creates a psychological barrier between people—one even harder to knock down when it's subconscious behavior.

To build rapport, you must remove such barriers. The first step to doing so is to allow yourself to be at peace talking with someone, even though you might disagree with them or dislike them altogether. That means finding a comfort in the moment, for yourself. Doc E's seismic gastrologic event worked because it helped him let go of the tension he was fighting. The overwhelming sense of relief was also infectious, which made it a double whammy. Doc E immediately felt more comfortable. The humor, along with him dispensing the power dynamic, allowed the Rice ballplayers to feel more comfortable as well.

Human beings are social creatures. Even the most reserved of hermits have an innate need to connect with other living souls. When we're relaxed around someone, we connect with them more readily, and vice versa; when we sense a connection, we feel more relaxed. Think of building rapport as establishing dual status: Comfort and Connection.

In chapters 6–10, we'll supply you with rapport techniques tailored to each Go-To Conflict Personality. There are universal strategies as well:

◡ **Arrange a Conducive Environment.** When you address a strained relationship or pressure-riddled collaboration, the setting you choose impacts everyone's comfort level. Whenever possible, sit in a peaceful, quiet place, away from foot traffic. Natural light is the most positive. If man-made illumination is necessary, go for bright but warm; give the Heisman to fluorescent light. Pick soft, cushiony chairs. Eliminate distractions. Checking your cell phone, letting it ping from your pocket, or innocently placing it in clear view on the table suggests to another person that you'd rather be with your device than with them and dampens a sense of connection.

◡ **Team Up.** People are generally uncomfortable when squarely faced off. That's a confrontational orientation. If you plop yourself down directly across from someone, looking right at them, they are likely to squirm in their chair a bit (be it physically or emotionally). Instead, sit side by side. There is a tangible sense of working together when seated on the same side of the table with someone, the two of you looking at a problem together versus looking at *each other* as the problem. If the available furniture isn't configurable for shoulder-to-shoulder positioning, or your relationship is relatively embryonic—such that proximity would feel a little too cozy—at least orient yourself at an angle to tap into an aura of being on the same team versus being opponents.

∿ **Tap into Humanity.** Being on an uneven playing field will block comfort or connection, or both. Notice how people act around celebrities? Awkward. You don't often see someone ask for an autograph and walk away with the digits of a great new friend. Though, some icons (e.g., Tom Hanks and Sandra Bullock) are extremely gifted at putting others at ease. From the second you meet them, it feels like you've known them forever. How do they do it? They dispense with pretense. They intentionally stumble or spill mustard on their shirt or tell a stupid joke to present themselves as just a regular Joe or Jane. They ask basic questions like, "What are you up to today?" You can do the same by dumping formality, titles, rigid rules, anything that puts you on a different plane. If you project humanity, you give others permission to do the same.

∿ **Smile.** It's amazing how something as small as a smile can be so effective. It's equally amazing how hard it can be, when Triggered, to pause and simply turn up the corners of your mouth. Of all movements, smiling is the single most impactful on our physiology and mood. Think of the most positive person you know, your life's Ted Lasso, seemingly always happy, their pearly whites ever gleaming. How long could you hold a sour disposition while spending time with them? How long could you remain down in the dumps hanging with Jason Sudeikis? Imagine how you feel around souls like this and allow the good feelings to wash over you. If nothing else, when you're in conflict, smile.

∿ **Match & Mirror.** Mirror neurons are communicators in the brain that are responsible for the interpersonal power of the smile. When you grin at someone, their brain is wired to want to grin back. Try it. See how many strangers you can get to crack a smile in response to yours as you walk by them on the street. Mirror neurons perceive all kinds of facial expression, plus posture, pace, tone, animation, openness, even breathing. You can influence any of these in another person by displaying what you want them to display. This rapport-building tactic is called Match & Mirror because it works best when it's bidirectional. In other words, invoke your *and* their mirror neurons:

- First, match what they are doing. If they're casually leaning back, you lean back too. If they're being animated, communicating with their hands, you should use your hands as well. If they're talking softly, you guessed it, match their tone. Note: this isn't apery. The objective isn't to mimic, which can come across as critical or poking fun. You merely want to, subtly, adopt similar mannerisms, voice, and articulations— the positive ones, naturally. Match the degree and depth of their candor. Borrow some of their language choices. And if you really want to take it over the top, match their breathing rate. It can be difficult to discern, but when you do, it'll blow you away how akin you feel to someone when your breathing is in sync.

- Second, exhibit optimistic, calming, confident, happy, or other comfort-producing facial expressions, posture, tone, pace, and gestures. The mirror neurons of the person you're interacting with will kick in, if you stick with the pattern. Soon, the other person will be reflecting the verbal and nonverbal bearings you're prompting and, since body language, tone, and so forth significantly influence emotion, you can introduce the comfort component of rapport.

Find Common Ground. You've probably spent a little time, somewhere along the way, with a truly gifted salesperson. Did you notice what they prioritized as they shook your hand, or maybe in the lead-up to the handshake (or high five or fist bump . . . or hug; talented connection-makers find a way to engage in distinctive touches without violating boundaries)? Chances are, in addition to offering an easy, warm smile, they were on the lookout for a shared experience—a shared relationship, hobby, value, preference, geography . . . an item of clothing, if that's what it took to find something the two of you had in common. "Sweet HOKAs! I bought my first pair last week. How are they working out for you?" They let the conversation flow naturally from there; they match your level of openness. They are genuinely interested in the common ground. They know that talking about common ground is a surefire way to build the connection ingredient of rapport. It's not rocket science; like a real pro, observe and listen. If nothing strikes you as a point of commonality, ask an innocuous, general question such as "Where are you from?" Draw on whatever modest connection presents itself. Unless you've never left your basement, it's pretty likely that you can find a tie to any place on the planet. "No way! One of my old buddies is from Milwaukee." Or, "You don't say! I'm going to be in Milwaukee this summer with my daughter. We're working through our bucket list of visiting every MLB stadium and we're hitting Miller Park."

~ **Appreciate.** Building rapport is infinitely easier when you genuinely care about connecting with people and helping them feel comfortable, particularly in the face of conflict, which is inherently *un*comfortable. For those with whom you'd like to foster rapport, you can demonstrate care by showing simple appreciation. Find one thing—just one thing—that you appreciate about them. A thing they did or said, an effort they're making, a good intention, a value they hold. Scale is irrelevant. Whatever it is, tell them you appreciate it.

Creating a conducive environment, tapping into humanity, discovering common ground . . . who'd have thunk a fart could accomplish all that? Whatever became of the flatulence-scaffolded rapport, you wonder? Doc E spent that offseason committed to the connection. He attended practices, a fixture in the dugout or behind the plate for hours on end despite other valuable things he could've been doing with his time. He stood out in the rain on terrible weather days. He ran wind sprints with (and, for fun, against) the guys—including one memorable day in a pair of wingtips because he'd rushed to the field from a conference at the Texas Medical Center that had run long.

Could Doc E have rolled the ball forward faster? Possibly. But after almost skipping over the rapport-building step, he was appreciative of the opportunity to hit the reset button and was determined to get it right. A winning relationship is almost always more valuable, in the grander scheme, than "winning" a conflict or "quick fixing" a problem.

Fall ball wrapped. A heck of a bond was in place. Some *very* funny holiday cards were exchanged. When the boys returned to campus for the 2000 campaign, they were ready to roll up their sleeves. Several of the players even started confiding in Doc E regarding highly sensitive subjects and deeply personal goals. *Serious* rapport. We were in business!

The season kicked off at Minute Maid Park, home of the Astros, with three top-ten opponents. Rice swept the tournament. The following weekend, number-one-ranked Georgia Tech, anchored by phenom Mark Teixeira, came to town for a three-game set. The Yellow Jackets boarded their flight home 0–3. A legit new powerhouse was brewing in Houston. Fourteen weeks later, the Owls hoisted a conference pennant. In the seasons to follow, they reeled off twelve consecutive conference championships, six College World Series berths in eight years, more weeks at number one in the nation during that span than any other school . . . and the coup de grâce: the 2003 NCAA Division I crown—Rice University's first national championship in any sport, ever. They also set a record that still stands: they are the only program in NCAA history to have three teammates picked in the first round of a draft.

Reflecting on these events always gives Doc E goosebumps. To be sure, the team had plenty of talent. But the leadership heroes weren't the big horses on mound. It was the role-players, like five-foot-eight Chris Kolkhorst, dubbed "Gritman," and Craig Stansberry, who became the first Saudi Arabian–born Major League Baseball player. What this group of young men had was chemistry. In spades. Their focus on great communication, a deep understanding of one another, and selflessness was second to none. In the final game, ahead 14–2 with only three outs left to go and Rice's starting pitcher, Philip Humber, still in, Coach Graham walked the length of the dugout to tell the team's closer, David Aardsma, who hadn't yet been in the series, to grab his mitt. A chance to throw the concluding pitch on this historic occasion, what an honor. Aardsma smiled. He said, "No. It's Philip's moment."

LEADING PEOPLE TO SOLUTIONS

When we're conducting a seminar, we'll instruct the audience to envision a great leader. "Picture them commanding their troops, their employees, their athletes or teammates, or their fans," we'll say. Then we'll ask, "How do they do it? How do they get people to follow them, at times seemingly blindly? In extreme conditions, such as charging into battle, playing through an agonizing injury, pulling an all-nighter to meet a deadline, how do they get people to do what they want them to do—to compromise, to make sacrifices, to give up something of personal value?" We let attendees contemplate this at length, after which we take an anonymous poll. Typically, the highest vote getters are the following:

"They lead by example."

"They reward their peeps lavishly."

"They punish their laggards severely."

"They use their charisma to be persuasive."

"Well, they're the boss so . . . "

What are the communal themes of these assumed leadership practices? For one, the leader. What *they* do. *Their* method for steering others. For two, none are effective when it comes to conflict prevention or resolution. All five actually tend to strain relationships, reducing instances of people-understanding communication and enhancing the possibility of conflict.

Certainly, those in positions of authority can strongarm others to take action, including those counter to the action-taker's own best interests. A sergeant can put a pistol to a private's temple to compel the soldier into combat. Pay raises and cattle prods can get a slug off the sofa. But only for so long, and only so far as there isn't a more attractive option. These instruments of leverage have a finite return and must be continuously applied to produce the desired result.

Which is why successful leadership doesn't orbit around the leader, or his or her resources or influence. Sustained behavior change comes about when a person has a meaningful desire to commit to the change. In scientific literature, we label this Intrinsic Motivation: force emerging from the inside out. Rewards, punishment, pats on the back, modeling, threats, media mentions—all fall into a category of psychology called Extrinsic Motivation: force applied from the outside in. You can rely on someone when they're Intrinsically Motivated. They'll do what they say; they'll follow through. You have to stay on someone when they're Extrinsically Motivated. You must supervise and "manage" them. Their heart's not truly in it.

So what does this have to do with Playing the Player? When you have a difference of opinion with a coworker or relative, when you find yourself fighting with a colleague or family member, don't coax. Don't clamor to convince. Don't try to twist their arm. Don't shock or spook. Don't bribe. Don't pull rank. Translation: don't engage in Extrinsic Motivation. Instead, lead properly. Lead people to get to acceptable solutions for *themselves*—because *they* want to, not because you want them to or because you're asking them for a favor. Help them find a good reason of their own—that is, an Intrinsic Motivation. Even better, help them feel that a conflict's resolution is their idea.

> "Tact is the ability to tell someone to go to hell in such a way that they look forward to the trip."
>
> **—Winston Churchill**

As with building rapport, we'll show you how to lead each individual Go-To Style in the upcoming chapters. Absent a Go-To assessment, however, you can utilize Leading Questions to begin to shepherd Intrinsic Motivation. Leading Questions are prompts that empower as they ask someone to make a decision or provide direction, rule on a matter, or otherwise have a sense of control of the conversation. Leading Questions elicit a sense of authority, but intentionally guided, framed so as to point toward a heading you wish to go. We realize this may seem diametric to Active Listening. However, when someone is Triggered, they are not seeing the blue sky for the clouds. They are stuck on positions or issues. If you've assessed well, you understand their underlying interest—where they need to get to for the conflict to be resolved. You can't just tell them, unfortunately. In the heat of dispute, instruction is almost always ill received. When people are upset, it's easy for them to complain about someone else's cooking. It's hard for them to complain about a meal they whipped up themselves. Cue Leading Questions. Use them to help the people you care about reach win-win solutions.

There are five basic types of Leading Questions:

~ **Suggestive.** A question that suggests a specific angle or answer by dint of language or tone. For instance, "Do you think that whack job Bob in HR should be let go?" The qualification of Bob subliminally indicates a "right" answer. Or, jockeyed with an excited facial expression, "Wow, how cool was that ride? Wanna go again?" Even if your spouse or friend didn't enjoy the ride, it's unlikely he or she will deny you staying at the carnival for another spin.

~ **Presuppositional.** A question that assumes a stance, thought, or feeling and asks for exposition on the assumption. A few examples: "Could you walk me through what you like most about the new product line?" directs commentary to support the launch. "How much damage to morale are we looking at if we press go on the policy restriction?" establishes that it's a bad initiative. "For Friday night, which restaurant sounds the yummiest, Durgin Park, Yard House Pub over by Fenway, or that new seafood place your sister recommended?" presumes agreement on going out for dinner.

~ **Coercive.** A request to confirm or reject an idea, proposal, or position that then makes it difficult to reverse direction, such as, "You'll support the new policy, right?" Coercive Leading Questions are the most aggressive type and, thus, should be used sparingly. If you don't already have some degree of buy-in, Coercive Leading Questions can Trigger the opposite of its intended effect—the other party shutting you down. Of course, if you *want* someone to slam the door on an idea, ask a totally absurd coercion for the answer you don't want! "If we cancel our summer trip to save a couple bucks, Susie won't be disappointed, will she?"

∿ **Interrelated.** Making a statement that contains a bias or irrefutable information, coupled with a related question, such as, "The survey data seems to indicate an overwhelming percentage of our fans are in favor of earlier game times on Saturdays. When do you think we should schedule them?" Chances are, you won't get a demand to hold the status quo. Or "We always come home feeling so refreshed from an unplug getaway. How about we play hooky and snag a hut on Kiawah next weekend?" Your significant other may object to cost, planning, traffic, or other variables but you're likely to score unplug time in some fashion and you sow the seeds for an island vacation happening sooner rather than later. In leveraging Interrelated Statements, make sure the lead declaration is entirely objective. Subjective references can backfire and instigate contentious debate.

∿ **Optionality Offering.** Asking someone to make a choice between two options—both of which you deem satisfactory. "If we were to do a renovation, would you prefer a new kitchen, or redoing the master suite?" gets your partner ruminating on home improvements. "We could bolster R&D funding or we could grow the marketing department. Which do you think is better?" If your goal is to infuse capital into the business, either election is a victory. A derivation of this strategy is to make one of the choices something you know the other person will hate. To give you a galvanizing example, "Do you want the scratchy, buttocks-chafing toilet paper or the plush kind?" Need we say more? Naturally, when implementing an Optionality Offering Leading Question, picking "neither" is always possible. But it's a covert alternative; people by and large put their mind on what is presented. Thus, choices that require contemplation work best. Occasionally, three or more options is fruitful, provided you don't paralyze someone with too much information.

When employing Leading Questions, do your best to use the language, phraseology, and expressions of the person whose logic you're escorting. Borrow their words. Put questions in their terms. Frame the questions around them; use "you" (or "we" if you're striving to engender teamwork) instead of "me" or "I" whenever you can. "Do you prefer A or B?" edges "Which is better, A or B?" Both crush "Should I go with A or B?"

Deep breath. There's a lot to digest here. Leading Questions take thought and foresight, and asking them is an acquired skill. Practice and planning make all the difference. We find the tool most effective when integrated into the broader conflict resolution process via the following steps:

1. Use chapter 3's Active Listening techniques to uncover the other party's underlying interest. Remember, interests can be intentionally disguised or unintentionally hidden in a haystack of positions and issues. Be patient. Actively listen. Refrain from jumping to conclusions or rushing to solutions. You need to develop a thorough portrait of what is fundamentally important to the other party—and why. If it takes multiple "slow cook" meetings, so be it; use that opportunity for rapport building as well.

2. As the interest picture comes into focus, cogitate on courses of action or solutions for the conflict that you are confident will help the other party realize their interest. On the materializing mental map, put a pin in the two or three that are of greatest benefit to you. If none work in your favor, keep deliberating (call for a time-out or lunch break as needed).

3. Administer Leading Questions to guide the other party to one of the pinned solutions.

The Holy Grail of conflict is to help someone feel like the answer to a problem—the path forward, the "Eureka!" moment—is one they generated, contributed, or recommended. You're the sherpa and they're the explorer who gets to plant their flag atop the mountain. For Leading Questions to succeed you must suspend your ego. You must be willing to do the work, without getting any of the credit. Like a world-class sherpa, you figure out the most advisable route; you let your "guidees" brag about the route *they* took.

While not earth-shattering or anything in the neighborhood of a patentable secret formula, one trick of the trade: juice Leading Questions with a whiteboard. If one isn't installed in your office or study, plan to be in a whiteboard-adorned conference room when you're going to turn to Leading Questions. Doc G was reminded of this power in a recent divorce settlement mediation.

Not surprisingly, a couple's separation proceedings had gone sideways. Despite nine years of marriage, they didn't know each other all that well. The husband was a frugal, old-fashioned homebody. The wife had lavish taste, liked to go out on the town, and burned the midnight oil on social media. The husband's heels were dug in that his wife's credit card bills belonged solely to her. She, in turn, wanted the house, a stipend to redecorate, and their new Lexus SUV. "He can sleep in that damn rusty pickup of his for all I care."

She'd been waging an Instagram campaign to discredit him and his frugal values. His lifetime social media authorship, on the other hand, was composed of one post. At the crack of dawn one morning, while she was still passed out from the evening prior, he pilfered her phone, guessed her password (in a single shot!), and uploaded:

"Sentenced to mediation. Shnookums says, 'If all I go home with is my toothbrush and my values, I'm walking away with the better end of the deal!'"

A line of inappropriate emojis was pasted at the end; we'll spare you that.

Doc G welcomed the feuding pair into his office's conference room less than six hours later. He'd not seen the husband's post. It turns out, he didn't need to; the wife had printed it out and brought it with her.

"Since the toothbrush is all he wants, we have a deal. So we're done here, right?" she said, shoving the printout into Doc G's hand as he offered a welcoming handshake.

"I can see you're eager to put this mess behind you," Doc G sashayed. "I bet you both'd like to be done with it as fast as possible. You don't want to be stuck in this stuffy dungeon a minute longer than necessary. Am I right?"

They both nodded.

"Great! I like the way you're thinking; I agree with you already," Doc G continued as he pulled up chairs for them to sit, side by side in front of his whiteboard. "Perhaps you can show me how the numbers stack up?"

Accord again (though, each eyeing an opportunity to justify their case).

The court had forwarded Doc G records of their depositions, filings, and hearing, along with copies of all their financial statements. The couple needed to approve a plan for distributing their financial holdings and obligations. In total, their assets were as follows:

$50,000 in cash

$175,000 in a stock portfolio

$25,000 in jewelry

$35,000 in deferred severance due from the husband's previous employer

$220,000 in home market value

$400,000 outstanding on their primary residence mortgage; they were upside down by $180,000 (guess the year)

$65,000 in credit card debt

$40,000 left on the Lexus loan, titled in her name

For months prior, the couple's yelling and screaming had grasped at every imaginable position and issue. Not allowing the other to reside in the house, who owes what to whom, duty to SUV carbon footprint offset, reputation reparations, suing over a cocktail napkin IOU (the wife promised, on their first anniversary, to freeze eggs for the husband, who was sterile), the monetary value of personal favors over the years, public apologies, who should "give in" first . . . it was *exhausting*. And not just for Doc G as an outside party; it was exhausting for the couple. While skimming over the legal transcripts, Doc G could see the underlying interest. The husband and wife both wanted to be free of any and all responsibility, whatsoever, for the other.

Now reread the balance sheet. A possible solution leaps off your calculator's screen, doesn't it? It's net *zero*. Keeping any of their property (house, auto, and jewelry) would saddle them with debt. Paying off their debts, conversely, would leave no valuables to stand up as straw tokens for continued disapproval, blaming, judgment, and claims of victimization. Piece of cake, eh?

Unfortunately, human obstinacy blinds us to solutions we would otherwise enjoy. People steadfast in "my way or the highway" will drive right past off-ramps to conflict. They'll ignore logic and reason. Had Doc G candidly explained the fair and painless expressway available to the couple, doubling down would have ensued for the same reason the estranged were ordered to his office—an unwillingness to yield.

Doc G walked to the side of the blank whiteboard.

"Forgive me. I'm terrible at math. I've got to write things down or I end up counting on my fingers and toes . . . and I've got *stinky* feet."

A slight snicker. Doc G was happy with any ounce of humor he could muster from the couple. He smiled back in a well-timed show of Mirroring.

"Will you help me out?" he invited. "How much was in the joint checking?"

He wrote the number on the whiteboard.

"And you had some stocks and bonds and stuff like that?" he asked, to which they gave confirmation. "A brokerage account? Gotcha. How much was in that?" Doc G inquired, careful in each iteration to feign the past tense. Present tense was likely to strengthen their emotional entanglement with the money. Doc G was using Suggestive Leading Questions to plant a sense that the money was no longer there to quarrel over.

He wrote the equity figure on the whiteboard, below the cash. One by one, he went through the rest of the assets, each time using a Leading Question to structure the exercise as the husband and wife directing. When Doc G arrived at the assets' total, he drew a line, scrawled the amount, and circled it.

"You had some charge cards, yes?" he inquired, Mirroring a positive head shake. "How much was on those?"

He added the credit card number to the whiteboard, starting a new column. Rinse and repeat, he iterated the process for each item of debt, showing his math until he got to a total. He drew a second line, put up the sum, and circled it. What a coincidence, it was right smack next to the asset total.

"I gotta hand it to you," Doc G complimented as he looked at the board, projecting approving body language. "Y'all were smart to agree to this session. Continuing it in court could take *forever*. And those guys love running the meter. How big do you think the legal bills would get?" Doc G asked, combining Presuppositional and Interrelated Leading Questions.

That hit a nerve, the husband and wife both suggesting massive figures. Doc G quickly inked a rough average of the two, in red beneath the debt total, while commenting, "Whew! I'm glad y'all decided not to pay *that* beast!" He then circled it.

"Thank you so much for walking me through all this. I really appreciate your patience with my lack of arithmetic ability," Doc G said as he sat down, sighing a happy, relieved sigh. Then he waited.

It took less than two seconds. The husband cocked his head and pointed. "You know, those two numbers are the same. Why don't we take the assets and put them toward the debt?"

"No $#!%, Sherlock," the wife quipped. "But you always point to the wrong thing. It's the red number, dummy. If we have to pay that, then it doesn't come out even."

Doc G cut in as fast as he could. "Wow . . . Pay the second column off with the first. And flat-out erase the red by telling the attorneys to take a hike . . . That's awesome! Want me to take care of the paperwork so you can blow this popsicle stand?"

Tandem agreement. Case closed.

Regardless of how glaringly obvious a conflict resolution plan may appear to you, regardless of how ubiquitously beneficial it is, it's worthless if the other party isn't on board. Devising and proffering plans is like yanking on a reluctant horse's reins to get them into a trailer. They're *much* stronger than you. You can tug with all your might; it ain't happening until it's their idea. We're assuming you've heard the related proverb "You can lead a horse to water, but you can't make them drink." The goal is not actually leading the horse to water; it's helping them realize they're thirsty and showing them that the water is right around the corner. Focus on the other party. Play the Player. Lead them to feeling like getting on board is their decision.

MOMENTUM VERSUS DOMINOES

We're on a mission to make conflict as painless as possible (dare we even say, fun at times), but no matter how readily applicable you may find our tips, no matter how much rapport you build or how intrinsically motivated you lead people to be, conflict resolution can be weighty. It can suck serious energy. You may find that simply managing energy—and helping others manage energy—can evaporate disagreements. To that end, a crucial consideration for Playing the Player is pace. The wrong pace of play for different opponents can zap their energy. And when they feel exhausted, overtaxed, or overwhelmed, conflict will escalate—not ebb.

The slickest recipe we've discovered for properly pacing interaction, based on who you are interacting with, also happens to be one of the most popular topics in our corporate seminars: Momentum versus Dominoes. In a nod to the overarching importance of Playing the Player, we tend to refer to proper pacing as Playing Momentum or Playing Dominoes.

Playing Momentum is about gradually compiling small wins, brick by brick, to build up to the big win: a resolution. You first identify and knock out the most inconsequential issues, one punch at a time. You dismiss smoke screens and irrelevant topics. Then you move on to relevant issues that represent low-hanging fruit—that is, maximally easy to address, fix, and put in the rearview mirror. This allows you to gain positive traction. You want the person you're in conflict with to feel a sense of progress. Hence the moniker "Momentum." You then proceed up the food chain, one level at a time, until you've tackled the largest issue.

Do you know someone who always tackles their honey-do list beginning with the least time-consuming items? They're Playing Momentum.

Momentum is smart with people easily overwhelmed, people who'd take a gander at a skyscraper schematic and react, "Whoa, that's a *big* undertaking." If someone is susceptible to getting the wind knocked out of them, has an aptitude for quitting prematurely, or doesn't like taking on a myriad of assignments or responsibilities, you will need to go slower, start smaller, and titrate their energy. If someone errs on the side of caution, needs to test ideas before committing, skirts around complicated topics, prefers chitchat over deep discussion, or insists on researching before weighing in, choose to Play Momentum. The same approach also works for competitive people who want to win—the quick and easy victories of this kind of pacing lend to a sense of triumph and a sense of progress. Momentum is ideal for Analyzers, Collaborators, and Accommodators.

Conversely, Playing Dominoes is about toppling the biggest cornerstone first, so the rest of the house can come crumbling down. With this approach, you identify the meatiest, most critical issue and hit it head on. Everything else can wait; push all those "satellite" issues aside and get to the elephant in the room. Once the biggest problem has been put to bed, the next in significance . . . well, it doesn't seem so significant anymore. And on down the line with many items dropping off on their own accord because of what's already been accomplished. You can see why the name Dominoes is apropos: everything snowballs to achieve a faster solution.

Did you have a classmate in school who'd always finish term papers ahead of time, oft even the day they were assigned (and then they'd be kicking back, sipping piña coladas while you pulled an all-nighter at the last minute)!? They were Domino Players.

Dominoes is a grand slam with impatient people. It works like a charm with those who don't like things hanging over their heads, are too busy to be bothered with little details, hate things that drag on and on, or take a "just get it over with" tact to unpleasant chores. Band-Aid rippers love Playing Dominoes. For people who like to "get their game on" and for people who peter out in extra innings, you'll be wise to implement Dominoes. Playing Dominoes is ideal for Avoiders and Competitors.

~~~~~~

The relationships we sustain during our spins lapping the sun are quirky, intimately unique, and ever evolving. Peppered with ups and downs, the best of them require our emotional investment—investment we're glad to make, in spades. Nevertheless, across the plethora personal connections that we value and want to foster for decades, it's an investment that will have plenty of challenges, many opportunities for mettle-testing to the nth degree. None of us is perfect. We're susceptible to the highs, the lows, and the bluffs; we can get flustered when we're dealt a bad hand. We have our moments when we're self-centered and fail to heed what our loved ones are communicating. We get stressed. We tire out. We lose perspective. We're "not ourselves" at times.

On the individual level, this book is about hacking into the best version of ourselves, about increasing self-awareness at junctures when we're apt to be the least self-aware—those times we just described, when we're not ourselves, when we wish hindsight could be conjured before it got to be hindsight. We hope you use *How to Get Along with Anyone* to gain an astute knowledge of your Trigger(s) and Conflict Personality Style; learn how to adopt other Conflict Personality Styles; recognize when you get distracted from your underlying interests or cloud them in positions and issues; lower your emotions when they're escalating to a point of compromising your logic and reasoning; and, when you're in the thick of it, get your mind off yourself, resisting the urge to focus only on the cards—that is, the conflict. If you enhance your skill in merely a couple of these areas, you'll be clutch under pressure. Ice water in your veins when others fall apart. Perhaps more importantly, you'll be inoculated against getting played yourself, wise to the piranhas on the dark side of the force who practice Playing the Player to take advantage of you when your buttons get pushed.

On the team level, this book is about awareness of how others act, react, and handle things when they're outside of their comfort zone, when *they're* not themselves. On this level, we hope you use *How to Get*

Along with Anyone to assist and guide others through conflict; to help them defuse emotion before it runs roughshod; to lead them to positive, productive solutions when they otherwise might get tripped up, or as our pro sport clients like to phrase it, "get in their own way." As you Play the Player, we hope you use the insight gained to strengthen your relationships, to build new ones and revive old ones. After all, *long*-thriving careers, friendships, and marriages are products of elite relationship management. Tapping a Matt Damon Play the Player *Rounders* soliloquy once more:

> "Why do you think the same five guys make it to the final table of the World Series of Poker EVERY YEAR? What, are they the luckiest guys in Las Vegas?"

There are a few things you can do to be one of them when it comes to improving your odds at the conflict resolution table. You're already favored if you ratchet up rapport, summon internal motivation, and ID the appropriate pace. From there, you can customize your approach from Go-To to Go-To. When you do, you become *heavily* favored.

Section II

Section II

6

The Avoider

Tiger Woods hoisted the 113-year-old US Open Championship Trophy in 2008—after hobbling around Torrey Pines on two stress fractures and a torn ACL, including walking an extra eighteen on his fifth day to edge out the tenacious Rocco Mediate in a playoff.

The first-ever Korean PGA member, K. J. Choi, won the 2002 Tampa Bay Classic by a hefty seven strokes—while suffering through wrenching abdominal pain. The next morning, he was in the operating room having his nearly burst appendix removed. "When I started out the day, I felt some sharp pain and uneasiness to be honest," Choi later shared through an interpreter. "I just said to myself, 'I'll take it hole by hole.'"

Vertigo forced J. B. Holmes to withdraw from the 2011 PGA Championship. It turned out to be *much* more than vertigo—a defect in his cerebellum known as a Chiari malformation requiring brain surgery. Adding insult to injury, unbeknownst to Holmes and his doctors, J. B. was allergic to the adhesive used to affix the plate they had to put into his skull; a month post-op he had to be emergency airlifted from his home in Kentucky to Johns Hopkins in Maryland for a lifesaving second brain procedure. The time line: August, PGA Championship; September, first brain surgery; October, second brain surgery; January, back on the links, playing in the Tour's Farmers Insurance Open.

From age eleven through high school, Stacy Lewis wore a hard, unforgiving, full-body brace—eighteen-plus hours a day, every day, no holidays or vacations. She suffered from severe scoliosis, her spine so twisted that coughing and laughing were often painful. Other movements, such as bending to touch her toes, were impossible. Her breathing was restricted, at times making Stacy feel as if the wind suddenly got knocked out of her. How did Lewis celebrate the few permitted brace-less hours? Getting rest? No chance; she wore the plastic armor at night so she could maximize opportunities to swing her golf clubs. Excruciating as it could be, Stacy loved the game that much. Seven and a half years of arduous therapy rewarded Lewis with graduation from the brace . . . only to wind up in the OR undergoing a spinal fusion that caused her to miss her first college golf season. Yet the very next year: SEC champion! The following year: another back injury, of all the disasters that could have struck . . . until she took an improbable swing at a late-season comeback. And won the NCAA title! Lewis then followed it up with a curtain call of twelve LPGA Tour wins, two Player of the Year Awards, a Rolex Athlete of the Year honor, and a number-one world ranking within five years of turning pro.

Extraordinary, for sure, but these are only a few of the inspirational treasures packing the sporting world's archives. What the above exemplars shared: a narrowing of focus when pushed out of their comfort zone; dodging of distractions and details and media and moment-to-moment performance undulations; turning inward for answers; then going *all* in when a huffing, puffing dragon of a problem reared its head.

And, of course, they all played golf.

Which leads us to why we call the Avoider Conflict Personality Style "The Golfer." We chose this nickname because of commonalities this Go-To has with mindsets, like those used by Woods, Choi, Holmes, and Lewis (and scores of others), that are instrumental in converting bad lies into birdies.

Whether you play an occasional weekend Nassau with your besties or you're a seasoned pro, you've likely had a few days when all you seem to be walking in is the deep rough. Sorry to say, reading this book probably won't lower your handicap, but we can tell you that getting out of trouble in the sport of golf is a whole heck of a lot easier when you downgrade the seriousness of the situation, when it's no biggie, when it's just another shot. Sport psychologists who have extensive, world-title-loaded résumés spend a significant percentage of their consultation hours with Tour winners training them to reframe conflict (e.g., mishits, hazards, bad weather, bogeys, etc.), coaching them on how to focus, purely and decisively, on the ball-striking task at hand. The advice, at its most succinct: under the scorching lamps of pressure, don't analyze, don't negotiate with your caddy, don't try to make up for anything that's now in the past, don't try to do too much or "fix" things (*especially* mechanics). In fact, treat it as if there is no conflict at all. It should take scant seconds. Pick out a simple strategy (club and swing) that you've practiced a zillion times. Pick out a clear target. See the ball go there in your mind's eye. Then just hit it with zero regard for anything or anyone else.

Sound familiar? Leaf back to chapter 2. Rescan the Avoider section, looking for dovetailing between LPGA and PGA clutch shot psychology and how people who fall under the Avoider Go-To rubric handle personal and professional conflict. It's a useful exercise for a couple reasons. One, it helps streamline your understanding of this Conflict Style, particularly its strengths. Two, it highlights that one-size-fits-all profiling is a formula for disaster. Not all folks who play the sport of golf have this Go-To, and vice versa. Remember, all five Go-Tos are specific to how people deal with interpersonal stress and strife. "The Golfer" label for an Avoider is a moniker of convenience, selected to help delineate the Go-To's characteristics, give them a functional frame of reference, aid in identifying them, and promote matching them to people in your life in a fun, positive manner. At the end of the day, though, when you are dealing with human friction, the ingredients of an Avoider Conflict Personality Style are all that count, not its name.

To that purpose, and lest it be assumed to be an elephant in the room, we should address the perhaps clinical feel of the term for this Conflict Personality Style: "The Avoider." Indeed, as a title it's more scientifically informative than Golfer. But we're confident you see why, at times, we avoid the Avoider tag. People generally associate avoidance with negative behavior. Avoiding responsibility. Avoiding the truth. Avoiding an in-law. All are counterproductive to your long-term well-being. Evasion, as it applies to this Go-To, however, has nothing to do with skirting accountability or dodging duties. Avoiding potholes is a more apt analogy.

Avoiders seek to keep their car humming down the road unimpeded by small bumps in the road. They view most conflict as an extraneous distraction to their goals, smarter passed than getting caught up in. Let someone else fill the pothole. Or, shoot, leave it as is; it's not hard to veer around. Those with the Avoider Go-To perceive there are more valuable things to do. The tendency to avoid, for this Go-To, is thus borne out of time and energy management—wise decision-making, in their opinion.

When a pothole wears to the point of backing up traffic, however, Avoiders get Triggered. They no longer avoid. They will rent an asphalt heater themselves, if they have to. They'll grab a rake and a tamper and get their hands dirty—no need to fuss around hunting for gloves. Stay out of their way.

The Avoider, like each of the other four Go-Tos, has strengths and weaknesses that can equally be leveraged to your advantage. There are circumstances when it's a boon to be an Avoider, or to have one on your team. Case in point: a newly installed fingerprint reading system at the manufacturing plant where you work contains an annoying "pothole." You must take your gloves off to enter the building. In Minneapolis. In winter. Plus, the scanner fails when it ices over and IT has to be paged to reboot it . . . a twenty-minute process while you wait in the cold since, brilliantly, employee key cards were destroyed and IT isn't authorized to screen entrants. Milk isn't the only thing getting whipped into a froth around the breakroom's espresso machine as employees air their frustrations. Complaints are falling on deaf ears of your COO, whose cybersecurity upgrades created the mess—and who, along with the rest of the c-suite (oh how conveniently), works out of corporate HQ across the river in Saint Paul. Your team's communication efforts have resulted in a singular, three-line interoffice memo:

SECURITY IS OUR #1 PRIORITY
Compromise is NOT an Option
Tolerance of Minor Hassles is the Price of Excellence

Minor hassles? You can surmise the notions your coworkers are bantering about. What do you do? Quit on principle? Cuss your COO as if you were legendary Yankees manager Billy Martin going after an umpire? Plead your case, trying to convince your COO to change his or her ways? Flood his or her e-mail inbox? Go around him or her, directly to the CEO? Be a "team player" and suck it up? Thankfully, you've crushed a copy of *How to Get Along with Anyone.* You figured out that your COO is an Avoider. You know that none of those actions would get you anywhere. They all treat the Avoider Go-To as a "problem." In doing so, you'd be the one to take a hit. The pothole wouldn't get patched. It's far better to flip the dance card, inviting the Go-To's strengths to the party. Schedule a series of 8:00 a.m. meetings at the Minnesota plant pertaining to crucial facility operations that mandate (by substance rather than demand) the COO's attendance. What a coincidence that your scheduling aligns with below-freezing weather forecasts! It won't take but a morning or two of icicled digits before the COO is thumbing (or thawing, ha-ha) through the yellow pages' "security systems and providers" listings.

TEE IT UP!

People with the Avoider Go-To are in their element when faced with three distinct conflict amalgamations: (1) inconsequential or low-importance disagreements, (2) slowly developing challenges that would derail if tackled prematurely, and (3) severely escalated, complex conflagrations or emergencies demanding problem-solving with laser focus and efficiency.

The first is a product of the Avoider's compulsion to stay out of conflict. Since they will avoid spats, friction, petty fights, and the like, they, by default, don't contribute to making small issues worse. Thus, any such conflict, which will naturally die out of its own accord, will end pretty quickly when one party is an Avoider. One might argue this isn't a direct "skill" of an Avoider—but it is an indirect benefit. Keep in mind, Go-Tos are sets of personality states that emerge when someone is Triggered—when tension is high, when reason and logic falter. When Triggered, an Avoider's talent lies in maintaining priorities, adhering to an agenda, ignoring distractions, relegating unimportant tasks to the back burner, keeping their brain free of clutter. For a lot of folks, that's hard to do when getting nagged. If there is someone in your office who tends to make the proverbial mountain of a mole hill, pair them up with an Avoider. The Avoider will use creative meeting, communication, and assignment tactics to neutralize the potential productivity drain.

The second scenario taps an Avoider's notably durable patience. This is a great match if the developing challenge isn't a ticking time bomb (i.e., if it requires ripening or slow baking to gain clarity or consensus). Unfortunately, interpersonal puzzles can, periodically, masquerade as the latter, preventing you from discovering TNT at the core. So only lean on an Avoider for the crockpot sort of conflict when you are certain it isn't destined to bubble over (escalate).

The third dish of conflict (perhaps more aptly, grease fire)—is of such severity, such an emergency, that time and energy are precious, rapidly evaporating commodities. At a juncture when the parties involved are at a loss for an answer and realize further debate will be disastrous, turn to an Avoider in the group. Give him or her the reins. *Completely*. Avoiders' ingenuity under pressure is a godsend for excising complexity with the swiftness of an EMT. If others aren't meddling or interfering. People with this Go-To disdain interruptions. Meddling or interfering will Trigger them, nullifying the benefit of turning to Avoiders for emergency kinds of scenarios.

Being strategically proactive means identifying when you have one of the above circumstances on your hands, knowing if one of the participants is an Avoider, and (a) if so, allowing the conflict to play out with confidence that the right personnel are in place, or (b) if not, making one of the following chess moves:

~ Should you be in the conflict, play the role of Avoider yourself.

~ Or, should the conflict be stirring in a group project, add an Avoider to the project team.

~ Or, proceed without the value-add of an Avoider's strengths by assessing the Go-To of the person whose Triggering initiated the conflict and then fast-forwarding to that Go-To's corresponding chapter.

Regarding the first suggestion, should this Go-To not be your natural state, there are a couple simple steps you can take to effectually approximate being an Avoider:

1. Resist urges! Remember when you were in junior high and had a crush on someone? What was surefire to drive them away? Coming on too strong, of course. Indeed, easier said than done, but the foundational rule of thumb in being an Avoider is to not engage. Ignore poking and prodding. Don't return incendiary e-mails. Turn on your "unavailable" autoreply. Just say no to nonessential requests for your time.

2. Create and follow a scorecard. Avoiders play Dominoes, so rank the issues on your plate from most important to least important. Cross off the bottom third. For the remaining items, affix dates by when they must be completed or resolved. Rank again, from soonest to latest. Again, cross off the bottom third. Attend only to what's left.

HOW TO GET AN AVOIDER BACK INTO THE FAIRWAY

As well attuned as you may be to the pluses of the Avoider Go-To, you may have to collaborate with an Avoider when the nature of the work feeds smack into his or her weaknesses. These occasions include times when frequent and voluminous communication is called for, there are no solo roles, rigid policies must be followed, or a wide-field view is paramount. An environment with these constraints will Trigger an Avoider to a degree that they become a liability—to your mission, to your family's or your company's mission, or to themselves. At some point you might have to negotiate with an Avoider over relatively trivial issues. Global-scale initiatives, for instance, entail a million moving pieces. As much an Avoider would like to, the little parts can't be skipped. Or maybe a loved one is an Avoider; maybe they're mired in a mud pit of a relationship characterized by blurred boundaries; who's-responsible-for-what accusation slinging, and heel dragging. Since they want to get out of the situation as soon as possible, their frustration and impatience can cause them to try to climb out of the pit too quickly. And you know what happens when you run too fast on a slick incline. Yup, onto your tuchus you go, sliding right back to the bottom.

So, milking the golf analogy, how do you get an Avoider back into the fairway? Whatever you do, don't invoke the Conflict Personality Style of the Analyzer! The Analyzer is an Avoider's worst nightmare. Analyzers creep cautiously, meticulously gather intel, explore every angle, and hit the brake pedal at the slightest hint of time pressure. When an Avoider is Triggered, they want the conflict crossed off their to-do list . . . *yesterday*. Analyzers love exploring. Open-ended questions are their favorites. All that probing will drive an Avoider batty. *Yak, yak, yak*, an Avoider will think. *What a waste of time.* Avoiders hate anything (or anyone) that wastes time.

If your own Go-To happens to be an Analyzer, you've got two options: (1) Grab the *soonest* opening you can to recuse yourself. Tap a tag team partner into the ring—an Accommodator. Accommodators are a great fit for Avoiders because neither wants to bother with conflict if they don't have to. They'll promptly dismiss issues. If dismissal isn't feasible, the Accommodator will, selflessly, noncompetitively, be concerned with the team's success while the Avoider will narrow in on the problem. As a result, the Accommodator will defer to the Avoider's solution. Neither's ego will factor into the equation. A match made in heaven. Alternatively, (2) find the nearest phone booth and pull your best Clark Kent transformation. Don an Accommodator cape, leaving your alter ego behind as you give flight to Accommodator strengths.

Not comfortable with portraying an Accommodator or don't feel practiced enough yet at the personality's conflict-handling approach? Can't logistically insert an Accommodator into a particular conflict with an Avoider or one isn't available to be plugged in? Then what?

Play the Player. When you know someone's Go-To Style, you know what Triggers them—what makes them anxious, what ticks them off. The converse calms the emotional spikes they experience. Reinforcing this central tenet of *How to Get Along with Anyone*, Playing the Player means treating conflict not as you versus them but, rather, as your words and actions influencing their words and actions. In Casey Ryback fashion, use the force *they* supply—their fervent desire to move away from anxiety, or from frustration producers, and toward emotion soothers—to aim them in a new direction.

> "There are some things one can only achieve by a deliberate leap in the opposite direction."
>
> **—Franz Kafka**

For an Avoider, the ace they're holding out for is conflict wiped off their plate. It's a pair of aces when the wiping is done in short order, or when they don't have to get involved at all. Condescending tones, hard negotiators, inefficiency, small talk, endless meetings, and inflexible rubrics are the chief stimulants for an Avoider to fold—that is, mentally check out. Practicing aikido with an Avoider, therefore, is the dance of (a) helping them see that their instinct to avoid will increase their irritants while (b) showing them how your plan will eliminate the conflict, allowing them to refocus on more worthwhile goals.

To accomplish this, capitalize on the Avoider's ability to narrow in. Target *one* issue. And play Dominoes; target the most vital, core issue. Don't wait for the Avoider to come to you or for an opportune "teachable" moment to arise. Such patience will feed into the Avoider's avoidance, a 180-degree heading from your intended finish line. As the old saying goes, "You cannot win a staring contest against the Great Sphinx."

Over the years, we've found a sequential series of three techniques to be most effective:

1. **Be a Speed Racer.** Move quickly. Don't go back and forth messaging and scheduling. Cut the chitchat; get straight to the point. No bull, no baloney. Communicate directly and clearly that your objective, your sole objective, is to resolve the issue forthwith. Let them know that by taking action, they will be saving time. You are happy to drop everything to do them the favor of getting this out of their hair.

2. **Roll Tide.** Regardless of how elegant your Speed Racer execution, an Avoider may still try to stiff-arm you or postpone problem-solving. Stay

persistent. Don't use e-mail, if possible. Avoiders have a penchant for ignoring; it's awkward to ignore a knock at the door. Continue to follow up
with what you want. The key is to emphasize, in every communication,
how your suggested tack will make the issue go away (and will get you to
go away too). Good waves with which to form a rolling tide include the
following:

> **Wave 1:** Begin with any variation of "I want to be respectful of your
> time. What specifically do you need from me to make _____
> happen?"

> **Wave 2:** "I hope your week is cranking. How are things coming along
> with _____? How can I help move things forward?"

> **Wave 3:** "I know you're extremely busy, so how about we get
> together to bang out _____? I can stop by at noon." An
> in-person meeting is the last thing an Avoider wants, which leads
> nicely to . . .

3. **Tip the Scales of Annoyance.** The Roll Tide step demonstrated that
you're going to be in the Avoider's kitchen. They either have to entertain you or entertain the problem. Avoiders almost always conduct an
opportunity-cost analysis of their time. To Tip the Scales of Annoyance,
show that dealing with you is going to be a lot more time-consuming
than ripping off the Band-Aid by simply addressing the conflict (which
also gets you out of the kitchen).

CHICKEN FEED

Doc G once had the pleasure of mediating a lawsuit between newly-
weds and a well-known fast-food chicken chain. What started out as a
typical honeymoon ended up as anything but (unless you count Chevy
Chase's antics as Clark Griswold in *National Lampoon's Vegas Vacation*).
That the lose-lose snafu almost didn't even make it to Doc G's office is

a cautionary tale about what can happen when you do not manage an Avoider wisely.

A wife and her husband had postponed their dream trip for two years following their nuptials. They were hardworking souls, committed to their jobs. Neither spent lavishly. Neither were prone to extravagant whims. They conscientiously lived within their means, so they were eager to cut loose for a change. Sin City was their ultimate "responsibility hiatus" destination.

To reserve their fancy-free funds for The Strip's shows and casinos, on the way to catch their flight, they stopped off at the nationally popular "Chicken Run" (we're not at liberty to share the business's actual name). No need to pay outrageous airport prices on a quick bite, they thought. The establishment was relatively empty, but the couple still received a clap and a "Congrats!" when they walked in. They'd decided to dress up to relive their wedding day, he in his tux, she in her wedding gown. They smiled, ordered their food, and sat down. The wife excused herself to go to the restroom.

Seconds later, a blood-curdling scream, "AIEEEEEEEEEEEEEEEE-EEEEK!"

Scattering their table and chairs in a jolt, the husband sprinted to the bathroom. The four other patrons were right on his heels.

There on the floor was his wife, clutching her arm and lying in the middle of a *huge* puddle.

"GET ME UP!" she bellowed.

He reached down and she screamed again when he grabbed her arm. "OWW!"

"Oh, I'm so sorry, hon."

He repositioned himself as one of the other customers helped, together lifting her by her torso. Her gown was soaking wet. And stained . . . *yellow.* A pungent ammonia odor was undeniable. The wife had slipped in a veritable lake of pee.

Just then, the restaurant's manager appeared, looking like a member of the Addams Family who'd recently discovered hair gel. What had also curiously just appeared was a "slippery when wet" sign, placed outside the bathroom's door. The manager, noticing what had happened, had gone to retrieve the sign during the commotion. He'd also pulled the restroom cleaning log from the stockroom, forged the signature of one of his employees, and hung it back up in the bathroom where it was supposed to be. Only, the manager wasn't the brightest bulb adorning the tree. All of his actions were caught on camera!

Slam dunk for the couple, right? She sues the fast-food chain for pain and suffering due to gross negligence and wins millions of dollars in a settlement. Except there was a problem . . .

She was an Avoider.

"Ma'am, I'm so sorry you didn't see the sign," said the manager. "Is there anything we can do for you?"

"Just get me my damn food."

"Um, coming right up," the manager responded.

Accompanying her back toward the dining area, the husband interjected, "Honey, shouldn't we go get your arm checked out?"

"No! I'm not missing Vegas because some idiot doesn't know how to mop a floor."

At that point, the wife was doubly Triggered—by the fall and by the prospect of her long-awaited trip getting grounded. Being clad in a ruined, urine-dripping wedding dress wasn't exactly shepherding logic either. The husband was at a critical conflict management intersection. What is the best pitch with an Avoider at a moment like this?

"Of course, dear," he said.

Oh, no! *Wrong.*

The husband went to the counter and picked up their food, to go, which they scarfed down on the remainder of the drive to the airport. Off they went to Vegas . . . where they proceeded to hemorrhage $10,000 on blackjack. Himself Triggered by the stress of dropping the funds they'd saved up for the honeymoon, mixed with plenty of liquor, the husband tabled any dialogue about his wife's arm. Besides, she'd picked up some painkillers from an unscrupulous bellhop, so she wasn't concerned. That is, until the flight home. Her arm was swollen. Her meds ran out. Her mood soured.

The husband took another crack at Avoider jockeying. "Babe, I really feel like we should get a doctor to take a look at your arm. We've got free

Wi-Fi with our ticket. I can book an appointment online. We can get in and out right on our way home from the airport."

Speed Racer, check. He articulated that the process wouldn't take up much time and he emphasized the minimal disruption to get it done, including his wife not having to tend to the details.

"Let's just let it go. I'd prefer to forget about it and move on," the wife replied.

"I hate to see you in pain, my love," the husband empathized. "At the very least, a nurse could give you a refill for the pain pills. If it's serious, the last thing I'd want is for it to get worse and you to have to have an operation."

Silence. The husband continued a bit more lightheartedly, "Who knows, we might even be able to get that restaurant to pay for the whole mess."

A pause, then the wife said, "I'll think about it."

Roll Tide, check. The husband didn't become discouraged; the silence didn't deter him. He provided the repeated—friendly—follow up necessary to elicit engagement, without being condescending or forceful. He planted in his wife's mind the idea of a monetary reward in contrast to a more painful, worsening arm condition. Which also kicked over the big domino, the fresh hole in their bank account. Granted, they'd set the money aside for a gambling vacation. But cost-conscious as they were, it still stung.

The husband didn't let the domino rock back. He powered on his laptop and surfed to their PCP's patient portal. He wasn't subtle about how easy it was . . . "Click, click," he narrated as he navigated the appointment page. "Annnd, click. Done, hon. I went ahead and booked a fifteen-minute checkup with Dr. Gil for you, just to be on the safe side if you feel up to going. I'll stop bugging you now. You get some rest. While you snooze, I'll do a little research on attorneys who specialize in slip-and-fall cases. It'd be great to find someone who's really good at knocking these things out of the park. If they think we've got an open-and-shut case, I'll take care of whatever they need to prepare the suit so you can focus on getting better."

"Okay," the wife agreed as she rested her cheek on his shoulder, adjusted her blanket, and closed her eyes.

Tip the Scales of Annoyance, check. The husband successfully juxta-posed the ease of an arm X-ray with the energy consumed by his ongoing worry, brainstorming, and suggestion-making. As well, he skillfully com-municated that he'd carry any time or emotional load of legal action, work-ing with lawyers to preempt any future conflict associated with the effort of filing a lawsuit.

With the Avoider pivoted, the couple saw Dr. Gil, who confirmed a broken arm. He cast it on the spot in less than twenty minutes. The wife decided to take medical leave from her job; as an Avoider, she didn't want the interruption of all her colleagues stopping by her cubicle to ask what happened, nor the bother of sending thank-yous for flowers and get-well-soon gifts. She relished the opportunity to get back to a painting she'd been wanting to finish. The husband, meanwhile, located a sharp attorney to submit their claim.

Alas, by this time, the fast-food chain had an ample runway to cover their @$$es. Their counsel took advantage of the wife's Go-To Person-ality Style, preying on her initial avoidance and her Triggered wish to exit the conflict zone (the restaurant) to discredit her story (and argue that she considered the honeymoon as more important than her health). The couple hadn't pulled out their phones to capture pics of the bath-room, which was out of sight of the security cameras. Unfortunately, for a jury (or, shoot, *Dateline*), the shock-and-awe value of a hi-res, glossy, blown-up photograph of a woman in a pee-covered wedding gown on the floor of a prominent eatery would have been powerful. Nor did the couple take a receipt for their meal, which would've had a time and date stamp. The company filed a response stating that the injury must have happened in Las Vegas. The company subpoenaed casino and bar tabs, filed a reputation-shielding injunction, and demanded deposing the wife.

Aggressive, hard negotiating is another Trigger for an Avoider. "I don't want to be in a room with all those vultures," the wife told her husband.

Which is just what the chicken chain wanted—spook an Avoider so dropping the claim is the more attractive route. The wife was inclined to do just that. The couple's lawyer, however, made up an excuse to stall in drafting a motion to withdraw—just enough time to get to the pre-liminary hearing and, fortunately, the judge saw through the restaurant's smoke screens. She ordered the case to mediation. It was assigned to Doc G.

Both sides had a ton to lose. The sheer ineptitude of the restaurant manager, the potential to round up witnesses, and the prospect of a disgusting bathroom-violation scandal going viral on social media meant even winning at trial would be a massive brand hit for the chain. On the other side of the table, mountains of discovery, seemingly endless depositions, and the meter running on a retainer were plenty to frazzle all the wife's Avoider predilections. And there was a risk a jury would call BS on account of her taking her food, living it up on vacation, acting as if nothing was wrong with her arm, and only later seeking to recoup a sizable gambling loss.

As a neutral third party, Doc G's job was to assist the parties in trying to arrive at a mutually agreeable resolution. He eventually settled it at $100,000. The chicken chain protected its image but paid a significant-enough sum to foster an internal examination of health code adherence. The newlyweds reversed their honeymoon fortunes without the Avoider getting pushed over a cliff. But mishandling the Avoider avoidance personality state at the very beginning (when the wife was the most Triggered) caused them to miss out on a golden payday. The couple's attorney later told Doc G that had he been able to spring into action on the day of the slip, he'd have been able to negotiate a settlement for $2 million, minimum.

Of the many applications to take home from this case, prominent is that much of conflict comes down to attending to timing. The husband finally landed on the correct Go-To strategy, which saved them from ending up broke. But by neglecting pace and not properly matching his approach to his wife's Triggers, he cost the couple a life-changing amount of money. ASAP is the name of the game for conflict with an Avoider. When you're working with or in a relationship with this Go-To, the longer you take, the greater their avoidance tendency. If you are not making a task a priority, they certainly won't. But if they can't avoid, their default behavior will be trying to swiftly put a conflict to bed. They want it off their calendar. Therein is the alignment of your interests. Get after it and get to that alignment.

Pro tip: for the Avoiders in your life, one of the greatest conflict prevention gifts you can give them is to keep your radar peeled for their Triggers. When you see one coming, jump on it. Don't placate. In the Chicken Feed case, this would have been attending to the wife's emotion spike in the restaurant and assessing that her curt reaction to the manager was her Go-To avoidance kicking in. That would have been the ideal time to Play Dominoes, Be a Speed Racer, Roll Tide, and Tip the Scales of Annoyance.

To recap, someone with the Avoider Conflict Personality Style thrives flying solo during pressure-packed stretches. They don't take kindly to micromanagement or rigid rule imposing. If given the opportunity, they'd never again attend a meeting or sit through a planning session. They absolutely cannot stand wasting time. They tend to communicate sparsely, so it's common to feel like they are not paying attention to you (or flat-out ignoring you). They'll avoid debates, arguments, tiffs, and clashes at every turn, if they can. If they can't, they'll strive for immediate disposal of a problem.

The keys to succeeding in a negotiation or conflict with an Avoider:

∿ Act! Don't fluff about.

∿ Be maximally time and energy efficient.

∿ Keep a narrow focus.

∿ Play Dominoes.

∿ Don't let a big issue fester but be willing to let little things go.

∿ Be persistent. Don't take it personally if they ignore you.

Getting through a rough patch with an Avoider is often a battle of wills. The Avoider, wanting to avoid the trouble, will resist getting in the pool. You have to get them to dive in. Stay committed to the swim! And if you're the one responsible for intervening in battles of will or preventing them in the first place—if you're the boss, or organizing a team or social group—be cognizant of Go-To matchmaking. Avoiders play well with Accommodators. For projects or events in which tensions might flare, refrain from pairing up an Avoider with an Analyzer.

For employers and managers, being considerate of the various Go-To Styles can make all the difference in reducing an environment's stress. It so happens that playing matchmaker with Go-Tos can also juice sales, a discovery that unfolded when a famous helicopter building firm hired Doc G to train its top executives. Doc G was swinging a pitching wedge, interactively teaching a lesson about the Avoider Go-To, when the global head of sales interrupted.

"Whoa! You're describing my guy, my Russia division sales manager. He usually kills it. But he's in a slump. I'm counting on him to close a monster account and here he is blowing off the buyer. That's an Avoider avoiding, isn't it? Doc, the buyer is one of the most powerful people in the world. I'm not $#!%in' ya! What do I do?"

Doc G licked his chops, ditched the rest of the session's Power-Points, and got down to business. Come to find out, the buyer was a Competitor . . .

7

The Competitor

A wild cauldron of conflict starts bubbling when you throw into the pot two multibillion-dollar corporations, a celebrity CEO, a "yes-man," Russian oligarchs, the owner of an iconic professional sports franchise, an IQ-off-the-charts salesperson, and end-of-quarter quotas. What did Doc G get himself into? When he boarded his flight, he was looking forward to conducting an educational seminar on winning team cultures. His slides, demonstrations, and exercises were all about preventing the day-to-day squabbles that get in the way of the kind of intraoffice bonding that juices both productivity and employee happiness. Doc G was prepared to discuss tips for things like open communication. Suddenly, it felt like a clandestine meeting during the Cold War. Here he was, in *Moscow*. Red Square and the Kremlin loomed outside the window of the Four Season's conference room. The head of global sales (nicknamed Hogs) for a company that, in addition to commercial helicopters, builds attack aircraft for the planet's superpowers was asking Doc G how to get a Russian operative—oops, we mean sales manager—to flip a faltering negotiation with one of the United States' wealthiest citizens, the chair of a tech empire selling software to governments across the globe. Spooky, to say the least. But it also presented an opportunity to facilitate international cooperation. Turning conflict into collaboration. Now you're talking—the whole purpose of *How to Get Along with Anyone*. Doc G was all in.

"Let's go!" he whooped, putting on his Active Listening cap and pulling up a chair in the middle of the audience to augment the team atmosphere, à la chapter 5. "Tell me everything."

Hogs laid out the backstory. He'd handpicked the current manager of Russian and Eastern European sales, hiring him into a junior position just a few years earlier. The young man, Yevgeny, was a self-starter with the endurance to toil for long, uninterrupted stretches. He assimilated technical knowledge at a lightning pace. He had a knack for focusing in on just the most salient details of customers' needs, bypassing middlemen, and directing clients' attention to the sexiest elements of helicopter buying. He rose up the firm's ranks rapidly, his consistent revenue numbers eliminating much need for supervision. Before long, Yev was selling helicopters to oil tycoons, rap artists, and movie stars. He was rewarded with his present title, the youngest manager of the prestigious Russian division in company history. When Hogs received a phone call from the uber-influential tech CEO, it seemed like a no-brainer. Put Yev on it. Yeah, Yev didn't have experience in the US market. *But*, Hogs thought, *he knows how to talk to these big-ego types*. Besides, American execs tend to go for jets over helicopters, so the firm's veterans in the United States were all in airplane sales. A month prior, the VP of that division had been assigned to finalize an eight-figure contract with the owner of an NFL team. It went sour. *Badly*. The NFL mogul made his dissatisfaction known publicly. The company lost the deal to its biggest competitor, a sting Hogs was determined to never feel again.

Yev hopped a plane to San Francisco, where an introduction had been set up during CES° (the mega annual technology innovation convention). Enter the yes-man. Expecting to sit down with a veritable rockstar of industry, Yev was met by an executive assistant.

"Where's the big dog?" Yev asked.

"Oh, he's in his suite, getting ready for his keynote tonight," the assistant explained.

"Sooooo," Yev pressed, "he's here, but he's not making time for this meeting?"

"Don't worry. I'm fully authorized to negotiate," the assistant said.

Yev was already Triggered. "This is a waste of my time. We're ready to custom build the most exquisite heli you've ever seen. If your boss isn't interested in that enough to come shake my hand, then there is nothing to negotiate." And with that, Yev stood up and walked out.

Yev had trades percolating with three Russian oligarchs. He was accustomed to being wined and dined. When buyers like those have their eye on a jewel, they spare no expense to get their way. They don't want people prying into their business, so they don't entertain "salesy" dialogue. Which was perfect for Yev—an Avoider.

By the time Yev got back to his hotel room, his phone was blowing up with texts from the executive assistant.

"I think you misunderstood, I'm the person charged with ironing out this purchase."

"Please come sit down so we can do business."

"Are you not getting my messages?"

"What am I supposed to tell my boss?"

"When I ask a question, I expect an answer."

"Do you seriously not know who you are dealing with?!"

"Reply!"

A migraine beginning to throb in his temple, Yev didn't stop to contemplate. This pissant (Hogs's choice of vernacular) represented endless back-and-forth. The executive assistant's job would be to screen all the conversations for his boss, while not delivering to him any information that the software magnate might not want to hear. As he mulled over this lack of efficiency and how protracted the next few days of negotiations would be, Yev could feel his migraine worsen. He had substantially larger contracts with the oligarchs awaiting him back home. Compared to them, an American CEO didn't impress him.

Delete, delete, delete, delete, delete.

Yev grabbed his suitcase out of the closet and haphazardly tossed in his clothes. "These guys are tire kickers," he told himself. "You don't send an assistant to buy a million-dollar aircraft. Unless you're going to nitpick every penny but don't want that hassle pinned on you. No thanks." Yev thumbed a Lyft and took off for the airport. He rerouted his itinerary through Helsinki and Saint Petersburg, making stops to see his other customers. He silenced text alerts and didn't check e-mail.

When he finally got home, his inbox was flooded with e-mails from the executive assistant. The oligarch visits ended up all party, no paperwork; those transactions were going to take longer than expected. What an exhausting trip. The last thing Yev wanted to do was wade through the humbuggery of a Yankee executive assistant who wasn't getting the hint. Over the weeks that followed, Yev continued ignoring messages from the United States.

"Has the buyer escalated it?" Doc G queried.

"Yeah! I got an e-mail *yesterday* from the assistant. How did you know?" Hogs exclaimed.

"Classic Competitor," Doc G shared. "What did the message say?"

Hogs pulled it up on his phone and handed it to Doc G. The body of the message was blank. There was a single attachment, a scanned letter from the EA, printed on the tech giant's personal stationery, with his initialing of approval. It read:

Dear Sir,

We've tried on numerous occasions to reach your associate. Regrettably, he has been unresponsive.

We wish to conclude our helicopter acquisition process. Is there someone else on your team we can speak with, or should we take our business elsewhere?

Sincerely Yours,

Mr. Cal Entoby
/ff FML

Doc G chuckled. "Perfect! You've got your Avoider and their two Competitors, all Triggered. There are a lot less risky ways to get to this point—you didn't have intel on the CEO's Conflict Personality Style; if he wasn't also a Competitor, he could easily have pulled the plug—but congrats, you've backed into a matchmaker's dream. Not only is there hope for the deal, you're in an even better position to negotiate a primo deal."

Doc G proceeded to explain that the Competitor Go-To is characterized by competitiveness and aggressiveness. Competitors are committed to getting a job done—and done *now*. We tap an American football reference in nicknaming this Conflict Personality Style since the speed and force this Go-To applies to overcoming challenges resembles a linebacker blitzing a quarterback. From the moment the play clock winds, they are all go, no stop, with everything they have until the whistle blows.

Alas, Competitors often get a bad rap. People can interpret "competitive" and "aggressive" as negatives, as insensitive, imposing, intolerant, too pugnacious. Not armed with an understanding of this Go-To, people can feel like a Competitor is assaulting them, but that's not a Competitor's intention. Their style springs from an unbridled desire to hit skirmishes, arguments, dustups, and controversies head on, to crush them as fast as possible. It's not machismo or one-upmanship for them. It's duty. Have you ever seen, in an NFL game, a Pro Bowl defenseman bust through the line, totally pancake a quarterback, and then extend a big paw to help the QB to his feet? That's the essence of this Go-To at its best.

The training session participants nodded along, getting the concepts. "The computer chair's executive assistant," Doc G proffered, "was Triggered the moment Yevgeny walked out on him. Not because he felt slighted. Competitors don't take things personally. His insistent texting was not geared at attacking Yev. When Competitors get Triggered, they become extremely persistent. They can dish plenty of poor word choices, for sure! Cussing, insults, threats—this Go-To isn't shy at using them, and such tactics can cause all kinds of problems for a Competitor. What you need to center on is what they're trying to accomplish. They're trying to engage you in order to resolve an issue."

"So the EA guy, he wasn't trying to get Yev to pick up the phone so he could rip him a new one?" asked Hogs.

"Well, given the amount of ignoring your Avoider did . . . yup, the executive assistant likely would have *come across* that way," Doc G clarified. "Pretty strongly, I imagine. Which is a great teaching moment. The first thing you need to do with a Triggered Competitor is take some punches. Are y'all familiar with Muhammad Ali's legendary Rope-a-Dope?"

"Heck yeah . . . the Rumble in the Jungle!" chipped in members of the troop.

Doc G smiled ear to ear. "Let the software corporation's Competitors release their steam. It'll lower their emotion while letting them feel like they've won. From their ranting, isolate a clear priority of theirs and, complimenting them, reframe it into a statement that achieves an objective of yours. Then be ready to seal the deal! Remember, people with this Go-To don't mess around. They want immediate resolution. Deliver it."

"This is awesome, Doc!" Hogs bellowed. "Do you mind if we wrap early today? I'd love to swing by the office and get with Yev on this."

"Of course!" Doc G agreed.

It was a two-part training split across two weekends. Doc G was psyched to log in the sightseeing on his docket. He'd look forward to getting an update from Hogs when the group reconvened. And what an update it was!

When Doc G walked into the conference room the following Saturday morning, he was greeted with applause. A bottle of Imperial Collection Super Premium vodka with a red bow was sitting on the lectern. Hogs walked up and wrapped his big, burly arm around Jimmy.

"I take it y'all sold a helicopter?" Doc G beamed.

"Magic, my friend," Hogs replied. "I taught Yev what you were teaching us, you know, about him being an Avoider, and how his avoidance was pressing the buttons of the EA. I told him all about Competitors: how they ratchet up their effort proportionally with their level of pissed, but it's huff and puff and underneath it all is a fierce desire to get results. Smart kid, that Yev, he got it like *that* [snapping his fingers]. His face lit up and he said to me, 'So tolerating that pompous @$$ will suck up less time than sticking him where he belongs.' Doc, you're gettin' to know me. Whether people like it or not, I'm a hugger. I gave that kid a Russian bear hug, then we hatched a strategy to bring it home."

"I'm on the edge of my seat," Doc G said.

Hogs kept rolling. "I figured, give in to his request to be granted a new sales rep and, sure, he gets a win, but we gotta restart the process, new introduction, new background check, their security clearance hoop jumping, yadda, yadda, yadda. Their CEO ain't forking out a huge sack of cash without all that. You're talkin' weeks, maybe a month. That timeline Triggers a Competitor even more, right? We need to go the other direction; speed it up. Give 'em another win that way, as well. Plus, I have no idea if the threat to buy from our competitor is a bluff. After the NFL deal fumble, *no way* I'm takin' that chance. We used your Ali move, Doc. Yev's got himself some hella-strong abs! He calls the guy, thanks him for the letter, and shuts up. The EA dove right in; he did all the lifting. He blustered on about his decades of calling shots for the 'most respected person in the United States' and how stupid it was for Yev not to jump at the opportunity to learn from him. Followed by, I kid you not, probably a half hour of fuming about his boss's disappointment in being unable to fly out from CES* in a brand-new helicopter, sporting the logo of an international leader in carbon footprint reduction, and that his boss had designs on a long-term partnership to tackle food distribution in impoverished nations. No $#!%, Doc; he laid out our whole pitch for us. Yev waited and fed it right back, but in sale closing terms. A stock model at full custom price with an added rush delivery bonus fee and a five-year fleet purchase option. They closed it on the *phone*, Doc."

There were pats on the back all around the conference room. Doc G suggested they celebrate and give a rouse to new friendships all around. Not much training took place that day. Doc G left Moscow with a retainer agreement instead.

THE LOVE CONNECTION

Go-To Conflict Style coordination in how you staff and organize your teams is an efficient way to prevent internal conflict. Work group synergy is paramount for an organization to thrive. Organizations must also navigate external conflict: negotiate tough deals, improve B2B partnerships, reverse customers' disgruntlements. The Heli Co. was keen to develop these talents. To that end, their leadership circle was riveted by the concept that specific pairs of Go-Tos foster more successful client relationships, particularly via rapport building, communication flow, and aligning interests—core fundamentals of sales. The strategies you're picking up in this book are ripe for that aim. Applying them with customers, clients, donors, and other outside stakeholders, however, is productive in an alternate way: engendering authentic, unsolicited enthusiasm to support you to serve as influencers or connectors for you. Such fervent desire is not for the widgets you sell. It's for *you*. It's a love of how you go about things, how you treat others. Human beings are wired to seek relationships that allow them to be heard, understood, and valued. Our biological need to connect on a deeper-than-surface level is pervasive. When you engage the mechanisms that allow people to sort out their differences—listening, validation, appreciation—you're cooking with the same ingredients that attract us to one another, that create bonds. You are fulfilling needs. You are gaining reciprocation. It's no surprise, therefore, that Go-Tos who are "best teammates" (as coded in chapter 2) tend to enjoy longer-lasting friendships, business affiliations, and marriages. Conflict Personality Style matchmaking (which is what connectors do) not only dissipates disputes; it builds better relationships.

A nice shortcut is to link up Go-Tos who are need-action complementary; in other words, the Triggered Go-To needs what the other Go-To is instinctively good at doing. The Competitor-Avoider pairing in the previous case study may seem counterintuitive. A Competitor charges; an Avoider avoids. Potential calamity. *Unless* the Avoider is also Triggered. A Triggered Avoider wants to resolve conflict as quickly as a Competitor. Both detest wasting time. Both gladly forfeit ego in favor of task completion. Thus, an Avoider won't care if a Competitor employs harsh or critical language, allowing the Avoider to channel Ali, to take blows and patiently listen (another Avoider strength). This makes the Competitor feel validated. Further, Competitors are uncomfortable deviating from a game plan, which is a weakness when facing complications or unexpected developments. Avoiders' creative problem-solving can come in handy when a Competitor is stuck in such a box.

In most instances, a Competitor's push, push, push perseverance will Trigger an Avoider. When the Avoider realizes the Competitor won't leave him or her alone, the Avoider will shift to addressing the matter ASAP to try to eliminate it. Exactly what the Competitor is seeking as well. The clear-it-off-the-calendar interests of both the Avoider and the Competitor are aligned. Be careful, though, not to assume the alignment is a lock. If it takes too long for an Avoider to reach Triggered go-mode, a Competitor may quit for greener relationship pastures or, worse, completely lose it.

HOW TO BE A RODEO CLOWN

If a Triggered Avoider isn't at the tee, or you're worried that your Avoider is too cozy avoiding the situation, how do you Play the Player with a Competitor?

First, the cautions: (1) Don't invoke the Analyzer Go-To. Analyzers are the worst teammates for Competitors. An Analyzer will refuse to make a quick decision. This will tick a Competitor off even more. The two are apt to get into a negative spiral, one which may become irreparable. (2) Don't apologize. While a Competitor's emotion is still heightened, saying your sorry is like a shark sensing blood in the water. Apologizing induces additional aggressiveness, further affixing the blinders a Competitor has on when Triggered.

Rather, be a rodeo clown! Be like host Mike Rowe on the television series *Dirty Jobs* when he voluntarily jumped in front of hoof-stamping bulls. In case you've never seen this for yourself, professional rodeo clowns dress up in loud colors and bright makeup, and run around wildly inside an arena, attempting to catch the attention of an angry bull. They can't try to escape the ring; their paycheck is earned by making the beast chase them. Bull-riding cowboys compete to see who can stay on the violently bucking creature the longest. No cowboy will mount up without a rodeo clown standing ready. Cowboys can't hang on more than a few seconds. They'll always get bucked. In that instant, they are incredibly vulnerable. The rodeo clown successfully distracting the bull can mean the difference between life and death, or severe harm. Crowds find the clown entertaining. The clown himself or herself? Gifted entertainers, but as serious as a heart attack. They know their job is, arguably, the most important component of the event's success. For everyone's safety, they dial in their attention to where the bull wants to go and steer him accordingly.

Resolving conflict with a Triggered Competitor is not all that dissimilar from being a rodeo clown (minus all the mauling and goring to contend with . . . usually; if those are of concern, call 9-1-1 immediately!). Thankfully, like Mike Rowe, you don't have to have previous experience (or a squeaky red nose). You just need determination and focus. For the best results, utilize three sequential techniques:

1. **Dance with Queen Elsa.** Competitors can stammer and holler and make a heck of a fuss. When that hurricane is aimed at you, biological instinct kicks in: shield, block, deflect, counterattack or run away. Yet, in an argument with a Competitor, somewhere in the flurry is a prized nugget of insight that you can use to disarm the disagreement. You need to be collecting, not discarding. To do so, to conquer human nature—to remind yourself that it's not personal, it's not really about you, even if the words on the surface suggest otherwise—visualize the scene as if it were a motivational aria in a musical or movie, the turning point for a downtrodden hero. We call this trick Dance with Queen Elsa, in applause of Disney's animated picture *Frozen*. In the film, Elsa breaks free of her societal shackles, belting out the song "Let It Go" (performed by the proclaimed queen of Broadway, Idina Menzel). We never get tired of singing along with our daughters and nieces:

   > *I don't care what they're going to say;*
   > *Let the storm rage on.*

   Queen Elsa's catharsis manifests itself in the form of a majestic ice palace, beautiful symbolism for what you can turn a Competitor's emotional spike into—if you *let it go!* You needn't use *Frozen* though. Pick a clip from one of your favorite movies in which the protagonist surges to transcend adversity. The goal is to leverage the imagery to refocus your lens, shifting your stance from being a combatant to being a rodeo clown, preparing to steer the bull. All the snorting and stomping contains valuable information regarding the direction that will be most effective to take the bull. Get comfortable with a Competitor's venting and *let it go!*

2. **Pan for Gold.** Competitors don't beat around the bush. Their fuming will always include their underlying interests. Those interests may be mixed up in the mess of verbal garbage, but not intentionally. A Competitor won't try to hide information from you, or play games. To find their interests, all you have to do is Pan for Gold. Get them to vent enough and the gold will be there. An excellent example of this is how Doc G's dad, Big Jim, earned his stripes playing college football for the Baylor Bears. He was a coveted recruit but as a freshman was at the bottom of the depth chart . . . at the same position as then senior Mike Singletary—NFL Hall of Famer Mike Singletary! Every day, Big Jim would get run over by Mike. Notoriously animated defensive coordinator Corky Nelson, known for screaming at players to toughen them up, singled out Big Jim. Coach Nelson made it his mission to test Big Jim's fortitude. Every drill, every practice, Coach Nelson tore into him like a drill sergeant at basic training. Big Jim never said a word. He kept hitting the field and kept taking beating after beating. Months went by. One day after a bitterly grueling workout, Corky held up Big Jim as the rest of the guys headed to the locker room. "Why can't I get a rise out of you, young man? How come you're still here?" Big Jim responded, "My father told me to always sift through BS to find a piece of information you can act on and then tune the rest out." Coach Nelson laughed and vowed to give Big Jim one new pearl of wisdom every day. Big Jim soaked it up, improving his football skill little by little, all the way into the starting lineup. They've been friends ever since.

3. **Reframe the *Mona Lisa*.** Keep Dancing and Panning until you've defused emotion. Reliable cues that emotion has dissipated are lowered tone of voice and calmer body language. A Competitor's underlying interest may be apparent before this, but you need to allow them to feel heard and validated. Once they get those psychological wins, Competitors are consistently logical and will be open to a rational suggestion. We've found that reframing is exceptionally compelling. We refer to this step as Reframing the *Mona Lisa* because Competitors maintain high standards. And they can be set in their ways. As cliché as it is, "their way or the highway" tends

to govern debates with them. In their noggin, their underlying interest is a *Mona Lisa*—precious, uncompromisable, in need of being hung. You can't convince them to throw it away or put it in the closet until later. But a Competitor doesn't care about the details as long as the artwork goes up on the wall, without delay. So house it in a new casing, mount it where the painting is enjoyable to you as well. "I love your idea of _____ " is the mother of reframing phrases. Fill the blank with an underlying interest they gave you in the Dancing with Queen Elsa and Panning for Gold stages. Then append it with your desired destination, making it appear to be the fruit of their idea. For example, a senior employee (a Competitor) bursts into your office, furious that, without consulting them, you reassigned their assistant (a talented analyst, unhappy in their position). You *let it go*! You let all their complaints pass you by. You pan through all their chest-puffing. It's evident that their concern is having reliable resources to support their initiatives. You Reframe the *Mona Lisa*: "You're right, what you do for this agency is priceless. I totally hear you that an admin is necessary for you to be at your best. We should hire someone who you can mold from the get-go. Do any candidates come to mind?" Listened to, appreciated, and victorious (they scored a hiring slot), the Competitor shakes your hand. Conflict resolved. Chances are, as a bonus, the relationship has been strengthened too. It wasn't personal to begin with and you confirmed that your employee can trust you to fix problems expediently.

WWE SCALPING THROWDOWN

We'd be remiss if we discussed how to maneuver with Competitors without sharing the crazy mediation case of World Wrestling Entertainment meets B-movie Western. Doc G was enlisted to settle an extended family conflagration. Two teenagers, despite vehement disapproval of their single-mother parents, secured fake IDs and eloped. The union lasted four months. It might have escaped the parents' notice (and the authority's) had the girl's mother not discovered that her daughter wasn't away at boarding school. Upon receiving a phone call from the school, inquiring about the girl's lack of attendance, the mom knew . . . "That no good young man, corrupting my daughter!" She marched into the local police station and filed a kidnapping allegation against the boy.

Investigating, the cops dug up a forged marriage license and tracked the youngsters to an out-of-town motel, where they were both arrested. The parents were summoned to the jailhouse. The mothers, squeezed into a tiny interview booth and having never met each other before, listened as a lieutenant began to spell out what was going on. Within seconds, the boy's mother leaped out of her chair into a flying body slam at the girl's mom. All hell broke loose. The "hot box" was a whirlwind of kicks and fist swings, toppled furniture, and blue uniforms rushing in to suppress the melee.

The parties separated. Accusation throwing, property claiming, and lawsuit threatening took over, eclipsing the room with a suffocatingly rancorous atmosphere.

"Your son cost me a fortune in school tuition!"

"*You* got my son put in handcuffs!"

And on and on. To try to smooth everything out and to get the file for the debacle the heck off his desk, the lieutenant offered to drop the criminal charges against the children and not issue any citations to the parents, in exchange for them accepting voluntary restraining orders along with mandated mediation to legally annul the marriage and dispense any claims of harm and financial duty to the other party.

Doc G swung open the mediation center's door. In walked the boy, barely 140 pounds soaking wet, his arm in a sling. He didn't say a word. The girl arrived next, kempt in her plaid school skirt, but with a *massive* chunk of hair missing from the top of her head. Her mother followed . . . carrying a sawed-off shotgun.

"It's okay. I've got a permit," she said, waving toward Doc G to remain seated.

For a *sawed-off* shotgun? Doc G explained that, nonetheless, no firearms were allowed in the meeting. She reluctantly relinquished it.

Shortly thereafter, the floor of the building started to shake. Down the hall came the boy's mother, no joke, appearing like an NFL nose guard; she dwarfed Doc G in stature.

"*Holy Competitors!*" Doc G thought. He escorted the participants to separate rooms so he could play man-to-man defense.

Doc G started with the girl and her mother and was surprised when it was the young lady who launched into a tirade. Doc G encouraged her to unload her concerns, to *let it go*!

She said that she wanted her "mother-in-law" put in prison, *that day*, for assault, chronicling that she'd gone to the mother-in-law's house to return (she went out of her way to emphasize "politely") some of the boy's belongings. The mother-in-law was on the porch drinking with a boyfriend, cans of beer littering the ground.

"I was trying to be nice. That ogre comes stomping down the steps, grabs me, throws me to the ground, and rips my hair out! She was high on cocaine. Reeked of alcohol. I was so scared. She went back up on the porch, jumping around, celebrating, showing my hair to her boyfriend. I ran to my car and got out of there. She's a violent psychopath who needs serious counseling. She needs to be locked up. She's a danger to everyone around her. I bet that sling is her doing. I'm afraid to even be in the same building with her today."

Doc G took careful mental notes, actively listening until the girl's emotion subsided. He then moved to the other mediation room to continue collecting information. Not shockingly, the boy's mother had a different recount of how the events unfolded.

"The little waif, she comes up to *my* house, acting all high and mighty. She was trying to plant her crap on our property to frame my son, so she could pull the wool over your eyes today. Nope, not on my watch. I stopped that hussy from shoving her way onto our porch and put her in her place," spewed the boy's mom.

"I appreciate your thoroughness," Doc G complimented. "Would you mind helping me understand what 'put her in her place' means?"

"I whupped that little princess's entitled @$$ and took her hair as a trophy. She isn't gonna get $#!% from my boy."

Dancing with Queen Elsa, check. By not allowing himself to be appalled, by not arguing with the mother or confronting her with the girl's version of events, Doc G allowed the boy's mom to feel heard while letting off steam.

"Thank you for that clarification," Doc G went on. "You know your son and what's best for him. Could you tell me specifically what you'd like to have happen this afternoon?"

She eagerly seized the invitation. "I want that rich bitch to keep her paws off my boy and I want her good-for-nothing mother thrown in jail so neither of them will ever bother us again. And I want everyone to know what two-faced scam artists they are."

Panning for Gold, check. By gathering and sifting through all the details, Doc G could see the parties' common underlying interest in ending things and going their separate ways.

"I appreciate where you're coming from," Doc G validated. "It makes sense that your main goal is to get this annulment settled as quickly as possible so you both can move on with your lives."

"You're damn right."

Reframing the *Mona Lisa*, check. All the hocus-pocus about imprisonment was Triggering residue. Doc G reframed that vitriol into a statement of the domino they most wanted to topple: attaining freedom from this ugly and unfortunate situation. Agreeing was then easy for two Triggered Competitors who ultimately wanted an end to the nonsense.

VINCE LOMBARDI'S PLAYBOOK

As we mentioned earlier, of the five Go-Tos, Competitor is the one most oft misinterpreted as a "bad" style. We must punctuate, *firmly*: there are no "good" or "bad" Conflict Personality Styles. Each has weaknesses that make the Go-To tough to interact with when Triggered. But each Go-To has strengths that give you an advantage in certain circumstances. Competitors' oak-strong commitment, willpower, and insistence on reliability and accountability contribute to them being fantastic coaches. Akin to renowned Green Bay Packers coach Vince Lombardi, people with the Competitor Go-To can be very motivational and bring out the best in others. If you stick to what you say you'll do, they'll have your back. They're fierce allies. And if a crucial deadline is careening toward you, you want a Competitor on your team.

"I don't believe in shrinking from anything, it's not my speed. I like to meet my adversaries head on."

—**John Wayne**

There are three distinctive scenarios in which it's a coup to exercise a Competitor Go-To. Delegate a Competitor to spearhead, or assume the Competitor style yourself:

1. When negotiating against an Accommodator. Accommodators despise heated confrontation. To escape it, they'll fold in a heartbeat. They'll give up their positions and take a loss before fighting with an aggressive, ultracompetitive negotiator. Who does that sound like? A Competitor, of course. Some may think this is cheating, by manipulating an Accommodator into succumbing. Rely on the context to determine what you deem ethical; consider what is at stake for all parties and how relationships will be impacted.

2. When time is of the essence. Nobody cuts through the fat better than a Competitor. If there are only a couple clicks left on the clock, if the solution to a quagmire demands blunt communication, if disaster has struck and no one has their wits about them . . . a Competitor's stewardship can save the day.

3. When the carrot doesn't work. You'll hear some pundits espouse a "carrot, then stick" approach. What they're saying, pertaining to handling conflict, is start with kindness. Be positive, supportive, and collaborative and then, if it doesn't get you anywhere, go "bad cop" to elicit an opponent's wish for the "good cop" to return. This is faulty advice. Being a jerk almost always costs you in the long run. Yes, meanies sometimes get their way, but at the expense of reputation and relationships. You don't want to "win the battle and lose the war." We harp on this point because Competitors are too commonly stereotyped as stick users. Using the Competitor Go-To is *not* issuing punishment. When carrots aren't effective, it's the Competitor's skill at being direct, no-nonsense, and assertive that is

needed to drop the hammer . . . *on the conflict*—that is, demand that the parties team up to defeat the problem.

Vince Lombardi was brilliant at identifying inner talent—dedication, fortitude, grit. He is heralded as one of the most inspiring coaches in history for drawing out these skills in everyone . . . tall and short alike, muscular and skinny, young and old, all races, creeds, and colors. Lombardi had zero tolerance for hatred, fear, and ignorance. He was a genius at getting people to drop their differences and work together. The Lombardi approach doesn't always come easily though. When you encounter one of the above scenarios, if you're not lucky enough to have a Competitor on your side, it's on you to insert a modicum of Competitor Style. Keep it simple. Do the following:

1. Pounce. Competitors are all about making progress. Pick your favorite proverb for being aggressive. "The early bird gets the worm. He who hesitates is lost. Do not be wise in words; be wise in deeds. There is no time like the present. The beginning is half of every action." To be a Competitor, prioritize baby steps today over monumental accomplishments tomorrow.

2. Swagger like Mick Jagger. Have you heard the expression "paralysis by analysis"? Elite coaches use the phrase in teaching their athletes to ditch second-guessing, to trust their instincts. The modern sports world is replete with *Moneyball*-made-sexy analytics. Analysis has its value and place. But under pressure, too much thinking causes you to freeze up, to choke. To be a Competitor, when life is messy, complicated, or stressful, find something to believe in and focus on it. Contrary to popular belief, true confidence is *not* having all the answers or being the best at something. Confidence is quieting your brain, being decisive, going with what you've got. Be like Doc G's wife, the consummate ER nurse. She comes through in the scariest of emergencies because, no matter what, she immediately tells a patient, "It's going to be okay." And then she does something, anything, to show the person that the wheels are in motion.

3. Trust. The same paralysis by analysis principle applies to teamwork. To imitate a Competitor, delegate with faith. Minimize meetings and managing. Refrain from constantly checking on people's performance. And if there is faltering on follow-through, act swiftly to make changes.

~~~~~~

The Competitor Conflict Personality Style is an all-go, no-stop, gun-the-accelerator-to-the-finish-line ambassador. That's not to say that people with this Go-To are "hard" negotiators in terms of lines in the sand. Competitors rarely walk away from the table. Quite the opposite, they'll get upset when someone leaves an interaction before the agenda has been furthered. If you want to work well with this Go-To, put your sensitivities in your pocket and put a premium on rapid resolution.

Remember that Competitors are passionate for a *good* reason. View their intensity as a beneficial commodity; use it to accelerate reaching an agreement. To swing the tide in your favor with a Triggered Competitor:

- Give them a reason to believe that the problem *will* be solved.

- Don't stall, slow down, or draw out the process.

- Give them an early win in the interaction.

- Allow them to vent.

- Don't take what they throw at you personally.

- Center on the most crucial issues. Play Dominoes.

- If there is an established playbook, stick to it.

- Adhere to deadlines.

- Say what you mean. Do what you say. Most importantly, *follow through*.

Competitors generally prefer tackling disagreements one-on-one. When there is a workplace altercation or controversy, the last place they want to be is a crowded conference room. From a Competitor's vantage, all those cooks in the kitchen bog things down. You'll be more successful with Competitors when you play them one-on-one. Competitors are all business.

But . . . they tend to not mix well with Analyzers, who *hate* actor Jay Mohr's line from the award-winning movie *Jerry Maguire*:

"It's not show friends; it's show business."

8

The Analyzer

S ea turtles do not do well in cold weather. Neither does the Texas power grid, which our nation learned the hard way in February 2021. The polar jet stream dipped abnormally far south, bringing with it a freezing vortex that spawned back-to-back-to-back severe winter storms. Arctic temperatures and howling winds ripped through an unprepared Texas. Sheets of ice engulfed roads, buildings, utility lines and stations. The state's energy infrastructure failed, leaving nearly five million homes without power, some for over a week. Food, water, and heat shortages resulting in needless loss of life on top of an estimated $195 billion in property damage—the most expensive disaster in state history.

En route to Mexico to give a seminar, Doc E was stranded on South Padre Island. Unable to cross the bridge and his hotel shut down, he decided to brave the elements. Thankfully, a beachside bistro was miraculously open. The proprietor had a generator cranked up and he was tending the bar, whipping up homemade hot cocoa. Doc E went in and grabbed a stool. The television on the wall was getting a satellite feed and *Jerry Maguire* had just started. Doc E struck up dialogue with the establishment's owner, a fit-looking late-fifties gent with a relaxed demeanor. No sooner did they start talking than the movie's dramatic opening climax rolled: Tom Cruise's tragic hero, the title character, getting fired—by his protégé, Bob Sugar—and spiraling into destitution as Sugar steals his clients. Comedian and actor Jay Mohr brilliantly infuses subtle but hard-hitting sarcasm into Sugar's persona. "Are you in or are you out? It's not show friends; it's show business," he punctuates as he pumps his fist in victory.

The men's conversation in the bar was abruptly paused. "I *hate* that line," the bartender exclaimed.

Naturally, Doc E's curiosity was piqued. "Why's that?" he asked.

"Success hinges on relationships," the proprietor replied. "You can't just walk over people like that," he said, pointing to the flatscreen. "Guys like Sugar . . . I've been dealing with them my whole life. They're 'takers.' They don't get it."

Doc E chuckled as he nodded in agreement. "Yeah. What're ya gonna do?" he rhetorically posited.

The barkeep was happy to elaborate. "You can't convince them to take a step back. They're in for a rude awakening when they're eighty and empty and have no friends and family around them. Heck, they can go through three divorces and still not get it. That's why I moved to this island. I'm done with Wall Street and trying to get the Bob Sugars of the world to grasp that business isn't all about making as much money as you can." He stopped for a second and refilled Doc E's mug, then continued, "But it's tricky, you know. Even here at this fantastic little joint . . . I've got to manage my staff thinking we can pour every penny into what our customers want. You can't ignore the bottom line either. It's a careful balance. You gotta deal with people on both sides of the equation getting frustrated."

What a fascinating, thoughtful person Doc E'd stumbled on. He was the only patron; the proprietor was happy to have someone to chat with. Doc E was happy to listen. It was freezing outside. For the next hour, Doc E was enrapt as the bartender shared his story. It turns out he was a recently retired, high-profile trader. He was fed up with the egos, the skewed almighty-dollar priorities, and, most of all, the recurring conflict at his firm over distribution of resources. Partners always wanted to line shareholders' pockets. Junior associates, idealism still intact, wanted profits reinvested into the business—technology upgrades, working-space improvements, funding for more frequent and robust client interaction, green initiatives, and other community service givebacks.

"Arguments would land on *my* desk," the bistro owner told Doc E. "I don't know why. I was the one who had to break up all the fights. I'd try to get them to see the value in compromising. I could get 'em back to work, but begrudgingly so. Nothing ever ended up changing. So here I am. I quit and bought a bar on a beach."

His Go-To was becoming evident: Analyzer. Congenial and well-liked by his colleagues, they would turn to him to solve problems. He'd listen to everyone and find middle ground that would settle dustups. But his methodical approach would Trigger all the Avoiders and Competitors (common Go-Tos on the NASDAQ floor), so ironing out one conflict would often beget the stirring of another.

It's an interesting catch-22. Analyzers are adept at the art of give-and-take. So it makes sense for them to be negotiators; companies and families turn to their Analyzers as intermediaries (albeit, rarely with a conscious understanding of why). Yet, the strengths that Analyzers bring to negotiation can be the very things that Trigger a conflict in the first place. As we discussed in chapters 6 and 7, and as our new friend in South Padre discovered, the slow, deliberate pace of Analyzers and their willingness to sacrifice productivity in order to minimize interpersonal friction make them poor teammates for Avoiders and Competitors. It's best to put Analyzers in the middle when trade-offs between the needs of an organization and the needs of its personnel are paramount (or those of a team and its members)—in short, when meeting in the middle is ideal. When middle ground is *not* indicated, when it's crucial to achieve wins in one direction or another, leave your Analyzers on the bench.

Back in the bistro, the owner was expounding on the similarities he'd found across industries, universal tensions that arise in managing people, from mom-and-pop shops to Fortune 500 companies. Employees on the front line go to their bosses with suggestions—pain points they've experienced interfacing with the public, or potential enhancements that have occurred to them. Those employees get Triggered when their ideas are not incorporated. They feel unappreciated in their jobs. They get disgruntled. They complain. Management gets Triggered, irked that their underlings are expecting them to divert budget, constrained or limited as it may be, without proof of concept or absent an opportunity cost analysis. Some leaders subconsciously interpret grumbling as directed at them, personally. They bristle. Conflict percolates.

"Take my place, for instance," the bistro owner offered. "My hosts and waitstaff fuss to me about how we need to add inventive microbrews, tear out the old smoke room and create an outdoor seating area, brighten up the bathrooms. They're voicing these criticisms because that's what they hear from the customers or what they'd like if they had their own bar. No spreadsheet can compete with what they feel. I have to humanize business decisions. I have to incorporate qualitative factors in assessing gains and losses and I sure as heck have to let my people know how valuable their input is, showing them how beneficial their ideas and feedback are, even in arriving at a no."

In the background, contract haggling was going belly up in *Jerry Maguire*.

"I am asking you for a *favor*," Maguire begs over the phone of the Arizona Cardinals' head coach, who had been ducking Jerry. In the scene, Cruise poignantly lays bare the intersection of professional and personal desperation, his character having been run through the wringer, still trying to salvage a deal. "I introduced you to your wife. We've spent Christmases together. Holiday cheer. Dennis—"

Coach Wilburn talks over him. "Jerry, you're reaching."

"Look, I'm . . . I'm asking you for a *favor*," Maguire pleads. "Don't do this to me. We have history, Dennis."

"Oh yeah, we got history, all right, Jerry. You drove the prices up on me for years. Now it's your turn to spend some time at the back of the line [*click*]." Wilburn presses the speaker-off button and emphatically hangs up the receiver. A classic portrayal of a Competitor reaching a boiling point with an Analyzer. At that point in the film, Tom Cruise's character is going through a midlife crisis of sorts, questioning the "almighty dollar trumps personal connections" value system of the sports agent world. He's wrestling with how to return to "love of the game" and how to achieve more meaningful outcomes—Analyzer natured, deeply philosophical pursuits that a Competitor, like Coach Wilburn, would see as too time-consuming and not immediately results-producing enough.

Suddenly there was a loud cheer from outside the bar. On the beach, a fishing boat captain named Henry Rodriguez had pulled up dockside. A small crowd had been accumulating, all wearing the same T-shirts pulled over their winterwear. The gatherers applauded as Henry tossed his spring line ashore.

"What's going on?" asked Doc E.

"They're rescuing sea turtles," the barkeep explained. "They started yesterday when the thermometer plunged below freezing. Henry's a legend around here. He takes vacationers out fishing, dolphin watching; whenever a surfer is in trouble or there's a storm, he's Johnny-on-the-spot. I'm open thanks to him. Heat and hot drinks for all those folks, on the house."

Doc E wasted no time, whipping on his coat and dashing out onto the beach. He was excited to witness the positive traits of the Analyzer Go-To Personality in action: decisive action based on a needs analysis, not allowing outside factors to sway commitment, and rallying others around the corresponding cause.

As he approached the group, he could make out the lettering on their shirts:

I SURVIVED
THE GREAT
COLD STUN
FEBRUARY 2021

They were all locals, members of a volunteer army named Sea Turtle, Inc., who'd rallied to aid Rodriguez and his deckhands. Inside Henry's boat, the hull was packed, shell to shell, with turtles! Cold-blooded creatures, they rely on the ocean's temperature to maintain body heat. When the water drops below fifty degrees, the reptiles become catatonic. They can't swim and float to the surface. Marine biologists refer to it as "cold stunning." If the surface air doesn't warm them up relatively quickly, the turtles perish.

What an inspiring mission! Doc E jumped in, helping lift the leathery cuties (each tipping the scales at seventy-five to one hundred pounds) onto handcarts and wheeling them from the pier to the volunteers' trucks. They were driven to the South Padre Island Convention Center, where dozens of kiddie pools had been set up.

The bitter sting of the storm's gale gave way to euphoria. Doc E carried a few turtles, manned hot beverage delivery, and dished out scores of hugs. The intrepid STI volunteers rescued, by the National Oceanic and Atmospheric Administration's count, fifty-three hundred Kemp's ridleys—the rarest and most endangered species of sea turtle.

Please join us in giving a rouse for Henry Rodriguez, an Analyzer extraordinaire. Analyzers get Triggered when they witness someone being taken advantage of. Henry demonstrated that "someone" includes furry and flippered friends, as well.

> "No matter what happens in life, be good to people. Being good to people is a wonderful legacy to leave behind."
>
> **—Taylor Swift**

THE DUNCUM METHOD

What we've gleaned from leaders like the bistro owner, Henry Rodriguez, and others is that a boots-on-the-ground approach is necessary at times to engender cooperation, to enlist the backing of folks with varied stakes in the undertaking at hand. Analyzers are excellent at this. They consider all perspectives. They take their time gathering everyone's viewpoints, weighing everyone's interests. As a result, when you have no time constraints and you're trying to sort out a complex situation, there is no better Go-To than the Analyzer.

What if you are staring at these conditions and you're not an Analyzer (and you don't have an Analyzer colleague or confidant to whom you can turn)? In the immediate-term, there are two things you should do to tap into an Analyzer's pressure-handling style:

1. Don't try to make bricks without clay. Obvious, right? You might be surprised (maybe not) at how many people make critical decisions without empirical evidence to support those decisions. One thing Analyzers do

well is putting aside gut instincts. They're information hounds. When you need to be an Analyzer, do the same; before you act, collect data. Data, data, data!

2. Pretend you're Nariyoshi Keisuke Miyagi—the sagely sensei, Mr. Miyagi, of *The Karate Kid* film franchise. With a Mr. Miyagi temperament, Analyzers take the time needed for careful, thorough consideration. They don't rush the process. "Patience, young grasshopper." Patience, patience, patience!

Longer term, we recommend taking a page from Doc G's mentor, John Duncum. Duncum is gifted at evoking Analyzer personality characteristics in his ventures' rosterees. Duncum made his first fortune in real estate, developing Waikiki Beach on Oahu after World War II ended. Understandably, American Japanese intercultural tension was palpable during that period. John was determined to be a uniter. Supporting diversity in his work crews, he thought, was a prime opportunity to do his little part in helping the world heal. He didn't make a commotion of it; he proceeded gradually. Rolling up his sleeves alongside his employees, Duncum focused on open communication, inclusiveness, respect—measuring architectural success both by the stability of his structures' foundations and the stability of his relationships' foundations.

One award-winning property led to another. Word got out that his teams had uncommon chemistry. Out of the blue, he received a phone call from the chair of the Toyota Motor Corporation, Taizo Ishida. Toyota was fresh off a nasty strike that resulted in a union-mandated resignation of the president, Kiichiro Toyoda, who was at the helm of the car manufacturing family's empire. Patriarch Sakichi Toyoda, raised by a farmer, believed strongly in education and expending one's own sweat to earn one's trappings. None of Sakichi's sons or grandsons were granted jobs at Toyota. All of his descendants had to prove their mettle, in school and then in other professions, before starting, at the bottom, of the family's businesses. Suddenly the reins had been passed to Ishida without the traditional Toyoda ascension process. Getting buy-in for Ishida's unconventional plans would be a tall order. On top of the need to save face for the Toyoda family: dissension within the ranks, general skepticism of innovation, big shoes to fill (Kiichiro was beloved by the company's board), and nationalistic fears about taking the business across the Pacific. Taizo knew he needed to expand his leadership acumen. He'd gotten wind of an American businessman scaling racial hurdles to foster commerce without conflict. He was eager to study John's process. John was eager to study the way of the samurai. A friendship budded.

Frequent trips across the Pacific ensued, with Taizo and John talking philosophy, morality, humanity, and kaizen—an emerging management concept that advocated continual improvement through organization-wide, collaborative participation. Harsh resource constrictions during the war planted the seeds of kaizen, which were watered by postwar reconstruction. The thrust was looking inward, relying on the depth and strength of people instead of leaning on financial or material drivers of growth—a notably Analyzer-ish way of tackling shortcomings. Duncum had been tinkering with kaizen ideology at his company. Motivated by his desire to predict and prevent conflict, he'd come up with a three-step strategy for practicing what he deemed turbocharged kaizen:

1. Empower members of an organization via regular meetings of working groups. Pair, in the groups, representatives from disparate units of the organization. For example, in a hospital, a financial manager, a lab tech, a food services manager, and a physician.

2. Require the working groups to remain in their meetings until they identify an existing or prospective Process Conflict within the organization.

3. Mandate that the group members brainstorm—and agree on—a minimum of three feasible game plans for eliminating or preventing the Process Conflict.

By implementing this technique monthly, Duncum enfranchised employees with a platform for contributing to real-time, communal stewardship, being part of *running* the company, together, not just workers in it individually. John gained a window into concerns and issues before they escalated. He gained valuable, already consensus-vetted ideas for improving the business.

Ishida loved it. He could see applications to the automobile industry that dovetailed with his desire to integrate brainpower across manufacturing and sales, particularly when it came to international operations. He wanted to open, before the 1950s was in the rearview mirror, dealerships in the United States supplied by plants in Japan. To get such units to work together seamlessly, he got busy designing and building a robust kaizen-driven system of communication. He turned around the internally bickering, sputtering auto industry in Japan. For his service to country, Ishida was bestowed the title "The Great Banto"—a Japanese honor reserved for only the highest esteemed merchants.

As for Duncum, he ended up owning multiple Toyota shops. He continued tweaking processes for implementing the strengths of the Analyzer. This Conflict Personality Style is ideal with kaizen as one of kaizen's overarching tenets is patience. The Analyzer is never rushed and will do everything in their power to gather all possible information before making decisions. Not long ago, John was presented with two authentic fifteenth-century samurai swords by the eventual Toyota heir, Dr. Shoichiro Toyoda, mastermind behind the Lexus brand as well as chair of the esteemed Japan Business Federation.

TRADING OUT OF CONFLICT

It was late July. The Major League Baseball pennant race was heating up. With three days to the trade deadline and a sliver of a margin separating nearly a dozen teams from playoff bids and an early termination of their runs, competition for "renting" one of the game's marquee sluggers was ferocious. That player's squad would have to leapfrog six other teams, including two division rivals to make it to the postseason. His manager, a beloved coach the guys called Skip, had just wrapped up a press conference following the team's sixth straight loss, a fourteen-inning heartbreaker at home. Reporters grilled him about the long odds of snagging a wildcard slot, their recent tailspin, rumors that he was going to get the axe, and the possibility that the franchise would deal their MVP to another contender. In no uncertain terms, Skip vowed that the fan favorite (we can't break confidentiality, so we'll call him "Moose") was not going anywhere, that he'd be proudly donning the city's colors until the day he retired. He stormed out of the press conference and into the elevator, headed for the baseball operations floor.

Cut to ten minutes later. "Are you *kidding* me!?" Skip screamed at the franchise's president of baseball operations. Pobo, as he was called, had closed the door but everyone on the floor heard it. The baseball guys always worked late after games, coding film, breaking down stats. They stopped what they were doing to listen. "You think you're going to trade Moose, throw me under the bus, put this team right in the cellar? Well, I've got news for you. He ain't waiving his no-trade clause without talkin' to me first. Go ahead. Watch what happens."

"I'm sorry, Skip. We are not having this chat again. That blinking light on my phone there . . . messages from nearly every GM in the league with trade proposals. No decisions have been made yet, but I have to take into account our barren farm system, our owner's checkbook—"

"Bull$#!%," Skip interrupted. "You're trying to cover your own @$$. You're the one on the hot seat. You're trying to spin the media to put this on me. Hang me out to dry, making it look like I was dishonest so the fans blame me when you let their hero go?"

"You know that's not the way we do things around here," Pobo replied.

"So you're *not* going to trade Moose?"

Pobo gritted his teeth. "As I said, no decisions have been made."

"Well, the press is getting this $#!% from somewhere," Skip pushed back. "You haven't included me in any discussions. You don't have any clue what's going on in that locker room down there. We've got a legit shot at catching up with our biggest rivals. But you can't get enough of your precious sabermetrics. You're crunching probability equations, calculating how much Moose's costing you per RBI. I bet you've got some risk-spending formula telling you the math doesn't add up. But we're going to be in the playoffs, and Moose is going to get us there. I'm tellin' ya."

"Let's be realistic here, Skip—"

"Oh no, no, no. That's total bull," the coach interrupted again. "I knew it. You're trying to work out a trade. You just haven't figured out how to tell me yet. That's it, isn't it?"

"No. There's nothing concrete, yet. A lot can happen in the next three days. But if we get the right offer, we'd be foolish to ignore it," Pobo said, dodging the question. "Now, I've got to get to work."

Pobo opened the door to his office and gestured Skip out. Skip desperately wanted to fire back, wanted to find something, anything he could say to shake some sense into his boss. He knew he'd better not though. He knew that last phrase, and that look. When Pobo got that expression, it meant he was done talking; he'd reached the limit of his tolerance.

The coach took the elevator down to the clubhouse. It was almost one o'clock in the morning. There was but a single dim light on in the laundry room, the dryers humming, full of uniforms. All the players had gone home. The clubbie had fallen asleep in the middle of the daily newspaper's crossword puzzle.

At home, Doc E's cell phone buzzed, waking him up. He looked at the screen to see who it was. Smiling, he tapped to answer. "Skip! How are you, big dog?"

"Doc. Glad to catch you. Man, I'm up against it here. The boss wants to trade our guy at the deadline. He doesn't think we'll be playing in October. He's talkin' loading up on prospects; no way has contract extension been put on the table. You don't pass on what I know other teams are throwing at him to then just go lose a guy to free agency. Either way, Moose's gone. And I kinda went off on Pobo. I blew it. Now he's all . . . what's the word you use? Triggered. It's a mess. How do I bring this thing back from the dead?"

Contemplate being in Doc E's shoes in that moment. How do you help?

The team's president of baseball operations had an Analyzer Go-To Style. He was an information hound in the middle of assessing a pending business transaction, for which more information was flooding in by the second. He was trying to use his skill for defusing tension, but there were deep and far-reaching relationships at stake—with his owner, his players and coaches, the fans, the media, the other executives around the league. And no matter what course he chose, someone would be upset. Large sums of cash were at stake. His field manager was uncompromising in his prioritizing of clubhouse chemistry. A hard deadline was looming. Trigger city for this Conflict Personality Style.

When Analyzers are Triggered, their propensity for conducting comprehensive homework and deliberation (wonderful endurances . . . when the clock is not *tick, tick, tick*ing) can lead them to stubbornness. They'll be resistant to engaging in negotiation or engineering solutions if they feel that they don't have all the relevant facts or if another party isn't showing a willingness to compromise. Any whiff of egos flaring or hounding them to speed up and they may shut down on you altogether. In their desire for fairness, striving to contemplate all angles, Analyzers can also get too far into the weeds. They can lose focus on the big picture. They can steer themselves into gray areas. If an issue isn't clearly differentiated from the person who's bringing the issue to the table, the lack of boundaries can hamstring an Analyzer's judgment, sometimes paralyzing their ability to reach a conclusion. Remember, this Conflict Personality Style has an innate craving to be in control. Analyzers genuinely feel that their process is the best way to make everyone happy. Which is why they get Triggered, poignantly so, when they see people freestyle.

Luckily, we have a lineup of effective techniques for getting a Triggered Analyzer out of the above ditches—nay, for Playing the Player with an Analyzer across the board. You may find that a couple of the following fall into place on their own, but think of these as a sequence of genie lamps to rub with an Analyzer:

1. **Lighten the Load.** In nearly 100 percent of conflict, there is potential for the relationship between the parties to wind up better than it was prior to addressing the conflict. How is that possible? Save for extreme, fight-to-the-death gladiatorial contests, whether a problem is fixed or not, whether people end up agreeing or disagreeing, doing business or parting ways, they can still gain an improved understanding of each other. Make it a priority, when you are dealing with an Analyzer, to communicate two things: (1) Separate the substance of what you are working on with them from your relationship with them. The substance is the "enemy," not each other. Attack it together, side by side. (2) Make a pact that, no

matter what happens, you'll enhance your relationship, even if only by an iota. Communicating these two things Lightens the Load of the conflict and leads to better problem-solving.

2. **X-Ray the Evidence.** Analyzers love to gather information, and they are skilled listeners. Recruit those characteristics to your advantage by x-raying the Conflict Agenda. Recall from chapter 3 that the Conflict Agenda comprises positions, issues, and interests. Positions are the obvious, surface elements of a contention—what one wants. Issues are justifications for those wants. Interests, often initially invisible, are the *whys*, the motivations beneath the wants. Underlying interests hold the key to resolving disputes. They can be satisfied without agreement on positions. For instance, you and your spouse are sitting in your living room, arguing about the window. They want it closed; you want it open. Positions. Switching the dialogue to interests, you uncover that they don't want a draft while you want fresh air. Winner, winner, chicken dinner: open a window in an adjacent room, letting fresh air in without it being drafty on the sofa. The goal of X-Raying the Evidence is to, like an investigator on the television series *CSI*, see through to underlying interests. An Analyzer's patience and penchant for analysis make them great X-Rayers.

3. **Deep-Six the Scorecard.** Cognizance of each other's underlying interests may cause answers to jump off the page. If not, you need to brainstorm. With Analyzers, you should seek multiple avenues for putting a dilemma to bed. Analyzers like to deliberate, so give them choices. Generate options. Deep-six the notion there is an ideal or one best path. Note: to make this step sing, it's pivotal to remove evaluation. Set the firm ground rule that, as ideas are concocted, they won't be judged. Get out pencils or dry erase markers and collectively jot down as many brainstorms as you can without assessing their practicality, affordability, or efficacy. Analyzers *love* lists, so success at this stage is filling up your pad of paper or whiteboard; it's not a "great idea" contest.

4. **Bake a Different Pie.** Unfortunately, most Triggered people get caught up in what's called Distributive Bargaining or a zero-sum game—but

especially Analyzers. They see a fixed pie; they focus on how it is to be distributed. For one side to attain something, the other side must give something up. If a buyer receives a better price, the seller makes less money. So Analyzers dig in their heels: anything other than a perfect 50-50 split is unfair in their eyes. But there is another way to negotiate: Integrative Bargaining. In Integrative Bargaining, the objective is to expand the view of the pie (and the utility of its components) or bake a new one (in short, integrate more or new strategies such that both sides benefit). For example, your neighbor is pissed off that your dog barks in the backyard at night and insists you keep your pet inside. Your spouse is allergic to canine dander. Seemingly, you are at an impasse. Until you find out that your neighbor has children who adore animals and would be ecstatic to have your dog cozy up with them in the evenings. Or say there's one piece of pizza left at family dinner and both of your teenagers want it. Try to cut it in half and they'll fight down to the nanometer of size inequality. You've got no shot to avoid a spat, unless you incorporate the fact that neither wants to do the dishes. You propose that the person who gets the last piece of pizza *also* must do the dishes. With Analyzers, center your conversation on how you both can end up in a superior spot relative to where you started. A helpful question to ask: "Of the items you penned in Deep-Sixing the Scorecard, which can't the parties attain on their own?" This type of thinking not only expands the list of possible solutions but also shows how conflict can allow both parties to end up in a better place than where they started.

When you're Lightening the Load, X-Raying the Evidence, Deep-Sixing the Scorecard, and Baking a Different Pie with a Triggered Analyzer, it's important to be present. If you attempt these techniques via an impersonal medium, such as e-mail, an Analyzer may consult other parties, go around you, or further muddy the waters. Endeavor to control the narrative by being as present as you are able. Don't "divide and conquer" with an Analyzer whereby you each go off to work on a subset of a problem by yourself.

Also, beware: do *not* bluff someone with the Analyzer Go-To. Analyzers are talented at flushing out "tells." They'll see through bluffs. They'll

The Analyzer | 185

become suspicious of your motives, making the bonding activities of Lightening the Load and X-Raying the Evidence nearly impossible, at least prior to substantial rebuilding of trust.

Doc E's ole baseball buddy was Triggered too. A textbook Collaborator, Skip was irked by the lack of recent communication and threatened by the specter of losing status. Doc E let him vent, allowing him to feel heard while defusing his emotion. Skip's a passionate coach, all-in and dedicated to his guys. He cares about them to such a degree that he can be blind to "cold" personnel decisions that might be beneficial to the franchise.

"You still play pickup hoops, right?" Doc E asked.

"Heck yeah," Skip replied. "Why?"

"The phrase 'same team' . . . You think you could walk me through what it means?"

Skip chuckled. "Ahhhhh; I got ya!"

Laughing along with him, Doc E began talking him through the techniques for Playing the Player with an Analyzer. In addition, he emphasized taking detailed notes.

"I'm not in school anymore," Skip joked.

"Do it, dummy," Doc E said. "Same team! You gotta show him you're on his side, that you respect his game and you're willing to play it. Write down his ideas. It'll validate the zillion hours he's put into arriving at those ideas. You don't need to agree with them. But you need them flowing if you're going to get him to X-Ray the Evidence, Deep-Six the Scorecard, and Bake a Different Pie with you."

Doc E was confident his friend was getting it. Skip's tone had completely changed. He was sounding like his usual positive self. Doc E complimented him, expressing that he knew he'd nail it, and asked him to touch base if any news broke. Of course, Doc E also knew that Analyzers and Collaborators are a great match. That is, when only one of them is Triggered. When they both have misplaced their marbles, the chore is to dissipate emotion and then refocus on commonalities or intersecting passions.

The next evening rolled around. Doc E tuned into the ball game and delighted in watching Skip make a string of bullpen moves to carry a 0–0 game to the ninth then walk it off with a pinch-hit bomb. Skip ducked the postgame interviews. Doc E's phone chimed.

"Skip! Congrats on a nice win," Doc E exclaimed.

"Thanks, Doc," the coach said. "Feels good to get back in W column. But the real win was this afternoon before the game. Doc, man, holy cow . . . what a 180."

"Talk to me, chief."

"I apologized," Skip related. "I made sure to catch Pobo in the weight room when he was getting in a light workout. He's always in a better mood when he's spinning. I jumped on a bike next to him and didn't mince words. I told him I was out of line yesterday and wanted him to know that whatever ended up being the right move for the club, I'd have his back. I told him I was peeved with this dang free agency business and players jumping ship all over the place these days. My frustration wasn't with him. But I took it out on him, and that was wrong, and I was really sorry about it. He said he totally got it, but appreciated me saying it. He reached over and gave me a pat on the back. Doc, I really needed that."

Lighten the Load, check. By sitting on cycles side by side, the two men looking in the same direction, Skip shifted the dynamic. He separated their relationship from the difficult task of making roster moves. He made it clear that free agency was the problem, not Pobo, and articulated a wish to collaborate on the problem. Analyzers need that sense of collaboration to move forward in partnership.

Skip continued, "He's been around me a while now. He knows I'm a passionate guy. I took that opportunity to share some more about how much I love this team and how loyalty and the bonds we've all formed matter to me more than anything. Everyone knows I want to win. I want to hoist another World Series banner as much as anyone, but because of what it means to the guys and to the city. I asked Pobo what was important for him. I mean, putting aside the contracts and the money and the media and the trade deadline and all that $#!%. It was great, Doc. You know, I realized we'd never had a heart-to-heart. He really opened up."

X-Ray the Evidence, check. The two talked about their core positions—Skip wanting to keep their star; Pobo wanting to trade him for top prospects—but how those positions were ultimately irrelevant compared to their underlying interests. What mattered to Skip was the franchise's culture: going to work every day in an environment of loyalty and love; being part of running a place that made a positive difference in people's lives . . . in the clubhouse, in the stadium, and in the community. Pobo valued those things too, but beneath it all, he was a self-professed economics geek. What thrilled him was engineering deals to skyrocket the franchise's fortunes, which would then permit the team to *really* move the needle in what they could do for their fans, both on and off the field. Skip and Pobo hit on a common interest: community well-being. Skip was trying to get there via baseball operations. Pobo was going about it financially. They acknowledged that their issues (winning games, making the playoffs, current and future payroll, fan sentiment, even their own employment), while all of major significance, were artifacts they should drive *from* their underlying interest, not the other way around.

The colleagues dismounted their bikes, grabbed towels and a couple bottles of water, and went to the scouting conference room where there were whiteboards full of player development and trade scenarios. They had a renewed enthusiasm to explore options and see if they could come up with some new ones. They agreed to withhold assessment. Skip busted a block of legal pads out of his handbag and they got to it. Deep-Six the Scorecard, check.

"Doc, it was great spending some time in his world; I've been so caught up on the field lately. It was refreshing. And *fun*," Skip shared. "We had an epiphany. We're getting together tomorrow morning to noodle on a whole new concept for roster construction. It'll take a while, beyond the trade deadline. But it's certainly making both of us think about upcoming moves differently. I'm jazzed, Doc."

Bake a Different Pie, check. Skip and Pobo widened the scope of the challenge to integrate wins in areas beyond merely baseball games and bank accounts. They ultimately surprised the pundits by making a big splash at the deadline . . . to *pick up* another all-star.

Reviewing, Analyzers are affable, fair-minded cooperators. They're peacekeepers. People with this Conflict Personality Style strive for work-life equilibrium and readily make sacrifices and compromises to achieve it. Analyzers value being fully informed before making decisions. To that standard, they work particularly well with the Collaborator Go-To, as Collaborators are profuse talkers and will happily answer any questions an Analyzer poses. Conversely, the Accommodator Go-To is an Analyzer's worst teammate. Accommodators' vagueness, resistance to revealing motives, and conflict avoidance will Trigger Analyzers.

A few quick no-nos with Analyzers:

∿ Don't try to strong-arm them.

∿ Don't get into a battle of egos.

∿ Don't impose tight or artificial deadlines for resolving a problem.

∿ Don't bluff.

∿ Don't flake. Don't constantly reschedule meetings or avoid discussion of issues.

When Triggered, people with the Analyzer Go-To may exhibit stubbornness and push to settle for easy compromises, for making people happy instead of reaching for optimal outcomes. They can get so absorbed in information gathering that they lose perspective. They are prone to blurring personal and professional boundaries. Considering these Achilles' heels, with Analyzers you'll be wise to keep in mind:

∿ They want to be informed. Facilitate them thoroughly exploring and understanding a situation.

∿ They are compromisers and appreciate the same in return. Show them you are willing to be flexible.

∿ They are much more comfortable being methodical and taking their time. Play Momentum with them, notching small wins at first before trekking up taller mountains.

∿ Once they feel that they've exhaustively considered all viewpoints and have arrived at a decision, they can get attached to it. Do your very best to be part of the process so you contribute before they reach a firm conclusion.

Armed with these guidelines and the Trading Out of Conflict techniques, you'll likely find Analyzers reasonable and engaging. Of course, if Analyzer is your own default Conflict Personality Style, you're familiar with these tools of the trade. You appreciate it when other Go-Tos make an authentic effort to join you in considering all viewpoints. You also appreciate working with Collaborators for their patience and their propensity for communication. Be forewarned, though! Collaborators' patience, and their amenability to answering all your questions, as we're about to reveal in the next chapter, can mask ulterior motives.

9

The Collaborator

Jean-Claude Killy was born in the French commune Saint-Cloud, a suburb of Paris, during the German Occupation of World War II. Though a restless tyke, he was not allowed to go outside to play. His mother lived in fear of bombing raids. His father, a Spitfire pilot, was off at war. Upon France's liberation at the conclusion of the war, the Killys moved to the Alps. Young Jean-Claude got his first ticket to freedom—a pair of old wooden skis being discarded from his father's shop. Jean-Claude was off to the races, as they say, tearing down the sloped, snow-covered roads of the small village of Val-d'Isère.

But his own liberation did not last long. His mother abandoned the family, leaving his father, with the meager resources of a small merchant, to raise the rambunctious Jean-Claude, his older sister, and his infant brother. A bit of a handful, Jean-Claude was sent to boarding school. He was shut inside once again, this time in a classroom by strict nuns who looked down their noses at frivolous recreations like sliding down a mountain. Of course, that didn't sit well with Jean-Claude. He didn't want to sit at all. Sneaking out became a regular occurrence. He'd hitch a lift on a farm truck to the nearest lake or slope—strapping on water or snow skis, it didn't matter which. Time after time, his father would pick him up and cart him back to school.

By Jean-Claude's fifteenth birthday, his father resigned himself to the fact that the lad's spirit would not be vanquished and permitted him to drop out. Less than a year later, Jean-Claude made the French national ski team. He was fast. *Very* fast. But it was a rare occurrence when he made it to the bottom of a course. He skied with utter abandon. Flamboyant and reckless, yet graceful, he captivated race-watchers. His crashes were spectacular. With fans holding their breath, his victories were even more awing. In one event, he literally skied out of his bindings. In another, two hundred yards from the finish, he hit a patch of compressed ice and tumbled hard. A broken leg not deterring him, he got up and swooshed to the line on one ski—with the fastest time of the day.

Killy made history when he won the inaugural FIS World Cup in 1967. He repeated in 1968 and then topped the year with a sweep of all three alpine gold medals at the Grenoble Olympics, the host country's hero schussing to the podium to capture skiing's triple crown in front of the largest crowds of the Games. There the story might end, the legend riding off victoriously into the sunset. If not for the equally gregarious Mark McCormack, the creator of the modern sports agent. At the time, most Olympic champions' retirements would be met by a small home-town parade and a rapid fade into obscurity. McCormack's then-recently-founded International Management Group (IMG) changed all that.

McCormack was everything sports fans have come to associate with agents. Fast-talking, jet-setting charm, hobnobbing with the hottest stars, a Rolodex to make even the most accomplished networkers jealous. Like Killy's, McCormack's DNA would not abide a sedentary lifestyle. After earning a JD at Yale, he *tried* to be a corporate attorney. He was at Arter & Hadden (one of America's oldest and most staid law firms) for only a few months before he started gazing out the window, longing to be on the golf course.

"I didn't really find law all that thrilling. There were all these eighty-year-old guys shuffling around the halls, and when someone died everyone moved offices. It was like my whole life was programmed. All I was really interested in was golf," McCormack told writer Ray Kennedy in a 1975 *Sports Illustrated* interview.

IMG was launched with what is called "The Golden Handshake." McCormack secured Arnold Palmer as his first client on the two gentlemen's words, no legalese, no contract. Shortly thereafter, he brought Gary Player and Jack Nicklaus into his fold. With McCormack pioneering the genius of off-the-course appearances, special events, endorsements, and brand development, "The King," "The Black Knight," and "The Golden Bear" revolutionized the game of golf, forever changing the sport's financial outlook. McCormack expanded to tennis, steering the careers of Chris Evert and Bjorn Borg. He moved into the auto racing business with three-time World Champion Formula One driver Sir Jackie Stewart, the "Flying Scot." Mark took the nickname to the bank.

In 1970, McCormack expanded to skiing. Fresh off his gold medal feats, Jean-Claude was not interested in settling down and taking over his dad's village shoppe. He partnered with McCormack. IMG had been enlisted by ABC to reenvision how the Olympics were showcased. McCormack campaigned for expanded coverage, pointing the camera at athletes' personalities, and Grenoble was the first Games broadcast in color. The larger-than-life Killy became a household name, worldwide. Mark spun the notoriety into earnings of $2 million. But over the ensuing two years, Jean-Claude's relevance to fans began to wane as his competitive days faded into the rearview mirror.

"We had to figure out some way to get Jean-Claude back on the slopes without tarnishing his winner's image," said McCormack.

They did it in confetti-raining style, cooking up the *Killy Challenge*. In the highly hyped television event series, Jean-Claude would give notable celebrities a head start on a parallel slalom course and then, in his famous wild-ride, fan-cheering-on fashion, chase them down the hill. Burt Reynolds, Farrah Fawcett, Joe Namath, and others joined the fun. Jean-Claude always won. His magnetic persona pervaded; people wanted to be a part of it. From promoting Schwinn bicycles to Chevrolets, Killy's influence continued well into the 1980s.

Killy and McCormack are role models of the Collaborator Go-To Style: socially tuned, effusive-communicating, charismatic extroverts who thrive on extensive and deep relationships. Like the classically profiled sports agent, people with the Collaborator Conflict Personality Style are markedly assertive. The degree to which they'll go to build and maintain friendships is second to none. They place a premium on group membership and status, and will devote copious time to preventing interpersonal discord whenever they can. They plan. They're in it for the long haul.

Naturally, these characteristics combine to form some attractive strengths. People with this Go-To are attentive to the needs of friends, family, and colleagues. They are dedicated to relationship management, so if "partner" is more important to you than "business" in a business partnership, seek to team up with a Collaborator. Because a Collaborator is observant, emotionally astute, and empathetic, they are also especially adept in arenas involving sales, client interfacing, and personnel management (though, you can find the Collaborator Go-To in all kinds of professions).

If such strengths resonate with you as personal or occupational requisites, or you want to encourage a Collaborator's attributes in certain people or projects, how might you go about tapping into this Go-To? You can get a leg up in scenarios ripe for a Collaborator's conflict approach by doing the following:

1. Place reading people atop your to-do list. Before taking action on a disagreement or disgruntlement, a Collaborator will look to establish someone's Go-To and their Conflict Type Trigger—whether they are Triggered by a task (Task Conflict), a process (Process Conflict), or a relationship (Relational Conflict). A Collaborator will make heavy use of tools such as the Water Bottle, Pen, and Staring Contest Techniques. (Flip back to chapters 1 and 2 for refreshers, if needed.)

2. Deflect, deflect, deflect! When in conflict, a Collaborator is reticent to spend much time talking about themselves. At every juncture they can, they try to turn the conversation back onto others. They focus on others' Triggers, not theirs. Often apt to come out of a Collaborator's mouth is some version of "It's not about me; all I care about is you."

3. Prioritize interpersonal connection over substance. Collaborators make it clear that their objective is to strengthen the relationship. They go to great lengths to understand where someone is coming from. Demonstrating empathy is central to a Collaborator's strategy for overcoming discord.

THE THREE-WAY LIGHT BULB

People with the Collaborator Go-To can poke and pry. On occasion, quite intensively. Their desire to dig into others' thoughts, feelings, and perspectives can be off-putting or prompt others to put up defenses. Collaborators will work hard to make things personal to get you to let your guard down. The more you clam up, the more likely it will be that you'll Trigger them and, thereby, the more aggressive or creative they'll get, milking different forms of communication and striving to break through. Of the other four Go-Tos, the Avoider will react the most severely. Someone with an Avoider Conflict Personality Style will try to avoid a Collaborator like the plague. Their opposing manners—avoidance and pursuit—will drive each other mad. Issues will escalate, in many cases unnecessarily. When conflicts arise, if you can help it, try to find a path to a solution that doesn't involve pairing up a Collaborator with an Avoider.

In addition to being substantially agitated by aloofness, guardedness, and avoidance, people with the Collaborator Go-To get Triggered when they feel their status or group membership is threatened, be it by another person or by circumstance. Note: Collaborators can perceive minuscule matters, things that might ordinarily go unnoticed by others, as jeopardizing to a relationship or their standing. Sports agents, for example, get neurotically skittish at the slightest of hints of client poaching. When working with a Collaborator, therefore, it is wise to not take things for granted. Make it a point to regularly check in with Collaborators. And don't be surprised when they're open to nontraditional or outside-the-box problem-solving if it fosters bonds or grows their network. We were reminded of this lesson recently in one of the most bizarre divorce mediations we've ever encountered.

A couple was splitting after discovering that they both were having affairs. They wanted to avoid lawyers, courts, and as many costs as they could. Thankfully, they didn't have any children, but they wanted to spare other loved ones any circus. While appreciably upset, feeling their trust mutually violated, they were both Collaborators, so they also held out a fragment of hope that their union could be ended amicably. They asked us to intercede.

Collaborators tend to engage in lengthier negotiation. They prefer Momentum to Dominoes. Knowing this, we did not rush the couple. We picked off low-hanging fruit concessions and assets. We cautiously kept returning the conversation to their situation, as their Collaborator habit of deflection caused them to inquire about us, our experiences, and our suggestions. They'd constantly say things such as, "Oh, we don't want to trouble you; what do *you* think we should do?" We can't decide for clients. Our job is to facilitate them reaching a satisfying conclusion.

As the mediation process gained steam, they found out that each other's affair had been going on for over a year. The husband was stepping out with a gal named Gertrude. The wife was also seeing a woman, and her name was . . . Gertrude! They were both sleeping with the same person. No longer were we in the realm of a common divorce negotiation.

They had been remarkably cordial to this point. Just one item remained to be sorted: what to do with their house, which they'd both acknowledged was in an exceptional neighborhood and would be ballooning in value in the coming years. Learning that they had been sharing a lover truncated their agreeability. Neither wanted to sell the house prematurely. Neither could afford to buy the other out at a reasonable markup. Neither was willing to give it to the other. Neither wanted the hassle of managing it as a rental property and they both were nervous about wear and tear or damage from tenants. Contemplating that the property might sit vacant while they awaited appreciation but concerned about the couple's finances in continuing to carry the mortgage, Doc G cast a brainstorming invitation.

"So who is going to live in the house?"

The dejected couple seemed stumped. They had nothing to offer.

And then suddenly, in spontaneous, miraculous unison they turned to each other, lit up, and simultaneously blurted out, "*Gertrude!*"

Their body language completely reversed. In pure Collaborator essence, they were collaborating. They were eager to see if Gertrude would be amenable to renting the house. We were able to patch her into our office's videoconference room. What we thought was already a lock for the next Nobel "Peace" prize then left the stratosphere. Gertrude was amenable. But then a pregnant pause.

"Um, just one thing," she said. "How are we going to do visitation rights?"

She didn't want to stop seeing either of them. She, too, hadn't known about all the interconnectedness. She, too, was a Collaborator! She didn't want to screw up the divorce, but we could sense that she was on the verge of becoming Triggered at the thought of losing her, shall we say, friendships with both the husband and the wife.

Astonishingly, the couple was quick to present a remedy: the husband would live in the house with Gertrude on odd weeks; the wife would live in the house with Gertrude on even weeks. They would split the cost of weekly maid service. And Gertrude would enter into a three-year lease at only 50 percent of fair market rent. They had us draw up the paperwork on the spot and invited us out to dinner with them and Gertrude.

Horrific conflict compromise? Or love affair extraordinaire? We'll leave that call up to you. All we know is that individuals with the Collaborator Go-To, when aimed at goals involving the people they care about, when spurred to implement their tendency toward empathy, when allowed to slowly open up and gradually progress toward resolution, are considerably collaboration minded.

CONFLICT FITNESS

What if you're dealing with a Triggered Collaborator? And what if you don't have a Gertrude who will ride in to the rescue? Invoke your inner Analyzer. Analyzers make the best teammate for Collaborators because they will not rush a Collaborator. They know there is more to a confrontation than what a Collaborator reveals (the Collaborator's tip of the iceberg). They'll be patient in getting to a Collaborator's underlying interests.

"Slow is smooth . . . and smooth is fast."

—Mark Wahlberg (in *The Shooter*)

If you're not a natural Analyzer yourself, you can adopt an Analyzer Conflict Personality Style by looking for opportunities to implement these three tactics:

- **Pulling the Goalie.** People with a Collaborator Go-To tend to be proficient at the art of cocktail conversation. In other words, they can dialogue without having to add anything substantive. In conversation, Collaborators focus on you instead of themselves. They'll keep handing you the mic. In conflict, you can't merely trade chitchat back and forth though. One, they'll get even more Triggered. As the adage goes, "You can't bull$#!% a bull$#!%er." Two, you won't get into any kind of depth regarding underlying interests, so you'll have no shot at effectively resolving conflict. You must draw out their true feelings. How? The more they talk, the more difficult it becomes to remain surface level. So create the impression that you are enrapt with what they are saying, verbally and nonverbally. Play dumb. For instance, "Wow . . ." you respond, "tell me more!" We call this technique "Pulling the Goalie" since it's giving them an open net, like in hockey or soccer. You're inviting them to go on offense.

- **The Boomerang Technique.** When a hot-button issue of a Collaborator gets pressed, they will initially try to deflect, to change the subject or swivel it to you. Picture the deflection as them throwing a boomerang. You want the boomerang to fly full circle and return to them, but it won't without a nice arc. If you cut a Collaborator's deflection off or instantaneously snap back to the sensitive topic, they'll duck with all their might. They may run away altogether . . . nowhere for the boomerang to land. Let the boomerang travel away from them—that is, allow them to switch subjects or you pick up the dialogue for a minute. When their tone or body language is more normalized, send the boomerang back. When a Collaborator deflects, it's your cue that you're getting to their underlying interest. With "rest" intervals in between, keep coming back to the matter that stimulated the deflection. Be persistent but patient. Chip away a little at a time. Remember that Collaborators are more comfortable playing Momentum.

- **Picking Red Tomatoes.** An old proverb advises, "Don't pick tomatoes when they're green." This sentiment can also be applied to Collaborators. Since it may take them a while to divulge what they really feel, think, or want, since they favor slow-baking negotiation, assess their readiness to problem solve. Yes, watering a garden can be tedious with a Collaborator. But don't turn the faucet on full force; it's counterproductive to expedite the ripening process with them. Wait until the tomato is red. Further, don't be afraid to take a time-out or walk away if you sense that you are being Triggered. A Collaborator isn't going anywhere; you don't need to be in a hurry to fix things.

A fantastic example of ironing out a dispute with a Collaborator comes from a custom retreat we hosted in Aspen. We have a blast putting on unique part-recreational, part-educational R&R getaways for small groups. They're particularly popular with companies that like fun year-end experiences to reward their top performers. For one of the world's leading fitness equipment manufacturers, we crafted a four-day weekend "decathlon" consisting of lawn games, pub games, and a culminating lake rope-swing contest. Mornings were packed with feisty yet laugh-a-minute competitions. Afternoons featured quality downtime and napping. Evenings were filled with rich conversation (and delectable food, not to mention a few stiff drinks) around an outdoor firepit, swapping stories and lessons about leadership, teamwork, and the healthy pursuit of excellence. On the second-to-last night, we got to chatting about how Go-Tos could be applied to facility owners. The participants, as part of their corporation's ongoing commitment to an employee-first learning culture, had all done Myers-Briggs, Enneagram, and StrengthsFinder workshops. Earlier in the year, they'd attended a conflict prevention training we did for the company. A concept that had stuck with them was the notion of Triggering—that making progress on an initiative with colleagues or customers can unexpectedly shift if someone gets Triggered, and that much of business success relies on, correspondingly, making adjustments. One of the retreat attendees, the company's top health club account manager, who'd been an elite, team-first minded soccer player in college, got to reminiscing about the amazing friendships she had developed with proprietors of gyms from Gold's to Anytime Fitness to YMCAs, and how learning those proprietors' Go-Tos was helping her further enhance the relationships. She'd been doing the Go-To Conflict Personality Style assessment together with her customers, as a team-building exercise.

"I've got this index card app on my phone," she shared with the group. "In it, I've now got Go-To notes for every one of my clients. When something goes wrong at their facility, an elliptical goes on the fritz, they have members complaining . . . or we screw up on an order or when a shipment is late or any of that stuff, I can take a beat before I call 'em. I feel so much more aligned in how I work with them. Honestly, I feel like I'm a better partner for them when everything *isn't* smooth sailing. I can be Catwoman, pouncing in to lower emotions and save the day."

With a tickled grin, she waxed on, telling us about the owner of a chichi NYC fitness-spa oasis. He'd purchased the building where his club was located and completed a massive renovation, ripping out walls to triple the fitness area footprint, and adding a café, juice bar, and mindfulness center. Two years and $8 million out the door, he was finally ready for a grand reopening. All over Manhattan, he'd publicized a big open house. Except . . . his new equipment didn't arrive in time.

"That kind of investment and our trucks don't show up when they're supposed to? Oy vey!" the account executive said. "I didn't find out until after the gala he'd planned. I got on the horn the second I knew. He was as cool as a cucumber. He said to me matter-of-factly, 'Look, it set me back a bundle. Your boss is going to have to eat the full cost of the order. Either the machines are free or I take your company to the cleaners. No hard feelings, though; it's not your fault. I like you. I'll keep your name off the suit.' Before I knew about conflict types, I would've been in nuclear panic mode and rallied every troop coast-to-coast. But now, you see, I know he's a total Collaborator. I'd have been jumping the gun, big time. And I'd have created a *monster* mess."

Picking Red Tomatoes, check. She realized that Collaborators typically don't lead with what's really bothering them, that Dominoes is not their game. She knew she needed to exert restraint, patiently seeking the club owner's true concerns. She could take a breath.

"How relieving, right?" she related. "I mean, we still had to correct the delivery debacle, that was a given, but I could basically play along and not really worry too much about the bill. So I agreed with him; I said, 'You're absolutely right. I think it's a brilliant idea to figure out how we can promote your sparkling new club while your club promotes a complimentary shipment of our shiny new models.'"

Pulling the Goalie, check. Like a seasoned pro, she invited him to charge forward. It hit a nerve right away, though, and he bristled, spinning the exchange back on her.

"He stopped me, saying, 'Whoa, hold on. I don't see you convincing your boss to do all that,'" she recounted. "I was definitely getting somewhere, because he turned it around to me. I played along a little more and then, Doc G and E, you'll be proud, I sent it back to him. I asked him why he thought our CEO would drop the ball. He released the hounds! He told me history he'd had with our chief and that he didn't trust him and that the only reason he was buying our equipment was because he liked working with people like me. That, in fact, he had contemplated not putting in any weight machines at all because what his members wanted was more flexible fitness space to begin with. Come to find out, his event was a huge success. Everyone oohed and aahed over the uncluttered floorplan!"

The Boomerang Technique, check. The account exec identified a Trigger source, let the spa owner deflect for a calming stretch, and then circled back. In this case, the Collaborator was primed to address his underlying interest faster than is characteristic for this Go-To, likely because of the proactive Go-To communication efforts the account manager had been logging. The two went on to craft a win-win arrangement: the equipment manufacturer sent, gratis, a select few prototypes they had in R&D, providing them field-testing data while giving the NYC club exclusive-use bragging rights without encumbering the new, opened up area. The rest of the machines in the original order were rerouted to other facilities, pleasing those customers, who happily paid sticker price for the sooner-than-expected fulfillment. And the CEO of the equipment company flew to New York to hand-deliver an apology with a $50,000 check from his personal bank account . . . which the club owner donated to charity!

The equipment exec was right about another thing too: we were very proud of her. You know the saying, "When the student becomes the master . . ." She's teaching her whole company the value of investing in understanding others. Her forbearance and determination to look for foundational interests were spot-on ingredients for resolving conflict with a Collaborator. Her dedicated, proactive notetaking set her up for expediently identifying those ingredients as winners for this particular type of conflict.

LITTLE RED RIDING HOOD MEETS J. EDGAR HOOVER

Collaborative resolutions such as the "Gertrude Generosity" and "Spa Spectacular" are, indeed, a strength of the Collaborator Conflict Personality Style. But take caution. The allure of empathy and easy-flowing rapport can hide a sneaky shadow side to this Go-To. Rather than using their skills for authentic bonding, some Collaborators can use them to gain an upper hand and manipulate you for selfish ends.

As you know, we commonly refer to Collaborators as Agents. Consider a different type of agent: black suit, crisp-starched white shirt, freshly polished sensible shoes, a neat crew cut, and dark sunglasses . . . the classic special agent. James Cagney topped the image with a fedora in his role as James "Brick" Davis in *G Men*. Kevin Costner rolled up his sleeves in *The Untouchables*. Keanu Reeves donned a wetsuit in *Point Break*. Gillian Anderson added a subtle touch of color in *The X-Files*. Will Smith tucked space-age technology into his jacket pocket in *Men in Black*. A tinkering here and there, but in nearly a century's passing since J. Edgar Hoover instigated the Bureau of Investigation overhaul in 1924, the role of the FBI agent has been synonymous with a loyal, trustworthy crusade for truth and justice.

Or has it?

Perhaps you are familiar with the secret life of Hoover. Maybe you've heard a cloak-and-dagger tale or two. The entanglement of espionage, the frighteningly Gestapo-like maneuvers, the cache of ill-gotten blackmail material that all but guaranteed a type of clandestine job security for J. Edgar, anchoring him as the country's top crime dog for forty-eight years. Hoover compiled mountains of dirt on prominent US citizens—politicians, diplomats, judges, activists, luminaries, actors and actresses, singers, athletes, you name it. In administration after administration, leaders feared Hoover too gravely, for what he might have on them, to attempt to remove him from office. Straddling parts of six decades, J. Edgar leveraged his unrivaled networking prowess, engendered an 80 percent public approval rating, and spared no expense to propagate the facade of the G-Man . . . all the while stocking his armory of information by contorting, circumventing, and breaking the law.

Hoover was the embodiment of a personality style we call "The Collector" (doubly apropos for J. Edgar). By outward appearance, every bit a Collaborator—an assertive but appealing, relationship-building, "in-crowd" figure. Behind the curtain, however, a manipulative power monger, flipping rapport into a "gotcha" weapon of control.

That's not to call the FBI or its members deceptive or underhanded. We're hyperbolizing, using the Bureau's entrenched, if film-embellished, profile to draw a pointed contrast between Collaborator and Collector. Between a Go-To that makes an outstanding teammate (a Collaborator genuinely values relationships) and a "Go-To wannabe" bad actor (a Collector only pretends to side with you, fronting connection only for his or her own gain).

You may be thinking, "Oh no! How can I tell a well-intentioned Collaborator from a bad-intentioned Collector? And what should I do about the Collectors that I'll encounter?" We're glad you asked.

In basic terms, a Collaborator is authentically interested in talking with you and getting to know you. They will do all the things we discussed earlier in the chapter because they feel that exploring and focusing on what others want is the ideal way to resolve conflict. When they are not Triggered, they'll prioritize relationship building, empathetic listening, and collaborating. A Collector, on the other hand, is an opportunist. They will give lip service to these things, but only follow through when of most personal benefit to them. Ask a person with whom you feel a sense of rapport to do you a favor. A Collaborator will try their best. If the person doesn't give it a shot or flakes out, they're likely a Collector.

Watch for consistency. Collaborators adapt their styles, their mannerisms and behaviors, to better relate to others and to encourage people to open up with them. They do this all the time. It's fundamental to their expression of empathy. If you notice someone acting this way only sometimes, particularly when they are Triggered—when emotions are heated—chances are they are a Collector rather than a Collaborator. And intensity level should make sense relative to the stage of connecting with someone. Recall, Collaborators are committed to their relationships. They'll marinate them slowly and appropriately. If someone you don't yet know well dives right into the empathy deep end or is nosy right out of the gate, be on red alert.

Fortunately, there is a method effective for both identifying *and* dealing with Collectors. If you want to ferret out a Collector or be shielded from one, do this:

~ **Gray Rocking.** Talk, talk, talk. Talk some more. And then keep talking. *But* don't say anything meaningful, colorful, or interesting. Be as bland and boring as you possibly can. Be the dullest human being on the planet. As the phrase goes, don't let them get a word in edgewise. If and when they do interject or pose a question, don't attend to what they say; don't answer. Simply resume your incessant, meaningless blather. A Collector will quickly get bored and move on in search of another target. Like the circling hawks they are, they will assess that you are unappetizing and they'll fly away.

The wolf in Little Red Riding Hood sums up Collectors nicely. If fairy tales aren't your thing, a brief summary: a little girl (in a red, hooded outfit), on her way to deliver wine and cake to her sickly grandmother, is met in the woods by a wolf. The wolf pretends to be concerned, recommending to Little Red Riding Hood that she stop to collect flowers, a gift that will surely please her granny. The girl takes the advice while the wolf uses the extra time to sneak to the grandmother's house (and eat Grandma or lock her in the closet, depending on the version you read). He disguises himself as Granny and awaits Little Red Riding Hood's arrival, hoping to eat her as well. Clearly, the wolf's "help" was not genuine; the wolf's offer of assistance was only extended to accomplish his own ends. This is a template for the Collector at work—an illustration that came to life in a child custody case Doc G was brought in to mediate.

A single dad, working three jobs and struggling to stay above the poverty line, was anonymously reported to social services. His work schedule was an impediment to complying with initial interview requests, resulting in a court summons. The judge was concerned. The father was late, came dressed in filthy work clothes with a dip can in his pocket, and his vernacular wasn't, let's say, "pleasant." The other family members, the child's uncle and grandmother, were cleanly adorned, polite, and pleaded for the opportunity to provide for the youngster. But evidence against the dad had some holes. The judge handed the case off to Doc G.

Mediation day arrived. The grandmother, punctual to the second, greeted Doc G with profuse appreciation. The father, tardy again, was not so appreciative.

"I just want what is best for that darling, precious girl," said Grandma.

"She's full of $#!%," the dad retorted.

Ignoring the comment, the grandmother said, "I'm willing and able to provide all the resources and assistance that my granddaughter and son deserve. Everyone needs a booster from time to time. I'm very happy that I'm here today, in a position to help."

"She's full of $#!%," the dad repeated.

Around and around it went, the sweet old granny presenting her and the uncle's case for being qualified, loving guardians, and the dad refusing to provide any rationale beyond cuss words for his stubborn, foul perception of his own relatives. Doc G's patience and Active Listening skills were being tested. Both sides were entrenched in their positions, but neither was Triggered. Unemotional, unwilling to answer any questions or participate in any dialogue, they seemed prepared to repeat their stance, ad nauseum, until the end of time. Shrewdly clever Gray Rocking by both sides, with *just enough* relevance to the mediation to, at first, seem meaningful.

Neither would take a shot when he Pulled the Goalie. None of his Boomeranging was producing a reaction. He could pick one of two courses: (1) Wait to Pick Red Tomatoes by terminating the session and rescheduling a series of follow-up meetings. When an opposition Gray Rocks you, but you must still find a way to work with them, filling their datebook is highly effective. They'll wearily scan across their calendar, cringing at the effort it will take to keep up the Gray Rocking, and eventually give up the ghost. Or (2) go full Competitor, pressing the issue by feigning to be Triggered, yourself, feigning to be confrontational in order to force an action—prepared, if it fails, to do a quick-save pivot back to option one.

With a child's welfare involved, it wasn't actually a choice.

He called out the father. "You know what? I don't think you want custody. I think you get a kick out of wasting everyone's time. I don't think you have any evidence to back up your claim that you're the better guardian. Prove me wrong or we're *done* here."

"%#@& you, Doc," deadpanned the dad as he stood up. He reached into his pocket, pulled out a thick stack of Polaroid snapshots, slapped them on the conference table, and walked out of the room without another word.

Picking them up, Doc G was *mortified.* They were photos of Granny and the uncle using heroin with drug paraphernalia strewn about them. One of the photographs depicted Granny injecting her arm while sitting in a beanbag . . . *in what appeared to be a children's bedroom.* Doc G could barely keep his composure.

"There seems to have been a development here," he said to Grandma.

"Thank you for your time, young man," she replied without the slightest change in tone as she rose and calmly strolled out of the office.

Before the elevator doors could close behind the grandmother, Doc G was on his phone to a dear friend of his at the FBI—in our opinion, *the* quintessentially noble G-Woman.

Merely typing the story makes our skin crawl. It was the most disturbing version of a wolf in grandmother's clothing we could imagine— Granny cunningly trying to fool social services, the judge, and Doc G by assessing their interests and playing to those interests as if she was wholeheartedly a teammate of theirs, entirely for her own gain. "My what colorful needle-mark-covering sleeves you have," we might have joked. But when the stakes are this high—in this case, the welfare of a child—it's essential to make sure you understand the motivations of all involved.

~~~~~~

It's important that we stress: Collaborators have some fantastic strengths that make them loyal partners. In digesting the Collector profile, we urge you not to pin those characteristics on a Collaborator. The Collector appears to be, feigns to be, a Collaborator but is an alien of a different, non-Go-To planet. People who are Collaborators genuinely seek to use their networks and relationships for the good of others. They are collaborators.

Those with this Go-To Style, though, can get frustrated when their colleagues, friends, and family members are not forthcoming, avoid engaging interpersonally, or shut down under pressure. Collaborators are Triggered by Relationship Conflict as well as barriers to their networking, relationship building, and inclusion. When you are in conflict with a Triggered Collaborator, when you need to Play the Player with them, be mindful to:

- Not take them at face value. They generally aren't direct about their interests.

- Be persistent in seeking to uncover what has Triggered them. Remember that they will deflect to try to focus on your interests rather than theirs. Patiently steer conversation back to them.

- Facilitate and validate their need to feel a sense of rapport and group membership.

- Start with minor issues; play Momentum.

- Avoid BSing them.

- Avoid rushing them.

- Avoid being "all business"—that is, understand that Relationship Conflict is their soft spot. Prioritize rectifying "people problems" with them, before moving on to other issues.

Owing to a natural emotional intelligence possessed by Collaborators, people with this Go-To can flourish as leaders. They can be intense, though, in the depth of dedication they pour into leading a team and juggling the needs of the people on the team. Be cognizant that they are susceptible to burnout; stand ready to aid them with time and energy management.

If, however, the possibility of a colleague's or love one's weariness stems not from an excess of their own commitment but from lack of a reciprocal level of commitment, they're likely an Accommodator rather than a Collaborator. You'll need a slightly different approach if they go bat guano for that reason . . . or, literally, livestock guano, as we'll see in the next chapter.

10

The Accommodator

Not long ago, a young woman was dazzling college basketball crowds with fancy footwork, Globetrotter-esque dribbling, and no-look passes. She was a point guard with an infectious smile and swagger, an ability to carry her team, and a seemingly bottomless reserve of endurance; some analysts were referring to her as the next coming of Magic Johnson. WNBA scouts populated the stands of her games. A top draft selection with a lucrative signing bonus should have been, yup, you know it, a slam dunk. There was just one problem. She had what scouting reports termed a "red flag" off-the-court history. Twice arrested in high school on drug charges, both times pleading nolo contendere, she was still on probation. The terms of the probation, combined with difficult family circumstances, meant that she had to pass up joining a Power Five program. Pro franchises were hesitant. Electric with the ball, yes, but she was still at a small school with limited exposure to the big time. Was she a prospective superstar? Or a PR nightmare waiting to happen? The risk of wasting a valuable draft slot, signing bonus, and large salary was considerable.

Draft Day arrived. The elite names started getting plucked off the board. The point guard tumbled down the list. Round 1 closed; she hadn't been picked. Round 2 went by. No takers. Round. . . . the point guard collapsed on her sofa, heartbroken. The draft concluded without her cell lighting up.

The phone that did ring was Doc E's. It was one of the WBNA team owners.

"Doc, we think at her core she's an amazing person. We did our homework. There's confidential intel that the public is unaware of . . . I'm sure it's the reason all the other clubs passed. But we really want to give her a chance. Would you be amenable to supplying her—and me, frankly—with some expertise to support her making a successful transition from college?"

"Absolutely!" Doc answered.

The team signed the point guard to a free agent preseason contract. It included a myriad of accountability measures and requirements, the pencil sharpened to the smallest of details such as strict times for arriving at every team scheduled activity. It was made clear to her that one slipup, even in the slightest, and she would be cut.

She was perfect. The model team member. She arrived at practice early and was always the last one to leave, dedicated to mastering the coach's game plan, a sponge of film on opponents. It was shaping up to be a plot Walt Disney Studios would salivate over.

Until the final exhibition, just before camp broke and season rosters would be ratified. The game was on the road. Players, coaches, trainers, front office staff, the owner and his spouse . . . everyone had boarded the bus at the team's practice facility. Except the point guard. Departure time was approaching; she was supposed to be there thirty minutes earlier. The team captain's iPhone buzzed in her pocket with a text from Doc E.

HEADED TO THE FACILITY NOW. NEED YOUR HELP!

The captain (affectionately called Cap) told the owner she'd be right back. As she exited the bus, Doc E's Porsche screeched around to the back of the gym, out of sight. Cap broke into a sprint. Rounding the building's corner, she was startled to see the point guard getting out of the car, her elbow wrapped in a blood-stained bandage.

"*Holy* $#!%," she screamed. But her mind immediately took pause. *Drugs*, she thought.

Doc E was concerned everyone would jump to that assumption. "It's not what you think," he said to Cap. "I'll handle the Big Boss. But you gotta get to the girls before they see this." He quickly explained. The point guard's nineteen-year-old neighbor had gotten mixed up with a bad crowd and had to appear in court that day. Her parents weren't at home and the kid accidentally locked the keys in the car. The point guard was trying to coat hanger it, but it wasn't getting anywhere and she was freaking out about both the kid and her being late. So she grabbed a rock, busted the window, and cut her forearm reaching in to unlock the door. She was afraid of breaking team rules and called Doc E for backup.

Cap took a huge breath of relief and put her hand on her teammate's shoulder. "You got the goods, girl," she said. "Don't worry about a thing. I got this. I got your back. Doc, get her to a hospital. I'll make sure the team is good."

One of the things that rocks about this story (in addition to the car window culprit) is that, at the start of preseason, the players had done a team-building off-site that incorporated the Conflict Personality Style Assessment. Kudos to the team captain; she had been working hard to use insight from the team-building session to improve the squad's communication and her own leadership. She knew that her teammate didn't have PG as merely a basketball position designation; the point guard in this case also had a Point Guard Go-To—as you'll recall, the synonym we affectionately use for the Accommodator Go-To. Cap therefore knew that, for her teammate, responsibility and accountability weren't about contract stipulations; they were fundamental to how she handled stress. And Cap knew that, as an Accommodator, her mate would be even more Triggered if her efforts to help her neighbor were questioned or criticized by her teammates. Like the champion she was, the captain validated her teammate's selfless actions and reassured her that her sacrifice would result in a positive outcome for the team.

We are very proud to share that Cap dexterously navigated explaining the situation to everyone back on the bus. Not only did the point guard end up cementing a lineup spot for years to come but the team nominated her for the league's prestigious WNBA Cares Community Assist Award honoring outstanding service.

The basketball frame of reference is convenient for discussing Accommodator Go-To characteristics. Someone with this Conflict Personality Style is an ultimate team player—accommodating, holding up others before themselves for the good of the group, willing to shoulder the load. When conflict arises for which there is a clearly defined task (or set of tasks), clear roles, and clear upside prospects, an Accommodator is who you want sorting it out. Within these parameters, Accommodators aren't likely to be Triggered, so they can bring to bear their substantial determination and creativity. When trusted to lead, when not interfered with, and when appreciated for their work, the Accommodator Go-To is a heck of an asset to have on your team.

If you're not intuitively an Accommodator but are keen to infuse a little of this Go-To Style into a difficult scenario that you are facing, a few tips come in handy:

1. **Turn the other cheek.** If a disagreement is making you feel overly emotional or irrational, take a time-out or walk away. You should have a good handle on what Triggers you. When a Trigger is looming, take a minute to decompress. A helpful tool for this is Thought Replacement: focus on filling your brain with calm imagery or relaxing music. Picture sitting on a quiet beach or swaying in a hammock, for instance. Hum a bar of your favorite chillax tune—perhaps even (appropriately) from Kenny Rogers's "Coward of the County" (written by Roger Bowling and Billy Edd Wheeler; United Artists Group, 1979):

   Walk away from trouble if you can
   . . . you don't have to fight to be a man

   Note: This doesn't mean you should universally dodge challenges or take the easy way out. One of the reasons Accommodators are intuitively adept at turning the other cheek is that they generally keep their head down. They are high-commitment people, which makes them dedicated problem-solvers.

2. **Be selfless. Accommodate.** Put loved ones' and colleagues' objectives above yours. Accommodators are good at making sacrifices. As the say-

ing goes, they embody the principle of "taking one for the team." To mimic them, aim your selflessness toward deeply cherished personal and professional relations, toward partnerships that accomplish meaningful outcomes.

3. Maintain standards. Before you conclude that the above advice sounds like getting walked all over, or teeing up an invitation thereto, consider that Accommodators believe in a devoted work ethic, the relentless pursuit of excellence, *and* the respect that both should garner. Give that respect. Expect it in return! Others may have dissimilar skill sets from you but, if they're going to be in your inner circle, in addition to contributing their skills, they'll contribute gratitude for yours.

TEAM NO TALK . . . TNT!

The general counsel of a well-respected company came to us a while back. The business had been expanding rapidly, transforming from a popular local mom-and-pop shop to a regional chain. But in that period of growth, the company had hit a speed bump.

The founders were a first-generation American immigrant couple with an age-old success story: they arrived in the United States with nothing in their pockets, busted their behinds to escape poverty, finally stashed away two nickels, opened a tiny market of their own, and worked around the clock to keep it afloat in its early years. They wanted to apply a personal touch in the markets they were entering; they opted not to franchise. Piece by piece, they built a management layer to oversee their vision systematically across all sites and implement the best practices they'd learned along the way. Their workforce grew, providing attractive jobs in many communities. Bottom-line profits told a happy tale. Yet the corporate headquarters atmosphere indicated a decidedly *different* narrative. A series of new employee policies had been rolled out, altering bonus structure, vacation time, and health care benefits. Some of the staff were excited about the progressive nature of the changes, particularly physical and mental wellness initiatives. A pocket of management was concerned about cost, potential for abuse of benefits, and operational complications.

"But all the complaints are pretty standard growing pains for companies," counsel explained to us. "Any decent consulting team would have it banged out in a week, tops."

"So you want us to recommend a good firm?" Doc G inquired.

"Oh, no, that's not why I'm calling you. That's not the problem," counsel replied.

"Ah, okay," Doc G said. "How can we help?"

"All the gray matter required is already in the building. We've got super smart people," he expounded. "But everyone is walking around on eggshells, afraid to bring up the elephant in the room. It's the owners. Well, their daughter. Well, actually, all three of them. About a year ago, as their idea of a college graduation gift, the owners gave the title 'Chief of Human Resources' to their daughter. She's green, no doubt, but she's sharp too. The new policies are her brainchild. She wants to demonstrate to everyone that she's not a free ride, trust fund kid, that she deserves her title and will add a lot of value. Her parents want her to follow their direction, listen, learn, and be an old-fashioned 'good employee.' It's your classic idealism versus experience clash. Except they haven't been addressing it. They act pleasantly, they nod and smile in the office, but they don't talk to each other! Guys, this thing's gonna blow."

The general counsel was describing Accommodators to a tee—*three* of them. Accommodators are great at empowering their teammates—for example, the company's owners giving their daughter opportunity, not intervening, and entrusting their managerial personnel with policy and program execution. But Accommodators are not pleased when their blueprints are not adhered to, are ignored, or are not fulfilled to their expectations. Thankfully, it takes a lot for them to become Triggered; they have a high Trigger tolerance. Accommodators are talented at sustaining their rationality when disgruntled, frustrated, tired, and so forth. Prior to succumbing to a Trigger, they'll typically pursue one of three paths: (1) Just do things themselves. They'll take on all the work of a job before they confront others. (2) Be passive-aggressive. They'll hint at what they want without directly bringing it up. (3) Bury the emotion. They'll dance around an issue or push it off to the side for as long as they can.

We gladly took on the assignment to visit with the company own-ers and their daughter. Recognizing that they were Accommodators who had not yet reached their boiling point and, therefore, might be reticent to roll up their sleeves face-to-face, we used the Caucus Technique: an intermediary holding separate meetings with the parties involved in a dispute. The Caucus Technique is an unobtrusive method for leading Accommodators to solutions.

Once we established rapport and tapped our Active Listening tools to get their underlying interests, the floodgates opened. The daughter launched into an impassioned speech on mental health, the unique needs of millennials, and research on contemporary productivity strategies. She cited feedback she'd been collecting from visiting with employees at all the company's locations. She emphasized how data driven her policies were. In a similar manner, the parents outlined staff complaints they'd received, particularly from an older demographic whose needs weren't being satisfied by the new policies. They referenced concrete examples from their four decades in business. At this point, we started trading information between the rooms. When the parents realized how method-ically thoughtful their daughter's process was, they readily agreed to a collaborative overhaul of HR. When their daughter got wind that her parents respected her empiricism, she became eager to figure out how to integrate their knowledge. Common goals diagnosed, and a couple hugs later, they were off and running.

The Caucus Technique is helpful for situations in which a third party is facilitative. It may not apply for you, it may not be feasible, or it might be too clunky or awkward. Regardless, when an Accommodator is a fam-ily member, friend, or coworker, it's essential to get out in front of irksome or sticky subjects. Accommodators will let things fester. Not because they are scared of conflict but because they feel that "their problems"—that is, their aggravation, their worries, and so on—shouldn't impact the team (or company or friendship or marriage). They don't want to put their burdens on others. We all know, while that may be noble in spirit, it can create bigger troubles down the line. Strive to take down conflict with Accommodators early, well before they snap. Otherwise, *they* may be humming the "you could've heard a pin drop" line from Kenny Rogers's ballad in which the title character, leaving the bar, suddenly stops, locks the door, turns around, and unleashes two decades of suppressed rage—and asking for forgiveness for not turning the other cheek.

Your mission with Accommodators is to identify their particular Triggers, keep an eye out for when they might be avoiding, overlooking, or burying an issue, and encourage them to engage. To the first step, an inventory of the most prevailing Accommodator Triggers is helpful:

- Irresponsibility or lack of accountability.

- Undefined job roles and duties.

- Protocols and game plans not being followed.

- Being unappreciated.

- Their commitment, effort, or team contribution being doubted or questioned.

- Competitiveness between teammates instead of cooperation.

- Moochers!

A minute on the last one . . . Accommodators, like most of us, dislike those who offer to pay for something but never do. However, Accommodators *cannot stand* people who try to ride their coattails without chipping in ample sweat, who try to take credit for something that is a result of the Accommodator's sweat, who loaf and let the Accommodator pick up their slack. To be sure, Accommodators are pleased to carry their team on their backs—when it's in service of teammates with integrity.

In addition, Accommodators can break down when they feel pushed around. They often struggle with Triggered Competitors, since a Competitor's mixture of ego, competitiveness, and aggressiveness can evoke a sense of being bullied (despite this rarely being a Competitor's intent). If an Accommodator and Competitor are working together and their opposing styles aren't coordinated in advance, an Accommodator will build up resentment until they either lash out or quit.

So what do you do? Armed with the knowledge that they despise confrontation, how do you recruit an Accommodator to resolve a conflict? Negotiating with a lot of Accommodators has taught us that the most effective approach generally proceeds through a four-part sequence:

1. **Validate Their Process.** The best way to start an Accommodator down the path of addressing conflict is to compliment their patience and restraint. Remember, they have a high Trigger tolerance. They can avoid, skirt, and bury issues with the best of them. If you try to *force* the opposite, you'll be criticizing one of their strengths. Attacking an Accommodator's process will kill any rapport you have with them. Instead, show appreciation. When you validate their approach, you are communicating, in a subtle and nonconfrontational fashion, your awareness of a possible issue while coupling it with a positive message.

2. **Steer Clear of the Ditch.** Once an Accommodator perceives that you "get it" and are supportive rather than critical, they'll be willing to open up. But be forewarned: when they finally get to vent, they'll vent about *everything*. The more bottled up they've gotten, the stronger their urge will be to get things off their chest when the dam eventually breaks. If you let them press ahead, there's a decent chance they'll drive themselves into a ditch—in other words, they'll get stuck wheel-spinning (complaining), unable to see past all the dirt flying. So don't let them ramble. Nudge them to focus. When they start to go on a tangent or veer to nonconflictual subjects, casually remind them of what you all were chatting about a moment ago. For instance, "That's interesting; it's like you were saying, _____." Or, "Yeah, you're right! It makes me think of _____." Keep in mind: when an Accommodator is Triggered, they *need* to vent; you are not shutting down their venting here, you are redirecting it back to topics that are relevant to solution finding.

3. **Disregard the Nail.** Credit for the header of this step goes to writer, director, and producer Jason Headly. His much-acclaimed (twenty-four million viewers and counting) 2013 short, *It's Not About the Nail*, is a brilliant depiction of the angst between two people trying to tackle separate topics. A woman wants to discuss coping and communication. A man, presumably her spouse, wants to discuss the nail that's physically embedded in her forehead. The two topics may be connected, but the failure to identify the distinction between those two topics is what leads the couple—and, too often, all of us—into argument and misunderstanding. Watch *It's Not About the Nail*, imagining that the nail cannot be seen, and consider the spouse still saying the same things. That misstep is the crux of this advice for handling Accommodators. Accommodators almost never immediately bring up their true concern. The presenting problem (be it obvious or an assumption you are making) is *not* the interest to attack. The rule of thumb with an Accommodator: disregard whatever jumps out first; continue Active Listening (and continue steering clear of ditches) until there is a distinct change in the Accommodator's body language or tone.

4. **Send Them on a Care Trip.** We could phrase it as a guilt trip, but caring is a far more appropriate descriptor for the goal here. Accommodators have an aversion to upsetting others, or to their teammates being ill-affected by something the Accommodator says or does. Bring their care to bear. Kindly suggest how their position or actions negatively impact you (or other team members) or how an alternate position or action will benefit those whom the Accommodator values. By way of example, Doc G's oldest daughter is an expert at this step. At age two, she figured out the utility of the phrase, "But, Daddy, I'm scared." His conscientiousness for her well-being overrides all else, so employing this phrase often works to her advantage. That she'll send him on a care trip for self-serving motives became apparent when she proclaimed, "But, Daddy, I'm scared to wear pants to church." The key to conducting care trips that are equally principled and productive is to align with an Accommodator's desire to put their team first.

Leaning on the basketball metaphor again, Accommodators, like point guards, are pros at assists. However, considering their priority for focusing on their teammates (both personal and professional), combined with their ability to stave off being Triggered, it's easy to infer that all is copacetic in their world. Check in on the Accommodators in your life and look for opportunities to help them—validate their hard work so they know you're open for a pass and exercise patience to filter through the horde of small frustrations they've been squirreling away.

"Every player wants to be acknowledged for what they have done; validation feels like Hall of Fame enshrinement."

—Barry Larkin

HOLY GUANO!

Two neighboring farming families, though owning competing businesses, had lived in relative harmony for nine generations. Both Charles's and Nory's respective ancestors headed west shortly after Thomas Jefferson's Louisiana Purchase at the dawn of the nineteenth century. Their forebears acquired hundreds of acres of fertile livestock-rich land, most of which made its way via inheritance to Charles and Nory. The families held on to their properties through westward expansion, war, economic downturns, natural disasters, and, of course, the occasional feud.

Only seven months apart in age, Charles and Nory grew up together, the best of friends. They played every imaginable sport together. They co-captained their high school's soccer, wrestling, and baseball teams. Wrestling was their favorite; they battled each other for state championship titles (some saying their success due to a sibling-rivalry level of passion). They went to college together and graduated with identical, lofty GPAs. Despite corporate recruiters coming calling and graduate school scholarship offers, Charles and Nory were farmers at heart. They returned home and took over the farms from their fathers.

Two centuries of tradition carried forward—with one big divergence: neither of the men married or had children. Their parents passed, not all that far apart, leaving Charles and Nory as sole heirs to the farms and, quite unexpectedly, a sizable monetary cache. Both families had a long history of stashing dollars away while living modestly. Charles and Nory were fortunate to never have lived in want. College scholarships, no debt, and now on top of the handsome scope of their two successful farms—leading producers for multiple top food brands—the men were sitting on millions in savings. Single and smart as whips, but with a lack of life experience tackling obstacles or failure, they both got itchy. And wound up in our office.

Nory reached out to Doc G, explaining that he and "an associate" had gotten sideways, complicated by a "small legal matter," and they were seeking expertise to avoid publicity. Hmm . . . the very thick FedEx package Doc G received the day prior from Charles, complete with medical records of head trauma and photographs of an enormous, burned-to-the-ground building, didn't exactly sync with Nory's presentation.

Doc G decided to tread slowly. He invited the men, individually, to sit-downs. In advance of the meetings, he also requested that they both take the Conflict Personality Style Assessment. They concurred. They both proved to be Accommodators.

Greeting Charles as he showed him into the conference room, Doc G was keen on getting firsthand accounts of the case. "Please, have a seat. Take me through your story and how I can be of assistance."

Charles began by relating the backstory of the two families. He emphasized how ardent the rivalry between the two friends had become since they each had become sole owners of their respective estates. Doc G noted the incongruous emphasis and encouraged Charles to keep talking. Charles then switched topics to brag about the two-hundred-year tradition of the families and the monopolistic success of the farms in the region.

Eyebrows raised and enthusiastic, Doc G responded, "That's incredible! The patience to build all that, the perseverance through all kinds of challenges . . . Amazon Studios should make a movie about you guys! I'd love to hear more about the rivalry. That would be a good twist for a film."

Validating Via Praising the Accommodator's conflict handling strengths, check. Steering Clear of a Ditch, check. Doc G picked up on how effusive Charles was about the family tradition but nudged him back toward the men's relationship.

Charles snickered, "A movie would be something. Maybe it would expose that S.O.B. I trust you got the packet I sent? That should tell you all you need to know about him, torching his own barn, breaking my nose . . . I got internal bleeding from that punch."

"I'm sorry to hear about that. It must have really hurt. What all caused it?"

Disregarding the Nail, check. The fact that Charles preempted the visit with documentation of his injury and brought it up immediately in conversation revealed to Doc G that whatever physical altercation the men had was probably not crux of their conflict.

Charles proceeded, "Well, about a year ago, I made the decision to do a total revamping of the farm. Everything was fifty-plus years outdated. The best way for me to ensure the future of the farm, and this industry to be honest, is to go high-tech. Automate everything; bring in AI. I've invested a little over $3 million so far. That includes a pretty massive marketing campaign to tout our farm's national leadership, innovation to supply cleaner, heathier food . . . Nory was a dear friend; I wanted to share the progress and all the media with him and have it help us both. But he got jealous. His farm does well, but everyone knows it's not the juggernaut that mine is, and I guess he felt threatened. Maybe he didn't get as big of an inheritance as I did? I don't know. He goes and starts selling off his entire inventory. And then one morning I wake up to his barn complex completely ablaze. He had to have made a bundle on his livestock; he had *good* animals. But setting fire to the barn? To try to collect insurance?"

Doc G politely interrupted, "Wow, that's a whole heap for you to watch your friend go through. Thank you for sharing. Did you try to put out the fire or . . . Could you help me understand where the assault charge comes in?"

Validating and Steering Clear of a Ditch, round two. Doc G sensed that Charles was headed down a rabbit hole by recounting these various incidents. It was becoming evident that the barn, livestock, money—none of those were truly hot buttons.

"That lunatic . . . His place is burning yet he comes storming over to my place and accuses *me* of setting the fire then, POP, shatters my nose!" Charles exclaimed. "I mean, he was my *best* friend. I don't it get; he's lost his marbles."

"Ouch! I can only speculate how painful that was. The nose, plus feeling like you're losing someone who's basically family and not knowing what to do about it," Doc G replied, finally seeing the conflict core that had been marinating for quite some time: Charles's worry and sadness regarding the friendship. Doc G knew a Care Trip opening was near.

Meanwhile, Doc E had gone to visit Nory. They shook hands and Doc E extended the same greeting as Doc G had provided to Charles. It was a near carbon copy of Charles's session. Nory began by pontificating about the two enduring, richly traditioned families. Doc E praised Nory's (and his family's) tenacity and dedication. Accommodator Validation, check.

Nory continued, "I am in total shock by what happened. I considered Chuckie my brother. I'm sure he told you about the livestock empire we manage, shepherd really, as we've been entrusted by our ancestors to protect their legacy. What I bet he didn't tell you is that we've taken a hit by the economy. The business has completely changed. Consumers want all organic. Whole Foods is king now. Unless you cater to more discerning markets and buyers, you'll be a thing of the past. Chuckie was going under . . ."

"Wow! I had no idea; that's fascinating," Doc E interjected, getting a hint that Nory might be driving toward a ditch. He Steered Clear, check, by turning attention to the relationship between the men. "An entire industry revolution like that had to have been brutal on you, watching your friend struggle."

"You bet," Nory said. "While he was hemorrhaging money on his renovation, I realized that the *real* future in serving the organic food market isn't the food. It's the fertilizer. Natural, biodiverse guano . . . Doctor

Eliot, I'm telling you, it's *gold*. It's okay, go ahead and hoot, but poop is the most valuable thing on a farm. It's the ultimate export."

"Holy $#!%," Doc E blurted in an amalgamation of astonishment and entertainment.

Nory let out a burst of laughter, "Exactly!"

Doc E could tell by Nory's neutral presentation when he telephoned us, plus all this talk about farming trends and economics: these topics were all Nails to be Disregarded, check. He pivoted back to Nory's references to the men's friendship.

"All those pressures on your farms, I can see how all sorts of frustrations or anxieties could end up in a nose punch. And the barn too?"

Nory nodded. "I wish Chuckie had asked for help. We always used to tag-team on everything. He must have gotten so crazy deep in a hole that he snapped. To take a match to my barn like that, though? I suppose it's possible he thought I was abandoning farming when I sold my inventory. Maybe he thought I was abandoning him?"

Care Trip, check—Nory was supplying the Accommodator assist of care tripping *himself*! Doc E geared up to guide this self-imposed Care Trip down the path to resolution. There was one more item though. The punch.

"What a difficult thing to go through. I can only imagine how upset you were, and then to have your friend accuse you of breaking his nose . . ."

"Oh." Nory sighed ruefully. "No, that was my fault. I lost my cool when I saw the barn going up in smoke and realized there was no saving it. I went over and socked him good. I feel terribly about it. If I had to do it all again . . . I mean, the fertilizer movement together with all that new tech he installed, if we hadn't gotten on such different pages, if we hadn't regressed back to our wrestling days, we could be unstoppable. But now Chuckie's suing me, he's dragging my family's reputation through the mud, and even trying to say I lit my own place on fire to commit insurance fraud. You can't just take that back."

Doc E pounced on the opportunity to bring it home with Care Trip number two. "What if . . . and humor me for a second, if you'd be so kind. What if Chuck's pride is all that's standing in the way of you two teaming up again like brothers? What if he just doesn't yet understand how your new business model will help him?"

"Well, I'd hate to miss the chance to do something about it. I doubt it's the case, but of course I'd want to figure it out," Nory offered.

"Thank you *so much*," Doc E offered in return. "If you don't mind, while I check in with my partner to see where things stand, could you sketch what a new business partnership might look like? Again, I really appreciate visiting with you. I'll be in touch as soon as possible."

"Sure, I can do that," agreed Nory.

Huddling up, we were completely jazzed about the underlying—albeit, initially suppressed—commonality: the men's positive feelings toward each other. After all, they were two Accommodators who'd essentially treated each other as teammates for over thirty years, their businesses operating in tandem thanks to the generational stewardship. However, a handful of twists had gotten them into conflict: (1) They both had lost the steady guidance of their elders and had to cope with a new phase of life. (2) Both had taken a leap out of their comfort zones: Charles bringing big tech into the livestock business, Nory transitioning into organic fertilizer. The funds they'd inherited, unfortunately, permitted too quick a leap for Accommodators who are more comfortable being methodical, playing Momentum. (3) When they misinterpreted each other's strategic moves as competitive, a classic Accommodator soreness, they got Triggered. (4) Since Accommodators are confrontation avoiders, they didn't address their misinterpretations with one another; they buried them. (5) They let frustration and resentment build up while toiling at their large-scale, expensive initiatives. All these variables created the perfect storm.

Doc G went back to Charles. "Thank you for your patience. Do you mind if I ask a hypothetical?"

"Not at all," Charles answered.

"Suppose Nory was in the process of completely reengineering his farm, shifting to an organic fertilizer operation," Doc G outlined. "With the complexity and the scale of changes, what if he got so caught up that he didn't come to you with the plan, or hadn't yet figured it all out yet so was hesitant to involve you prematurely, but his intention was for it to be synergistic with all your plans?"

"If that were to be true, that would explain a lot of things," Charles said cautiously. "It doesn't excuse arson and assault though."

"Of course," Doc G said. "I realize you're very upset; anyone in your shoes would be. But I'm hopeful we can produce a positive result here which would make your asking us for assistance worthwhile. Would you be open to considering a proposal—out of respect for us—to settle the dispute amicably while structuring an agreement for your two evolved farms to increase each other's revenues?"

"Well, of course," Charlie replied, his demeanor softening and his curiosity percolating.

A meeting of the minds was on the horizon. We went to town on the details and logistics. It turned out that the fire was a result of an electrical failure; the authorities ruled no fault. Nory received his full insurance coverage and used a portion of it to pay for all of Charles's medical bills. The reunited friends got to work modernizing and expanding their joint empire.

~~~~~

We're incredibly fortunate to have been able to live through a great number of "Happily Ever After" tales. Some demand a *lot* more sweat than others. They're all worth it. Fortunately, Accommodators will match that energy, as they're happy to expend it on those whom they care about deeply. Accommodators, despite the elbow grease required to deal with their Trigger tendencies, are "Same Team!" believers, through and through. Unless you hammer them with a big ego, self-absorption, bullying, or mooching, their commitment to their team winning will be unwavering.

To reiterate the most salient components for Playing the Player with Accommodators:

~ Demonstrate your dependability and reliability.

~ Stick with the game plan they are anticipating.

〜 Tasks for which an Accommodator is counting on you: get them done!

〜 Be patient. Play Momentum.

〜 Show appreciation for their dedication, perseverance, sacrifices, and selflessness.

〜 Don't get in their kitchen or make things competitive between the two of you.

〜 Get out in front of small disharmonies, discord, or disconnects.

〜 Don't take them for granted.

Keep top of mind that colleagues or loved ones of yours who are Accommodators will be loath to confront you and may hold things inside. When they come to you with a complaint, it's likely to not be what is really bugging them. If you don't spend the time and energy to listen for their underlying Trigger, you can expect them to repeatedly return with similar or other trivial annoyances. In this way they are like what ER staff call "Frequent Flyers"—people who repeatedly find (make up, even) minor reasons to ask for attention. Recognize that, for Accommodators, such behavior is a veiled request for help with a more significant concern. Take advantage of these openings to give them an assist.

At the end of the day, Accommodators accommodate. They are fully invested in their relationship with you. That investment translates into a knack for—and willingness—to put your needs before theirs. But they can continue accommodating for only so long if their effort and care is not acknowledged and reciprocated in some manner. Unresolved irritants and aggravations will store up until eventually an Accommodator can't take it any longer and must let the steam escape. Learn your Accommodator friends', family members', and colleagues' Triggers and be tuned in to them. If you do, your relationships with Accommodators will be rock solid and sustained.

Revel in the benefits of having an Accommodator on your team—while maintaining an awareness of how valuable diversity is in all conflict. All five Conflict Personality Styles have rich upsides and value. They all have their weaknesses and challenges too. Every Go-To can be a tremendous ally if you do your homework. If you take the time to learn the Go-Tos of the people in your world, you will know when to lean on their unique strengths and when to shift your approach to efficiently and effectively manage their weaknesses.

We're always glad when we do. We know you will be too!

Epilogue

Whew! Those were some pretty packed chapters, dense with goodies for predicting and preventing conflict, for getting out of sticky situations, for resolving differences. We know, a lot to digest. We've found, in our seminars and trainings, that it helps to summarize the material into three pragmatic statements. If, at first, what you do is just carry these three nuggets with you, you'll gain a healthy advantage in the quest to reduce the discord around you:

1. High emotion and reason don't cooperate in the human brain when it is stressed. Land the emotion plane.

2. Humans are rarely "themselves" when their buttons are pushed. Assessment is half the battle. Solve people, not problems.

3. While you have a Go-To Conflict Personality Style when you are Triggered, you can learn to adjust. Play Go-To matchmaker!

Naturally, the tools and techniques we armed you with in the discourse of three hundred plus pages require practice to master. As you seek to move from the three prescripts to conflict Jedi knighthood, we recommend taking it one case at a time. View this book more as a "choose your own adventure" handbook than an all-encompassing set of rules. Trying to use the entirety of the information we've provided in every walk of your life is an effort destined to fail, or at least to leave you *way* short of your potential. Start with one disharmony or one person with whom you want to strengthen your relationship. Apply what you now know about Conflict Types. Layer on what you now know about Go-To Personalities. Then flip to the chapter, based on the scenario or individual in question, that is the logical next piece of the puzzle. We think you'll be pleasantly surprised how easy it is to use *How to Get Along with Anyone* as a kind of playbook pocket reference, helping you skip past the distractions, smoke screens, misperceptions, and missteps that we're all prone to in the heat of a tense moment—helping you pick out a positive new play to run. As Hall of Fame running back Emmitt Smith once shared with us, "All that fancy juking, head faking, and hip swiveling . . . a whole lot of movement in the same place; a good step forward wins."

Be like Emmitt. Be like Coach Boone in chapter 1. Or Dr. Brick in chapter 3. Be like Matt McConaughey or Jimmy Kimmel (chapter 4); Matt Damon or David Aardsma (chapter 5); Stacy Lewis (chapter 6); Yevgeny, Muhammad Ali, or Queen Elsa (chapter 7); Skip, Henry Rodriguez, or Taizo Ishida (chapter 8); or the Catwoman fitness executive (chapter 9). Be like Cap in chapter 10.

But most of all: be like the best version of yourself—the you who values understanding others, who recognizes that conflict elicits distinct patterns of emotionally driven behavior. Be the you who seizes this opportunity for performance enhancement *and* relationship strengthening!

"Why fight . . . when you can negotiate?"

—Jack Sparrow

What's Next?

We'd like to extend a parting invitation to you. As you put your newfound wisdom into practice, if you run into obstacles or uncertainty, give us a call. We love fielding interesting questions and hearing about the wide spectrum of situations for which our work might be of assistance. We were blessed with the opportunity to write this book across twenty-six states, eight countries, three continents . . . and seemingly every plane, train, beach, mountaintop, and hole-in-the-wall restaurant in between. Throughout our travels, inspiration was gifted to us from conversations with remarkable people from remarkable backgrounds, willing to open up about their personal stories of conflict, their pet peeves, their relationship complications. The fundamental things uniting humanity have never been clearer to us— our differences among them. Siblings fight. Spouses fight. Coworkers fight. Countries fight. As ironic as it may sound, we're connected by our common experience of disconnect. Everyone has tales of interpersonal tribulations, times they wish they were treated better, tensions they'd relish in eliminating. Everyone would prefer there to be less violence, more harmony, more neighbor appreciating neighbor.

So many people, though, dislike talking about conflict, let alone wading into the muck, that it gets dismissed, buried, handed off . . . lipstick is applied and relationship problems fester. "I have great coworkers, Doc. My company's a great place to work," we hear. Come to find out, when we follow up, they feel all they do is put out fires. We've found this happens, by and large, due to the universal discomfort with conflict combined with people feeling unequipped or unskilled at handling conflict. You're not one of those people. Thank you for picking up this book!

As you've learned about us by now, we're passionate about flipping the script on this narrative—converting our common discords into common victories. We hope you'll lean on us when a challenge crops up for which you'd appreciate an assist. We hope you'll share your success stories with us! So hopeful, in fact, that we're planning a sequel to *How to Get Along with Anyone*, a compilation of firsthand accounts of the principles in this book in action, used for a marvelous myriad of applications, large and small, wild and crazy. From haggling with a car salesperson to getting out of a speeding ticket to divorce-turned-happily-ever-after to a monster job promotion to a ceasefire, we want our next project to be a rip-roaring ride of practicable anecdotes. *We want you to be included!*

To that aim, please reach out to us. Log in to **www.theconflictdocs .com**, shoot us a message . . . heck, come catch a ballgame with us at Fenway. The dogs are on us! We look forward to it. Until then, we wish you all the very best in your personal and professional *How to Get Along with Anyone* adventures.

HUZZAH!

Acknowledgments

Our gratitude has no bounds for all those whose contributions, mammoth and microscopic alike, led to *How to Get Along with Anyone* being in your hands right now. That said, our first and most important thank-you goes to *you*. Thank you for picking up a copy of this book and joining us in the journey to try to make the world a nicer place to live. If every reader like you makes just one little stride to reduce conflict . . . that's a whole lot of big, hairy conflict we can collectively eliminate. To you, our greatest appreciation.

Of course, this project wouldn't have reached the light of day without some serious giants who let us stand on their shoulders. *Thank you* to our literary agents, Jim Levine, Courtney Paganelli, and Kirsten Wolf, the very best of the best in this business. Your vision and support—unparalleled. *Thank you* to the absolutely amazing, world-class team at Simon & Schuster: to Jon Karp, Priscilla Painton, Irene Kheradi, Emily Simonson, Brittany Adames, Julia Prosser, and everyone on the publishing and marketing frontlines; to Stephanie Frerich, our editor, who should be in the Hall of Fame, in our opinion, for her quarterbacking skills . . . on top of the countless hours of insightful, dedicated, sleeves-rolled-up manuscript polishing. *Thank you* to all our clients over the years, to all the coaches and athletes we've been blessed to work with and call friends—shining lights of patience, resilience, cooperation, humility, and the most wonderful of values; you've taught us so many lessons that we're honored and humbled to share. *Thank you* to our brilliant compadre and leader extraordinaire Dr. Matt Walker; to our ever keen and crafty, indefatigable colleague Michaela Dylag; and to our selfless, community-first colleagues who make up the Texas A&M University Sport Management faculty and staff.

At the risk of our Oscar speeches rambling on too long (Chris Rock, if you're reading, please spare us), we'd also like to extend our deepest appreciation to all the people behind the scenes who've encouraged us, opened doors for us, helped us through adversity, and so much more in shaping our lives . . .

For Doc G, *thank you* to: my personal Lord and Savior Jesus Christ, who provides me the greatest example of how to handle conflict; my amazing wife, Chelsea, and daughters, Blair and Caroline, for making every day a joy and teaching me, more and more every day, what life is really about; my parents, for all your prayers, patience, and wisdom; my brother and best friend, I love you and will do anything for you and thanks for being there for me no matter what; and the Dallas Cowboys for teaching me patience and giving me a place to direct my emotions so I can remain calm resolving conflict.

For Doc E, *thank you* to the very dearest friends in the history of mankind: the Goffman, John Goff; Johnny Katen, the genius, single-celled organism scientist; Terry "Big Daddy" Davison; Dr. Gilly "theCarDoc508" Sustache (the detailing retreats are the best therapy ever!) and the whole Brown University baseball crew; "The Fleming Draft" Carlton Fleming; Tony Apollaro; Lauren "LA" Anderson; Dr. Melissa "The Missy" Antman; Dr. Seth Alpert; Hansy Mallalieu; Paraag Marathe; Pennsylvania state champion coach Jeff "Hurricane" Hoke; Larry Domingo; combat sports guru Nir Moriah at www.streetsmartstv.com; Dr. Susie "Thoos" Wootton; "Pharmacy Doug" Paige; Dr. Chip "Say" Hay; Shawn Tester; and the entire Santa Clara Stogies and Charlottesville Blues rosters. *Thank you* to coaches Willis Wilson, Scott Layden, John Emery, Bill Reinhart, Mike Walsh, and Nigel Topping; mentors Dr. Bob Rotella and Dr. John Corson; and inspiration Roy Hobbs. *Thank you* most of all to my rock, my family: Gramps; Mom; Dad; Wheatie and the M&Ms; my cousins, Elisabeth, Roger, Kevin, and Collette; my endlessly loving sister, Anner; brother-in-law, Norm; and rock star Tar Heel niece, Amelia.

To *all* of you, our love.

Notes

Introduction

xii **real-world work and family illustrations:** Throughout the book, names, locations, and other facts that could identify the real-life participants of the case stories presented were altered where necessary to adhere to confidentiality requirements.

xv **why isn't this a required course in school?:** We're on it! Thanks to several visionary teachers, principals, and school district administrators—in tag team with the amazing people at Simon & Schuster who've made this book possible—we're rolling out innovative curriculum to equip young folks with conflict prevention and resolution skills. If you are in education and want to get involved, please reach out to us at **www .theconflictdocs.com.**

1. Identify the Trigger

4 **Lou Ferrigno and Edward Norton:** Fictional character Bruce Banner (originally David Banner), and actors Lou Ferrigno and Edward Norton, are in reference to the Marvel Comics–based graphic arts books, 1977–1982 television series, and 2008 film *The Incredible Hulk* in which a highly intellectual MD/PhD scientist routinely gets Triggered, morphing into an enraged, justice-seeking, "stand up for the little guy" monster. We'd be re-

miss if we didn't also give a nod to Mark Ruffalo, who turned in another excellent portrayal of Banner and the Hulk in *The Avengers* (2012).

9 **Mr. Spacely–esque:** For those unfamiliar with 1980s Saturday morning cartoons, Mr. Spacely was George Jetson's arrogant, autocratic CEO on *The Jetsons*.

16 **self-fulfilling prophecy:** The self-fulfilling prophecy, known as the Pygmalion effect (for the mythical Greek sculptor who fell in love with one of his statues), was brought to mainstream prominence in 1968 when Harvard psychologist Robert Rosenthal teamed up with South San Francisco school principal Lenore Jacobson to reveal the profound impact teachers' expectations of students have on students' subsequent classroom performance. In the five decades since, their studies have been replicated widely, from sports to office settings, demonstrating the power—both positive and negative—our beliefs have in influencing the behaviors of others. Authority figures (teachers, coaches, bosses, etc.) must be vigilant to prevent their expectations from creating treatment inequities.

17 **fixated on one small detail:** A particularly poignant example of this uniquely human propensity comes from a fascinating line of research in the field of cognitive psychology regarding eyewitness testimony. When witnesses—highly credible witnesses—testify about a crime that involved a gun, greater than 80 percent of the time the only facts they can accurately recall are about the gun. They draw blanks or give wildly erred testimony on all other details, such as time of day, the number of people involved, races and genders, clothing (even their own), etc., leading to poor conclusions, including wrongful convictions.

2. Predict Behavior

33 **most deeply ingrained behavior patterns:** Have you ever noticed that your spouse gets on you more frequently for biting your fingernails (or another habit of yours) when your in-laws are visiting? Or that you seem to need to go to the bathroom right when you're in a rush to get someplace? These aren't accidental coincidences. Research on "Psychological Load" has shown that marked increases in emotional stress bring forth positively correlated increases in homeostatic or thalamic drives. Though an explanation of the subcortical nature of nail chewing is beyond the scope of this book, the take-home lesson remains just as valuable: the stronger the pressure we face, the more ardently we revert to our ingrained habits.

34 **Ted Williams:** The Docs always enjoy sharing their expertise with great artists who produce works to promote learning, education, and com-

munity awareness. Join us in giving a rouse to MLB Network producer Gary Waksman. Of the scores of projects he's given the world, he did a marvelously insightful piece on Ted Williams, highlighting the variables (such as his Personality Go-To) that led to the Splendid Splinter's success. Check out Gary's film "*The Immortal*" *Ted Williams*: https://vimeo.com /127507843.

40 **"meeting in the middle":** For further insight on why the top conflict resolution specialists consider "meeting in the middle" to be an undesirable result (with both sides losing), we highly recommend *Never Split the Difference* (Harper Business, 2016) by our friend Chris Voss, one of the most decorated hostage negotiators in FBI history.

42 **oration virtuoso:** If you haven't seen *The Blacklist*, it's worth a watch. Actor James Spader's genius for soliloquy delivery is, understatedly, a thing to behold. Prefer legal dramas to crime thrillers? Spader infuses similar speech artistry into his role as Alan Shore on *Boston Legal* (David E. Kelley Productions and 20th Century Fox Television, 2004–2008).

48 **Aces aren't born with this range:** On the oft occasion, a talented pitcher will arrive in the Big Leagues still relying on their fastball. To become an all-star, they must add new range or improve the ineffective pitches in their arsenal. This means their pitching coach must tweak the mechanics the pitcher has had since junior high. Talk about resistance to change! "Coach, they're paying me a million dollars a year. I think my stuff works."

48 **help you uncover your Go-To:** To take the Conflict Personality Style Assessment to learn your Go-To, visit **www.theconflictdocs.com**. You can also use this site to arrange team assessments for your business or organization (or for family fun), stay abreast of current research, take a variety of skill-enhancement courses, gain continuing education credits, schedule customized on-site training, and more.

59 **alter egos:** The tried-and-true playbooks of Marvel Entertainment and DC Comics sell movie tickets, streaming subscriptions, video games, and comic books by the truckload. Why are they so popular? They draw us in by allowing us to feel a commonality with these characters of mystical powers. They have quirks and fallibilities, just like us. They aren't deterred. Good wins in the end. Just as is the proposition for us: you, too, can overcome conflict; you, too, can be the hero of your story.

3. Get to the Underlying Interest

63 **starting prop:** If you are unfamiliar with the sport of rugby, or new to its lexicon, the World Rugby Federation offers marvelous resources. Visit

www.world.rugby/the-game/beginners-guide/safety. The US National Team also provides an excellent graphical tutorial for quickly learning the basics of the game. Check out usa.rugby/rugby101.

67 **between all primates:** Legendary ethologist Jane Goodall likes to tell stories of her COVID-19 adventures attempting to Zoom with chimpanzees. She jests, "Homo sapiens aren't much better! We're not designed to talk without touching." From our ancestors, we inherited relating to each other holistically, not relying on vocabulary.

68 **our five senses, to a degree, compete:** Have you ever heard someone bragging about how good a multitasker they are? On occasion, are you the braggadocious one? Check your pride at the door. Being an "expert multitasker" means perceiving that you can excel at multiple things simultaneously. You can't. Neuroscientists such as Earl Miller at MIT (we highly recommend his 2017 podcast) have demonstrated that, in this state, one is purely Task Switching without realizing they are Task Switching. Frequent and rapid Task Switching causes increased error rate—on all the tasks—as well as a residual performance decline ripple effect. Even toggling from a job for a scant thirty seconds to read a text message can lead to a subsequent *half hour* of subpar work!

74 **John Belushi–esque confidence:** The Belushi reference, of course, to the actor's notorious line, "We can do anything we want; we're college students!" Incidentally, *National Lampoon's Animal House* is based on the experience of one of its screenwriters, Chris Miller, as a member of the Alpha Delta Phi fraternity (the rugby frat, no less) while a student at Dartmouth in the early 1960s.

4. Defuse Emotion

85 **Bale as the highest-grossing male performer:** Aggregated from *Forbes's* series titled *Top-Grossing Actors*, December 2008–2012.

88 **a "rational" lens:** From the Greeks' development of philosophy through the Age of Enlightenment we have pointed to reason as the defining feature of our species. But inquiry into Rational Expectation Theory has revealed that insistence on this characteristic, oxymoronically, leads to substantial irrational thinking and behavior (particularly in fields such as economics in which we significantly underestimate nonrational forces). As University of Paris professor Justin Smith says in his book *Irrationality: A History of the Dark Side of Reason*, "The desire to impose rationality, to make people or society out to be more rational than they are, mutates into spectacular outbursts of irrationality."

90 **escalated into a full-blown dispute:** In formal mediation terminology, dispute is defined as conflict that has developed into an impasse or has spawned a counterproductive motivation by one or more parties. Conflict itself, on the other hand, is a disagreement or opposition of views that isn't inherently negative.

91 **inherent bias for speed over substance:** In fact, the American corporate workforce is so familiar with this tendency that a surefire line to get some laughs at the start of a meeting you are leading (and to break the ice in a manner also teeing up a productive brainstorming environment) is to ask, "Before I state the problem, are there any solutions?"

93 **survival mechanism:** All primates have a collection of brain cells whose sole function is to copy things like intonation, hand gestures, accents, tone, and other nonverbal communication. They're aptly named mirror neurons. Located in the oldest parts of our brain, mirror neurons developed as a protection instinct, allowing us, when in perilous situations with neighboring or warring tribes (or with the dominant members of our own tribe), to appear as friends and not foes.

96 **The power of empathy:** For further insight into the concept of empathy, we recommend looking up Brené Brown. Brené has done incredibly uplifting work helping people help other people feel heard and understood—what decades of psychological research has demonstrated to be a rudimentary human need. Of course, when it comes to helping others, we also encourage you to read Doc E's book with Indiana Pacers' president Kevin Pritchard, *Help the Helper* (Penguin Portfolio, 2014).

98 **change blindness:** The legendary duo Penn & Teller, true masters of psychology, take change blindness to a whole new level in their shows by heightening the audience's emotional state with crazy stunts, shock and awe (such as spurting fake blood and guts), and entertaining dialogue that encourages fans to feel like they are "in" on the trick, only for the bit to be about something else. The genius is that using emotion, from humor to horror, as the change blindness agent allows viewers to look squarely at Penn & Teller's ruses and still be fooled. The sentiment, "I knew they were going to trick me . . . and it was AWESOME" is brilliant artistry. For entertaining insight, check out https://www.youtube.com/watch?v=_fisK6scpns.

99 **Milgram experiments:** A psychologist at Yale, Stanley Milgram, devoted his career to studying acts of genocide and justifications offered for them, such as the claims of obedience ("I was following orders") on display during the Nuremberg Trials. Milgram's experimentees were given the role of "teacher" and instructed to deliver increasingly powerful electric shocks to

incorrectly answering "students" (who were confederates in the study, and unbeknownst to the experimentees, not actually shocked). Results horrifically revealed a human propensity to seriously harm, even kill, innocent people, if directions come from an accepted authority figure. In a series of replicated variations, the very worst of the damage delivered—and an untethered willingness to do so—occurred in two conditions: (1) when the "teacher" could not actually see the "student" and (2) when the "teacher" could delegate the shocking to an "assistant."

104 **batting 1.000:** For those who aren't familiar with baseball statistics, perfection at the plate (one hit in one attempt, ten hits in ten attempts, etc.) is referred to as "batting a thousand." It's represented in a box score as 1.000, as batting averages are ratios, calculated by dividing a player's number of hits by his number of times at bat.

106 **strengthen your understanding:** Hopefully you are familiar with Daniel Goleman's groundbreaking discovery of a specific kind of intelligence— Emotional Intelligence, EQ. Since his seminal work was released (1995), it's been well established that one of the strongest predictors of successful leadership is high EQ. Thankfully, unlike IQ, Emotional Intelligence is something we learn; it can be developed. Which is another reason why making the upfront investment in your relationships that we've been discussing in this chapter is so valuable.

5. Play the Player

107 **is a window:** Figuratively *and* literally. The picture begins with Damon's character, Mike McDermott, descending below the streets of New York City into a murky hallway, sealed off by a massive block of a steel door. A Damon voice-over spells out the risks of playing cards for money, the sharks trolling the waters of the unregulated poker industry. A security slit opens. McDermott is eyeballed. The slit slams shut and then the door creeks open. "This is KGB's place. You won't find it in the yellow pages." In we follow . . .

107 **cult classic:** The same year *Rounders* came out, a Canadian company, Planet Poker, launched the first online real-money poker game. ESPN broadcast the World Series of Poker (WSP). Texas Hold 'Em, the version of poker featured in both the movie and the WSP, began gaining mainstream popularity. Today, the WSP is an international phenomenon composed of over 150 tournaments, 8,000 entrants strong, culminating in the Caesars Entertainment–sponsored grand finale in Nevada. The champion takes home over $10 million. Matt Damon, himself, once finished as a

runner-up at a finals' qualifying table. He got knocked out by two-time world champ Doyle Brunson, the first person to amass over $1 million in career poker earnings.

112 **give the Heisman to fluorescent light:** Fluorescent bulbs refresh at a high rate. This "flickering" is normally not outwardly visible (until a bulb is on its last legs and the refresh rate begins to slow), but your brain still senses it. The electromagnetic signal is, at best, subconsciously distracting. At worst, it causes eye strain, headaches, fatigue, and frustration—all conditions that reduce comfort and exacerbate conflict.

113 **Jason Sudeikis:** We're huge fans of Sudeikis's art. He's thoughtful, grounded, coming to character development from tribulations to which most people can relate. He cares profoundly about improving people's day-to-day lives—and in more meaningful ways than transient "mental getaway" entertainment. If you haven't yet watched his sixty-one-Emmy-nominated, thirteen-Emmy-winning series, *Ted Lasso*, please treat yourself. Figure out who your "biscuits with the boss" compadre is—or make it you!

114 **engage in distinctive touches:** Research on the NBA has revealed a strong, positive correlation between the frequency with which teammates physically touch one another and the winning percentage of their team. In MLB, the correlation is even more poignant relative to hug frequency.

115 **talking about common ground:** Untrained salespeople (or those who've eschewed rapport-building training), on the other hand, screw this up. They try waaaaay too hard to pretend they have all the same likes and ideals that you do. They fake it, and not slightly either. They pry too vigorously into your personal affairs. You hold them at arm's length as a result. Or you walk away. Don't make those rookie errors.

129 **"get in their own way":** From Major League Baseball dugouts to NBA and WNBA locker rooms to World Cup pitches, athletes and coaches we've worked with have all used some iteration of the words "getting in one's own way." It transcends sports, gender, race, age, experience, and résumés. Staying out of your own way, and helping your teammates and coworkers stay out of their own way, is an essential ingredient of success.

6. The Avoider

134 **the above exemplars shared:** Speaking of golf, the stories we selected are also prime representatives of the Ben Hogan Award—given annually to a sportsperson who has heroically overcome a grave illness or disability. The recognition, as you may know, is in nod to its namesake, who won sixty-three professional golf events despite the career interruptions of World

War II (Hogan was a US Army Air Forces pilot) *and* being struck, head-on, by a Greyhound bus, leaving him with a double-fractured pelvis, a fractured collar bone, a fractured ankle, chipped ribs, a life-threatening blood clot condition, and evermore physical limitations due to circulation problems. As scary and life-altering as it was, the vehicular crash would have been fatal for Hogan—if not for his courageous lunge to protect his wife, who was riding in the passenger seat of their car. They were on the way home to Fort Worth, Texas, from the 1949 Phoenix Open (in which Hogan finished tied for first but got nosed by Jimmy Demaret in an eighteen-hole playoff). Thick fog had set in that morning, drastically reducing visibility. As Ben and Valerie were crossing a constricted, no-breakdown-lane bridge, the driver of an oncoming bus, despite being unable to see, crossed the center line to pass another car. Seemingly from nowhere, out of the fog, the Greyhound barreled right at them; no place to turn. In a flash, instead of attempting to maneuver, Hogan threw his body in front of Valerie. It saved both of their lives. The steering column rammed clear through and out the other side of Ben's vacated seat.

135 **Sport psychologists:** FYI, while journalists are fond of writing sensational stories about the field of sport psychology to dramatize "behind the curtain" practices or paint color around certain celebrities and their accomplishments—or failures—the growth of the profession is largely academic. Yes, there are now hordes of degree-touting counselors, therapists, professors (and nondegreed, yikes, "gurus") claiming expertise in the mental game. Yet, within the inner circles of elite sport, there are only, roughly, a dozen people whose phones ring, unsolicited, when the top athletes and coaches want to talk shop about the brain. They're referred to as "The Utopias" and they practice many of the skills explained in this book, including the sherpa-referenced effort to give others credit. They work intently to remain under the radar.

136 **Stay out of their way:** Stay out of their way . . . or brace for the *Terminator*. Arnold Schwarzenegger made headlines in April 2023 for doing exactly this: filling a pothole in his Brentwood, California, neighborhood. "Today, after the whole neighborhood has been upset about this giant pothole that's been screwing up cars and bicycles for weeks, I went out with my team and fixed it. I always say, let's not complain, let's do something about it. Here you go," Schwarzenegger wrote on X (at the time, Twitter).

137 **figured out that your COO is:** For any of your friends, family, or workmates, if chapter 2's six-point Go-To inventories (Common Triggers, Strengths, Weaknesses, Ideal Conflict Scenarios, Main MOs, Nicknames, Best Teammate, and Worst Teammate) don't immediately spark a light

bulb, run a Big 4 Checklist or let the assessment tools at **www.theconflict docs.com** do the heavy lifting for you.

137 **personality states:** Neuroscientists distinguish psychophysiological and behavioral patterns that are situationally linked, provisory, and malleable, called "states" from those that are enduring, omnipresent, rigid, and unchangeable, called "traits." As the former, Go-Tos are learnable and trainable. Everyone has a predominant default, which they'll initially be inclined to respond to conflict with, but with training and ample practice, you can learn to implement an alternate Conflict Personality Style as various situations demand.

140 **Casey Ryback:** At the heart of J. F. Lawton's *Under Siege* trilogy, Casey Ryback is the soft-spoken, pacifist-spirited Navy SEAL aikido master portrayed by iconic martial artist Steven Seagal, a seventh-dan (degree) black belt in aikido himself. Known as the "Art of Peace," aikido was founded by Japanese guru Morihei Ueshiba with a visionary philosophy of harmonizing and unifying combatants. Aikido practitioners don't attack. They redirect force. The "ki" in the name means "life energy" (and, fascinatingly, was a foundational concept George Lucas built upon when he created "The Force" for *Star Wars*). Ueshiba believed that opponents should be steered to safety rather than "defeated," using ki for everyone's benefit—including ours, as aikido is a shining illustration of healthy conflict resolution strategy. Worldwide, champions of peace and harmony have gravitated to the art of aikido, including Sean Connery and Joan Baez, black belts both.

7. The Competitor

156 **Muhammad Ali's legendary Rope-a-Dope:** The rope-a-dope is a defensive boxing maneuver made famous by Muhammad Ali. In training, Ali would let his sparring partner hit him in the stomach as a toughening method so he could take punches in a bout without sustaining injury. One day before the 1974 heavyweight championship in Zaire against George Foreman, photographer George Kalinsky, while capturing Ali's preparations, commented, "You should try that against Foreman. Sort of like a dope on the ropes." To which Ali chimed in poetic fashion, "Big George, he thinks he's the Pope; but he can't beat me, I'm a Rope-a-Dope." Foreman, the reigning undisputed champion of the world, an undefeated 40–0, was colossally favored. In front of an estimated global TV viewership topping one billion, Ali delivered Foreman's first career loss, knocking him out in the eighth round. We credit Ali as one of the masters from whom we

cobbled together techniques that work like a charm when you're in conflict with a Competitor.

156 **bottle of Imperial Collection Super Premium vodka:** Imperium Collection's Super Premium is a twelve-times-distilled, fresh spring water vodka that uses the recipe created in 1721 for Russian tsar Peter the Great.

158 **serve as influencers or connectors for you:** Connectors, a label coined by Malcolm Gladwell in *The Tipping Point* (Little, Brown, 2000), are people who sync well across the entire spectrum of Go-To Conflict Personality Styles. Not because they're entirely different cats. Like all of us, they have a dominant Go-To of their own. But they've practiced adopting the other Go-Tos and strive to select, consciously, how they respond to pressure— seeking to mesh with those around them—as opposed to reactively relying on their natural Go-To. This vaults the perception of them as special glue for connecting people.

158 **need to connect on a deeper-than-surface level:** As an aside, you've probably heard someone pontificate, "I love my dog; he totally gets me!" Emotional support animals provide tremendous benefit for a reason. They don't commit the conflict-escalating communication errors to which humans are prone (interrupting, not listening, assuming, talking over, disrespecting, dismissing, etc.). As a result, they soothe Triggered emotions.

159 **television series *Dirty Jobs*:** Airing for nine seasons (2003–2012) as *Dirty Jobs*, and recently revived as *Dirty Jobs: Rowe'd Trip* (2020–present), the five-time Emmy-nominated Discovery Channel show gained popularity for its hilariously gasp-eliciting portrayal of the strangest, messiest, most arduous, most disgusting jobs imaginable. One certainly gains a refreshing perspective on their own profession after watching a few reruns. Of the 179 and counting episodes, Rowe ranks the rodeo clown adventure among his most thrilling.

160 **biological instinct kicks in:** Undoubtedly, you know the fight-or-flight response, the sympathetic nervous system's cascade of hormones in reaction to a perceived danger. It's an autonomic process, happening without conscious thought. It can be a gift (such as when you come upon an alligator . . . *RUN*), or it can hamstring you. Don't leave it to chance. Much of our success with elite athletes and special forces units has come from helping them shape challenges—not as beating someone else but as "Winning the Inner Battle." Win the Inner Battle in conflict with a Competitor by resisting the fight-or-flight response.

166 **Being a jerk almost always costs you:** A few years back, Doc E had the pleasure of sitting in on a consultation conducted by a former CIA interrogator. The session was for one of Doc E's NBA clients, to gain some goodies

for communicating with difficult people. Entirely eye-opening! The retired agent shared with us that torture, from withholding sustenance to water-boarding to worse, proved to be the least effective interrogation methodology. The CIA's trump cards? Finding common ground, active listening, and validation. Go figure. It's such a shame that Hollywood has spent so much celluloid dramatizing what doesn't work.

8. The Analyzer

171 **brave the elements:** By now you're probably figuring out that we're a bit nuts. We were probably storm chasers in a previous life. In 2008, Doc E decided to go Rollerblading through the ghost-town-like streets of Houston in the middle of Hurricane Ike. How he convinced his girlfriend, Jenny, to join him in the seventy-plus-mile-per-hour winds is a conflict resolution story for another time. Stay tuned for the *How to Get Along with Anyone* sequel!

177 **Toyoda:** Folklore has it that the Toyoda family attached the alternate spelling to the company for the 20 percent conservation of pen strokes and ink in writing the automobile's name, in Japanese, with a T instead of a D it would save them.

178 **implementing this technique monthly:** Duncum's experimentation led him to land on monthly mini retreats. Optimum frequency for kaizen, however, varies based on type of industry, business scale and age, and of course the Go-To Personality Styles of the personnel involved.

179 **two authentic fifteenth-century samurai swords:** Yes, Doc G has since wielded one of the swords, showing off his best impersonation of Ken Watanabe in *The Last Samurai.*

179 **Dr. Shoichiro Toyoda:** True to family values, Shoichiro earned a doctorate in engineering and commenced his career by starting in an entry-level position at a fishcake-processing plant.

182 **gain an improved understanding of each other:** Winston Churchill famously said of Hitler, "Those who have met Herr Hitler face to face . . . have found a highly competent, cool, well-informed functionary with a disarming smile, and few have been unaffected by a subtle personal magnetism." In *no* way was Churchill admiring or condoning Hitler. Winston was making a profound statement regarding the importance of respecting that even one's most vile adversaries have positive or effective qualities. There will be individuals you "hate." If your hatred blocks you from seeking to evolve your understanding of them, then, chances are, you'll be the one getting the short end of the stick.

9. The Collaborator

192 **everything sports fans have come to associate with agents:** It's suspected that some of McCormack's exploits were woven into both the characters Jerry Maguire and Spencer Strasmore, the retired NFL-player-turned-financial-manager in Dwayne "The Rock" Johnson's HBO series *Ballers*. McCormack's stunts, in many ways precursors to those of today's promotional baron Richard Branson, are generally credited as the catalysts for the sports industry becoming the multibillion dollar juggernaut it is today. For nearly three decades, Mark was dubbed the most powerful man in sports. He put Laura Baugh's infectious, dimple-booked smile on golf-themed Ultra-Bright toothpaste boxes—six months before she was old enough to join the LPGA. He organized a high-roller "play with the champ" spectacular in Monte Carlo for Philip Martyn, with Cartier picking up the tab. Who's Philip Martyn? A backgammon player! Mark turned Kiwanis picnics into paparazzi destinations. He took popes on barnstorming tours! He wrapped a bow on ABC's *Superstars* to get it on TV, packaging the show, in which athletes from a broad spectrum of sports competed in contests mostly out of their indigenous element, with the most unexpected of storylines. Olympic pole vaulter Bob Seagren took home the maiden trophy, but it was McCormick's boxing client, Joe Frazier, who stole the limelight. Nearly drowning in the kickoff event, a fifty-meter pool lap, it turned out that Joe didn't know how to swim! Furiously dog-paddling, Frazier made it to the wall and, as he climbed out of the water, opined to the camera, "That Mark Spitz is a tough mother&#@%er!"

194 **if "partner" is more important to you than "business":** The most common professions where we see the Collaborator Go-To propelling success: coaching, sales, counseling, and human resources.

198 **"Pulling the Goalie":** For those not familiar with net-guarded sports like hockey (lacrosse, soccer, etc.), when the game clock is nearing expiration and one team is a single goal behind, predominant strategy is for that team to take their goalkeeper out of the game, replacing the goalie with an extra offensive attacker in a last-ditch effort to score. In these instances, an open net gives opposing teams free rein to fire away if they get the puck (or ball). As discussed in this chapter, an interesting twist of relevance is that, in resolving disputes, there are proactive times when you *want* people to take shots.

199 **custom retreat:** We welcome inquiries about producing events specifically tailored to organizations' most pressing needs—be those needs relating to conflict reduction or prevention . . . or an entirely different application of

performance enhancement. We are passionate about creating opportunities for people to learn how to harness psychology while simultaneously having a total *blast*. Fun is the best platform for sustainable learning. Give us a call!

202 **the role of the FBI agent:** Ratification of the Eighteenth Amendment to the US Constitution in 1919 put law enforcement squarely in opposition to most of the American public. Federal prohibition operatives were the enemy; bootleggers the heroes. Gangsters thrilled newspaper readers and moviegoers, who applauded the likes of John Dillinger, Pretty Boy Flood, Bonnie and Clyde, Baby Face Nelson, and Machine Gun Kelly rising up against a freedom-snatching government, "sticking it to the man." The Great Depression plummeted trust in authority. For FDR to lead the country out of despair, to enlist widespread support for his New Deal agenda, he needed a positive avatar of social order. Enter the unbridled power granted to Hoover for his revamped, dare we say sexy, G-Man [*sic*] brand of policing.

10. The Accommodator

215 **The Caucus Technique:** When there are more than two parties in conflict (or if you are serving as an intermediary between people arguing), a strategy that can be helpful, particularly in removing Triggers and diffusing emotion, is to separate the parties and work with them individually. If it's you that's in turmoil with someone, you can implement the Caucus Technique by handing the Go-To management reins to a neutral third party. If you need assistance, we're always happy to help; ping us via **www.theconflict docs.com.**

218 **Jason Headly:** We encourage you to tune into Jason's art. To watch *It's Not About the Nail,* here is the YouTube link: www.youtube.com/watch?v=-4EDhdAHrOg. Please also join us in applauding actress Monica Barbaro for her skilled portrayal of the kinds of nonverbal cues exhibited by people who are Triggered but who are trying to remain calm.

219 **Barry Larkin:** Larkin was inducted into Major League Baseball's Hall of Fame in 2012. His on-field performance spoke for itself in validating the sports writers' votes. His clubhouse caretaking of staff and teammates alike, and his off-field community contributions, in our opinion, are what truly separates him from his peers. Join us in applauding Barry for his unwavering commitment to bringing people from all walks of life together.

225 **"Same team!":** In case you are unacquainted with the phrase, it's originally a basketball reference to two teammates unintentionally fighting each other for a rebound. One of them (or another teammate or coach) shouts

out "Same team!" to interrupt the simultaneous effort that is getting in the way of securing possession of the ball. In applicable terms for this book: sometimes, you run into a conflict in which you and another person are, ultimately, seeking the same objective. Squabbling has gotten in the way of seeing that. One of you, or a friend or colleague, needs to interject (in a positive tone and fashion, of course), "Same team!"

Acknowledgments

234 **"theCarDoc508":** The good doctor Gil Sustache, a family physician, is the undisputed world champion in the caring-people category. We are so blessed that he is part of our extended family. If you'd like to see a true artist at work—both in trade craft *and* community building, please check out https://www.instagram.com/thecardoc508. On the off chance that you are a fan of babying your ride, Dr. Sustache also provides exceptionally valuable tips for you.

234 **combat sports guru Nir Moriah:** Tae Kwon Do national champion Nir Moriah is a dear friend and the CEO of Street Smarts, LLC. We highly recommend that you check out his work at www.streetsmartstv.com.

234 **Roy Hobbs:** A shout-out, as has become a custom in all of Doc E's books, to Robert Redford's character in *The Natural* (Tri-Star Pictures, 1984). Thank you, Bobby, for all your work on and, especially, off the screen.

Works Cited

Adair, W., Brett, J., Lempereur, A., Okumura, T., Shikhirev, P., Tinsley, C., & Lytle, A. (2004). Culture and negotiation strategy. *Negotiation Journal, 20*, 87–111.

Adler, P. S., Goldoftas, B., & Levine, D. I. (1999). Flexibility versus efficiency? A case study of model changeovers in the Toyota production system. *Organization Science, 10*(1), 43–68.

Agarwal, P. (2018). How does lighting affect mental health in the workplace. *Forbes*. December 31.

Anderson-Lopez, K., & Lopez, R. (2014). Let it go (recorded by Idina Menzel). In *Frozen* [Film]. Wonderland Music Company & Walt Disney.

Avildsen, J. G. (Director). (1984). *The Karate Kid* [Film]. Delphi II Productions & Jerry Weintraub Productions.

Bain, L. L., & Wendt, J. C. (1983). Undergraduate physical education majors' perceptions of the roles of teacher and coach. *Research Quarterly for Exercise and Sport, 54*, 112–118.

Beersma, B., & De Dreu, C. K. W. (2002). Integrative and distributive negotiation in small groups: Effects of task structure, decision rule, and social motive. *Organizational Behavior and Human Decision Processes, 87*, 227–252.

Benetti, S., Ogliastri, E., & Caputo, A. (2021). Distributive/integrative negotiation strategies in cross-cultural contexts: A comparative study of the USA and Italy. *Journal of Management & Organization, 27*(4), 786–808.

Biddle, B. (1979). *Role theory*. Academic Press, Inc.

Bielby, D. (1992). Commitment to work and family. *Annual Review of Sociology*, *18*, 281–302.

Bokenkamp, J. (2013). *The Blacklist* [TV series]. Davis Entertainment, Universal Television & Sony Pictures Television Studios.

Bošnjaković, J., & Radionov, T. (2018). Empathy: Concepts, theories and neuroscientific basis. *Alcoholism and Psychiatry Research*, *54*(2), 123–150.

Bowling, R., & Wheeler, B. E. (1979). Coward of the county (recorded by Kenny Rogers). On *Kenny* [Album]. United Artists Group.

Brett, J. (2000). Culture and negotiation. *International Journal of Psychology*, *35*, 97–104.

Brown, A., & Sieben, N. (2013). The elephant in the classroom: Examining the influence of athletic coaching on secondary pre-service teachers. *Teacher Education Quarterly*, *40*(3).

Buck, C., & Lee, J. (Directors). (2013). *Frozen* [Film]. Walt Disney Pictures & Walt Disney Animation Studios.

Camiré, M., Trudel, P., & Bernard, D. (2013). A case study of a high school sport program designed to teach athletes life skills and values. *Sport Psychologist*, *27*(2), 188–200.

Campagna, R. L., Mislin, A. A., Kong, D. T., & Bottom, W. P. (2016). Strategic consequences of emotional representation in negotiation: The blowback effect. *Journal of Applied Psychology*, *101*, 605–624.

Capra, F. (Director). (1946). *It's a wonderful life* [Film]. Liberty Films.

Ceruzzi, P. E. (1999). *A history of modern computing*. MIT Press.

Childs, B., & Harold, D. (2003). Assessing the perceived and experienced role conflict of the community/junior college teacher/coach: Factors affecting role performance. *Humanities and Social Sciences*, *56*(5), 1704.

Cohen, B. P., Chow, C. C., & Vattikuti, S. (2019). Dynamical modeling of multi-scale variability in neuronal competition. *Communications Biology*, *2*, 319–330.

Conan Doyle, A. (2014). *The sign of four*. Penguin Classics.

Crowe, C. (Director). (1996). *Jerry Maguire* [Film]. TriStar Pictures, Gracie Films, & Vinyl Films.

Dahl, J. (Director). (1998). *Rounders* [Film]. Spanky Pictures & Miramax Films.

Davila, J. (2016). Stop trying to fix things, just listen! Do you give practical or emotional support? It's the classic couples' dilemma. *Psychology Today*, June 17.

Davis, A. (Director). (1992). *Under siege* [Film]. Regency Enterprises, Le Studio Canal, & Alcor Films.

Deffenbacher, J. L., Filetti, L. B., Richards, T. L., Lynch, R. S., & Oetting, E. R.

(2003). Characteristics of two groups of angry drivers. *Journal of Counseling Psychology, 50*(2), 123–132.

Delvecchio, S., Zemanek, J., McIntyre, R., & Claxton, R. (2004). Updating the adaptive selling behaviours: Tactics to keep and tactics to discard. *Journal of Marketing Management, 20*(7), 859–875.

Díaz-García, J., González-Ponce, I., Ponce-Bordón, J. C., López-Gajardo, M. A., Ramírez-Bravo, I., Rubio-Morales, A., & García-Calvo, T. (2022). Mental load and fatigue assessment instruments: A systematic review. *International Journal of Environmental Research and Public Health, 19*(1), 419–434.

Dickinson, D. L., McEvoy, D. M., & Bruner, D. M. (2022). The impact of sleep restriction on interpersonal conflict resolution and the narcotic effect. *Journal of Economic Behavior & Organization, 194*, 71–90.

Drake, H., & Herbert, D. (2002). Perceptions of occupational stress and strategies for avoiding burnout: Case studies of two female teacher-coaches. *Physical Educator, 59*(4), 170–183.

Duxbury, L., Higgins, C., & Lee, C. (1994). Work and family conflict: A comparison by gender, family type, and perceived control. *Journal of Family Issues, 3*, 449–466.

Elgoibar, P., Munduate, L., Medina, F. J., & Euwema, M. C. (2014). Do women accommodate more than men? Gender differences in perceived social support and negotiation behavior by Spanish and Dutch worker representatives. *Sex Roles, 70*, 538–553.

Eliot, J. F. (2004). *Overachievement: The new model for exceptional performance.* Penguin Portfolio.

Eliot, J. F., & Pritchard, K. (2012). *Help the helper: Building a culture of extreme teamwork.* Penguin Portfolio.

Faisal, A. A., Selen, L. P. J., & Wolpert, D. M. (2008). Noise in the nervous system. *Nature Reviews Neuroscience, 9*, 292–303.

Festinger, L. (1957). *A theory of cognitive dissonance.* Row & Peterson.

Festinger, L. (1962). Cognitive dissonance. *Scientific American, 207*, 93–107.

Figone, A. (1994a). Origins of the teacher-coach role: Idealism, convenience, and unworkability. *Health Source, 51*(3), 148.

Figone, A. (1994b). Teacher-coach role conflict: Its impact on students and student-athletes. *Physical Educator, 51*(1), 29–34.

Fillo, A. J. (2019). Poof! Science reveals how easily a magician can fool you. *NOVA*, July 10.

Fisher, R., Ury, W. L., & Patton, B. (2011). *Getting to yes: Negotiating agreement without giving in* (3rd ed.). Penguin.

Fletcher, S. (2013). Touching practice and physical education: Deconstruction of a contemporary moral panic. *Sport, Education and Society, 18*(5), 694–709.

Fuqua, A. (Director). (2007). *Shooter* [Film]. Paramount Pictures & di Bonaventura Pictures.

Gaete, J., Couture, S., Smoliak, O. (2018). Reflexive questions as constructive interventions: A discursive perspective. In T. Strong & O. Smoliak (Eds.), *Therapy as discourse: Practice and research* (pp. 117–140). Palgrave MacMillan.

Galinsky, A. D., & Schweitzer, M. (2015). *Friend and foe: When to cooperate, when to compete, and how to succeed at both.* Penguin Random House.

Garcia, A. (2015). Understanding high school students' sports participation. *Sport Science Review, 24*(3–4).

Geher, G. (2019). Are humans rational? How evolution shaped the human mind to only sometimes be logical. *Psychology Today,* November 26.

Gehring, V. V. (Ed.). (2004). *The Internet in public life.* Rowman & Littlefield.

Geiser, C., Götz, T., Preckel, F., & Freund, P. A. (2017). States and traits: Theories, models, and assessment. *European Journal of Psychological Assessment, 33*(4), 219–223.

Gelfand, M. J., Leslie, L. M., Keller, K., & de Dreu, C. (2012). *Conflict cultures scale.* American Psychosocial Association.

Gifford, R. (1991). Mapping nonverbal behavior on the interpersonal circle. *Journal of Personality and Social Psychology, 61,* 398–412.

Giorgi, A. (2009). *The descriptive phenomenological method in psychology: A modified Husserlian approach.* Duquesne University Press.

Gladwell, M. (2000). *The tipping point: How little things can make a big difference.* Little, Brown.

Goleman, D. (2005). *Emotional intelligence: Why it can matter more than IQ* (10th anniversary ed.). Bantam.

Goleman, D. (2017). *Achievement orientation: A primer* (audio). Key Step Media.

Gonzalez-Franco, M., & Slater, M. (2019). Would you give a virtual electric shock to an avatar? *Scientific American,* April 12.

Goodall, J., & Grant, A. (2021). Jane Goodall on leadership lessons from primates (interview). *TED Conferences,* March 2.

Gordon, A. M., & Chen, S. (2013). The role of sleep in interpersonal conflict: Do sleepless nights mean worse fights? *Social Psychological and Personality Science, 5*(2), 168–175.

Greenhaus, J., & Beutell, N. (1985). Sources of conflict between work and family roles. *Academy of Management Review, 10,* 76–88.

Guidi, J., Lucente, M., Sonino, N., & Fava, G. A. (2020). Allostatic load and its impact on health: A systematic review. *Psychotherapy & Psychosomatics*, *90*(1), 11–27.

Gundmundsdottir, S. (2006). *The Teller, the tale, and the one being told: The narrative nature of the research interview*. Sage Publications Ltd.

Gunnison, H. (1985). The uniqueness of similarities. *Journal of Counseling and Development, 63*, 561–564.

Hagel, J., III. (2021). Good leadership is about asking good questions. *Harvard Business Review*, January 8.

Hale, J. D., & Connare, C. (Eds.). (1793). *Old Farmer's Almanac* (periodical). Yankee Publishing, Inc.

Hall, J. A., Coats, E. J., & LeBeau, L. S. (2005). Nonverbal behavior and the vertical dimension of social relations: A meta-analysis. *Psychological Bulletin, 131*(6), 898–924.

Hall, J. A., Horgan, T. G., & Murphy, N. A. (2019). Nonverbal communication. *Annual Review of Psychology, 70*, 271–294.

Hanna, W., & Barbera, J. (1982). *The Jetsons* [TV series]. Hanna-Barbera Productions.

Harinck, F., Kouzakova, M., Ellemers, N., & Scheepers, D. (2018). Coping with conflict: Testosterone and cortisol changes in men dealing with disagreement about values vs. resources. *Negotiation and Conflict Management Research, 11*, 265–277.

Havens, R. A. (2005). *The wisdom of Milton H. Erickson: The complete volume*. Crown.

Headley, J. (2014). *It's not about the nail* [Film]. *Jason Headley Tells Stories*, YouTube: https://www.youtube.com/watch?v=-4EDhdAHrOg.

Heerey, E. A., & Gilder, T. S. E. (2019). The subjective value of a smile alters social behaviour. *PLoS One*, December 2.

Holcombe, M. (2023). How being a "gray rock" can protect you against narcissists. *CNN*, August 7.

Hritz, A. C., Royer, C. E., Helm, R. K., Burd, K. A., Ojeda, K., & Ceci, S. J. (2015). Children's suggestibility research: Things to know before interviewing a child. *Anuario de Psicología Jurídica, 25*(1), 3–12.

Hughes, D. E., & Ogilvie, J. L. (2020). When sales becomes service: The evolution of the professional selling role and an organic model of frontline ambidexterity. *Journal of Service Research, 23*(1), 22–32.

Hurt, A. (2021). What magic can teach us about the human mind: Why do we fall for magic? The secret lies in clever psychological tricks that exploit gaps in our brains. *Discover*, April 5.

Ivankova, M. (2014). *Qualitative research and evaluation methods* (4th ed.). Sage.

James, G. (1987). *The Tao of programming*. InfoBooks.

Jiang, Z., Jiang, Y., & Nielsen, I. (2021). Thriving and career outcomes: The roles of achievement orientation and resilience. *Human Resource Management Journal, 31*, 143–164.

Johnson, S. R., Pas, E. T., & Bradshaw, C. P. (2016). Understanding and measuring coach–teacher alliance: A glimpse inside the "black box." *Prevention Science, 17*(4), 439–449.

Johnstone, K. M., Chen J., & Balzan R. P. (2017). An investigation into the jumping-to-conclusions bias in social anxiety. *Conscious and Cognition, 48*, 55–65.

Jones, R. (1999). Where sport meets physical education: A systematic observation of role conflict. *International Journal of Physical Education, 36*(1), 7–14.

Jussim, L., Soffin, S., Brown, R., Ley, J., & Kohlhepp, K. (1992). Understanding reactions to feedback by integrating ideas from symbolic interactionism and cognitive evaluation theory. *Journal of Personality and Social Psychology, 62*, 402–421.

Kaye, B., & Giulioni, J. (2012). *Help them grow or watch them go: Career conversations employees want.* Berrett-Koehler.

Kennedy, C. W., & Camden, C. T. (1983). A new look at interruptions. *Western Journal of Speech Communication, 47*, 45–58.

Kerwin, S., Walker, M., & Bopp, T. (2016). When fault lines are created: Exploring the conflict triggering process in sport. *Sport Management Review, 20*(3), 252–260.

Konukman, F., Agbuga, B., Erdogan, S., Zorba, E., Demirhan, G., & Yilmaz, I. (2010). Teacher-coach role conflict in school based physical education in USA: A literature review and suggestions for the future. *Biomedical Human Kinetics, 2*, 19–24.

Kosa, B. (1990). Teacher-coach burnout and coping strategies. *Physical Educator, 47*(3), 153.

Kostić, A., Chadee, D., & Nedeljković, J. (2020). Reading faces: Ability to recognize true and false emotion. In R. J. Sternberg & A. Kostić (Eds.), *Social intelligence and nonverbal communication.* Palgrave Macmillan.

Kraus, M. W., Huang, C., & Keltner, D. (2010). Tactile communication, cooperation, and performance: An ethological study of the NBA. *Emotion, 10*(5), 745–749.

Kubota, S., Mishima, N., & Nagata, S. (2004). A study of the effects of active listening on listening attitudes of middle managers. *Journal of Occupational Health, 46*(1), 60–67.

LaMotte, S. (2023). Ban spanking in all schools, pediatrician group urges. Do this instead. *CNN*, August 21.

Landis, J. (Director). (1978). *National Lampoon's animal house* [Film]. Universal Pictures.

Leo, F., González-Ponce, I., Sánchez-Miguel, P., Ivarsson, A., & García-Calvo, T. (2015). Role ambiguity, role conflict, team conflict, cohesion and collective efficacy in sport teams: A multilevel analysis. *Psychology of Sport and Exercise, 20*, 60–66.

Leterrier, L. (Director). (2008). *The incredible Hulk* [Film]. Marvel Studios & Valhalla Motion Pictures.

Levinson, S. (2015). *Ballers* [TV series]. Closest to the Hole Productions, Leverage Entertainment, Seven Bucks Entertainment, Film 44, & HBO Entertainment.

Lewin, K. (1951). *Field theory in social science*. Harper.

Lewis, M. (2003). *Moneyball: The art of winning an unfair game*. W. W. Norton & Company.

Livingston, S. (2003). Pygmalion in management. *Harvard Business Review*, January 1.

Locke, L., & Massengale, J. D. (2013). Role conflict in teacher/coaches. *Journal of Teaching in Physical Education, 7*(2), 162–174.

Loftus, E. F. (1979). *Eyewitness testimony*. Harvard University Press.

Lohrenz, C. (2021). The shocking truth about multitasking in the age of distraction. *Forbes*, June 15.

Lucas, G. (1977). *Star wars* [Film]. Lucasfilm Ltd.

Malhotra, D. (2016). *Negotiating the impossible: How to break deadlocks and resolve ugly conflicts (without money or muscle)*. Berrett-Koehler.

Mann, R. D. (1959). A review of the relationships between personality and performance in small groups. *Psychological Bulletin, 56*(4), 241–270.

Markovitz, D. (2020). How to avoid rushing to solutions when problem-solving. *Harvard Business Review*, November 27.

Martinez-Conde, S., & Macnik, S. L. (2008). Magic and the brain: How magicians "trick" the mind. *Scientific American*, December 1.

Mathes, E. W. (2024). The effects of trait and state affect, on affect-consistent, emotional regulation. *Current Psychology, 43*, 6217–6224.

Matsumoto, D., Frank, M. G., & Hwang, H. (Eds.). (2012). *Nonverbal communication: Science and applications*. Sage.

McCallum, B. T. (1980). The significance of rational expectations theory. *Challenge, 22*(6), 37–43.

McG (Director). (2009). *Terminator salvation* [Film]. Halcyon Company, Wonderland Sound, & Vision.

McLeod, S. (2023). The Milgram shock experiment. *Simply Psychology*, November 14.

Mellalieu, S., Jones, C., Wagstaff, C. R. D., & Kemp, S. P. T. (2021). Measuring psychological load in sport. *International Journal of Sports Medicine*, *42*(9), 782–788.

Merton, R. K. (1957). *Social theory and social structure*. Free Press.

Milgram, S. (1963). Behavioral study of obedience. *Journal of Abnormal and Social Psychology*, *67*(4), 371–378.

Milgram, S. (1974). *Obedience to authority: An experimental view*. Harper Collins.

Miller, E. (2017). Multitasking: Why your brain can't do it and what you should do about it. *Hack Your Mind*. Radius (in partnership with MIT Community Wellness).

Millslagle, D., & Morley, D. (2004). Investigation of role retreatism in the teacher/coach. *Physical Educator*, *61*(3).

Milne, A. A. (Author) & Shepard, E. H. (Illustrator). (1926). *Winnie-the-Pooh*. E. P. Dutton.

Mobley, J. (2005). The relationship of the dual role assignment to the level of perceived burnout by secondary teachers. *Humanities and Social Sciences*, *55*(9), 2765.

Moore, D. A. (2004). The unexpected benefits of final deadlines in negotiation. *Journal of Experimental Social Psychology*, *40*(1), 121–127.

Morin, A. (2015). 7 Surprising ways your emotions can get the best of you . . . and how to take back control. *Psychology Today*, October 5.

Morris, L. S., Grehl, M. M., Rutter, S. B., Mehta, M., & Westwater, M. L. (2022). On what motivates us: A detailed review of intrinsic v. extrinsic motivation. *Psychological Medicine*, *52*(10), 1801–1816.

Niemivirta, M., Antti-Tuomas, P., Anna, T., & Heta, T. (2019). Achievement goal orientations: A person-oriented approach. In K. A. Renninger & S. E. Hidi (Eds.), *The Cambridge handbook of motivation and learning* (pp. 566–616). Cambridge University Press.

Nolan, C. (Director). (2005). *Batman begins* [Film]. Warner Bros. Pictures, DC Comics, Legendary Pictures, Syncopy, & Patalex III Productions.

O'Connor, A., & MacDonald, D. (2002). Up close and personal on physical education teacher's identity: Is conflict an issue? *Sport, Education and Society*, *7*(1), 37–54.

Overbeck, J. R., Neale, M. A., & Govan, C. L. (2010). I feel, therefore you act: Intrapersonal and interpersonal effects of emotion on negotiation as a function of social power. *Organizational Behavior and Human Decision Processes*, *112*, 126–139.

Patterson, K., Grenny, J., Maxfield, D., McMillan, R., & Switzler, A. (2021). *Crucial conversations: Tools for talking when stakes are high* (3rd ed.). McGraw Hill.

Patterson, K., Grenny, J., Maxfield, D., McMillan, R., & Switzler, A. (2021). *Influencer: The power to change anything*. McGraw Hill.

Phillips J. (1993). Nonverbal communication: An essential skill in the workplace. *Australian Medical Record Journal, 23*(4), 132–134.

Pool, E., Brosch, T., Delplanque, S., & Sander, D. (2015). Stress increases cue-triggered "wanting" for sweet reward in humans. *Journal of Experimental Psychology: Animal Learning and Cognition, 41*(2), 128–136.

Raymond, E. S., & Steele, G. L. (Eds.) (1996). *The new hacker's dictionary* (3rd ed.). MIT Press.

Richards, A., Templin, T., Levesque-Bristol, C., & Blankenship, B. (2014). Understanding differences in role stressors, resilience, and burnout in teacher/coaches and non-coaching teachers. *Teaching in Physical Education, 33*(3), 383–402.

Richards, K., & Templin, T. (2012). Toward a multidimensional perspective on teacher-coach role conflict. *Quest, 64*(3), 164–176.

Ritter, K., Matthews, R. A., Ford, M. T., & Henderson, A. A. (2016). Understanding role stressors and job satisfaction over time using adaptation theory. *Journal of Applied Psychology, 101*(12), 1655–1669.

Robertson, A. S., McInnes, M., Glass, D., Dalton, G., & Burge, P. S. (1989). Building sickness: Are symptoms related to the office lighting? *Annals of Occupational Hygiene, 33*(1), 47–59.

Robertson, K. (2005). Active listening: More than just paying attention. *Australian Family Physician, 34*(12), 1053–1055.

Rosenthal, R., & Jacobson, L. (1968). *Pygmalion in the classroom: Teacher expectation and pupil's intellectual development*. Holt, Rinehart and Winston.

Rotella, R. J. (1999). *Life is not a game of perfect: Finding your real talent and making it work for you*. Simon & Schuster.

Rotella, R. J. (2015). *How champions think: In sports and in life*. Simon & Schuster.

Rouse, S. (2021). *Understanding body language: How to decode nonverbal communication in life, love, and work*. Rockridge Press (from Simon & Schuster).

Rowe, M. (2003). *Dirty Jobs* [TV series]. Pilgrim Films & Television.

Ryan, R. M., & Deci E. L. (2017). *Self-determination theory: Basic psychological needs in motivation development and wellness*. Guilford Press.

Ryan, T. (2008). Antecedents for interrole conflict in the high school teacher/coach. *Physical Educator, 65*(2), 58–67.

Saatchi & Saatchi UK (2018). *Stuck on an escalator: Take action* [Film]. Vimeo: https://vimeo.com/232982301.

Saffici, C. (2015). Teaching and coaching: The challenges and conflicts of dual roles. *Sport Journal*, 19.

Sage, G. (1987). The social world of high school athletic coaches: Multiple role demands and their consequences. *Sociology of Sport Journal, 4*(3), 213–228.

Sanchez, S., & Dunning, D. (2021). People who jump to conclusions show other kinds of thinking errors: Belief in conspiracy theories and overconfidence are two tendencies linked to hasty thinking. *Scientific American,* October 15.

Seidman, I. (1991). *A structure for in-depth, phenomenological interviewing: Interviewing as qualitative research.* Teachers College Press.

Senécal, C., Vallerand, R. J., & Guay, F. (2001). Antecedents and outcomes of work-family conflict: Toward a motivational model. *Personality and Social Psychology Bulletin, 27*(2), 176–186.

Shafa, S., Harinck, F., Ellemers, N., & Beersma, B. (2015). Regulating honor in the face of insults. *International Journal of Intercultural Relations, 47,* 158–174.

Sharma, S., Bottom, W. P., & Elfenbein, H. A. (2013). On the role of personality, cognitive ability, and emotional intelligence in predicting negotiation outcomes: A meta-analysis. *Organizational Psychology Review, 3,* 293–336.

Sharma, S., Elfenbein, H. A., Sinha, R., & Bottom, W. P. (2020). The effects of emotional expressions in negotiation: A meta-analysis and future directions for research. *Human Performance, 33*(4), 331–353.

Sheldon, K. M., & Kasser, T. (1995). Coherence and congruence: Two aspects of personality integration. *Journal of Personality and Social Psychology, 68,* 531–543.

Short, D. (2020). *From William James to Milton Erickson: The care of human consciousness.* Archway Publishing (from Simon & Schuster).

Silliker, A., & Quirk, J. (1997). The effect of extracurricular activity participation on the academic performance of male and female high school students. *School Counselor, 44*(4), 288–293.

Simon, H. (1955). A behavioral model of rational choice. *Quarterly Journal of Economics, 69*(1), 99–118.

Simons, D. J., & Ambinder, M. S. (2005). Change blindness: Theory and consequences. *Current Directions in Psychological Science, 14*(1), 44–48.

Simons, D. J., & Chabris, C. F. (1999). Gorillas in our midst: Sustained inattentional blindness for dynamic events. *Perception, 28*(9), 1059–1074.

Sisley, B., Capel, S., Gloria, S., & Desertrain, B. (1987). Preventing burnout in teacher/coaches. *Journal of Physical Education, Recreation & Dance, 58*(8), 71–75.

Smith, J. E. H. (2019). *Irrationality: A history of the dark side of reason.* Princeton University Press.

Soebbing, B., & Washington, M. (2011). Leadership succession and organizational performance football coaches and organizational issues. *Journal of Sport Management, 25*(6), 550–561.

Spradlin, D. (2012). Are you solving the right problem? *Harvard Business Review*, September 1.

Staff (2014). Road rage: What makes some people more prone to anger behind the wheel. *American Psychological Association*, February 1.

Staff (2015). *Identifying the culprit: Assessing eyewitness identification*. National Research Council.

Staff (2020). Do you speak therapist? 50 expressions that never fail. *Mind Remake Project*, May 6.

Staff (2022). What is gray rocking? *Medical News Today*, September 12.

Staff (2024). How the grey rock method can protect you from abusive people and toxic interactions. *Cleveland Clinic*, January 23.

Staffo, D. (1992). Clarifying physical education teacher-coach responsibilities: a self-analysis guide for those in dual roles. *Sport Journal*, 19.

Steinel, W., & Harinck, F. (2020). Negotiation and bargaining. *Oxford Research Encyclopedia*, September 28.

Steinfeldt, J., & Vaughan, E. (2016). Masculinity, moral atmosphere, and moral of high school football players. *Journal of Sport & Exercise Psychology, 33*(2), 215–234.

Stevenson, S. (2012). There's magic in your smile. *Psychology Today*, June 25.

Sudeikis, J., Lawrence, B., Hunt, B., & Kelly, J. (2020). *Ted Lasso* [TV series]. Ruby's Tuna Inc., Doozer, Universal Television, & Warner Bros. Television.

Sulfaro, A. A., Robinson, A. K., & Carlson T. A. (2023). Modelling perception as a hierarchical competition differentiates imagined, veridical, and hallucinated percepts. *Neuroscience of Consciousness, 2023*(1).

Swaab, R. I., Galinsky, A. D., Medvec, V., & Diermeier, D. A. (2012). The communication orientation model: Explaining the diverse effects of sight, sound, and synchronicity on negotiation and group decision-making outcomes. *Personality and Social Psychology Review, 16*, 25–53.

Templin, T., Levesque-Bristol, C., & Richards, A. (1980, October). *An analysis of occupational role dysfunction* [Presentation]. Association for Health, Physical Education, Recreation, and Dance.

Thomke, S., & Reinertsen, D. (2012). Myths of product development. *Harvard Business Review*, May 1.

Trousdale, G., & Wise, K. (Directors). (1991). *Beauty and the beast* [Film]. Walt Disney Pictures, Walt Disney Feature Animation, & Silver Screen Partners.

Vallerand, R. J. (1997). Toward a hierarchical model of intrinsic and extrinsic motivation. *Advances in Experimental Social Psychology, 29,* 271–361.

Vallerand, R. J., & Bissonnette, R. (1992). Intrinsic, extrinsic, and amotivational styles as predictors of behavior: A prospective study. *Journal of Personality, 60,* 599–620.

Van Boekel, M., Bulut, O., Stanke, L., Palma Zamora, J. R., Jang, Y., Kang, Y., & Nickodem, K. (2016). Effects of participation in school sports on academic and social functioning. *Journal of Applied Developmental Psychology, 46,* 31–40.

Van Dijk, E., Van Kleef, G. A., Steinel, W., & Van Beest, I. (2008). A social functional approach to emotions in bargaining: When communicating anger pays and when it backfires. *Journal of Personality and Social Psychology, 94,* 600–614.

Van Kleef, G. A. (2016). *The interpersonal dynamics of emotion: Toward an integrative theory of emotions as social information.* Cambridge University Press.

Van Lange, P. A. M., Otten, W., De Bruin, E. M. N., & Joireman, J. A. (1997). Development of prosocial, individualistic, and competitive orientations: Theory and preliminary evidence. *Journal of Personality and Social Psychology, 73,* 733–746.

Verbinski, G. (Director). (2006). *Pirates of the Caribbean: Dead man's chest* [Film]. Walt Disney Pictures & Jerry Bruckheimer Films.

Voss, C. (2016). *Never split the difference: Negotiating as if your life depended on it.* Harper Business.

Waksman, G. (2015). *"The Immortal" Ted Williams* [Film]. MLB Network, the Smithsonian, & Manhattan Place Entertainment.

Weber, B., (2023). How to prevent fluorescent light headaches. *Medical News Today,* May 9.

Wedell-Wedellsborg, T. (2017). Are you solving the right problems? Reframing them can reveal unexpected solutions. *Harvard Business Review,* January 1.

Weiland, S., Hewig, J., Hecht, H., Mussel, P., & Miltner, W. H. R. (2012). Neural correlates of fair behavior in interpersonal bargaining. *Social Neuroscience, 7,* 537–551.

Whedon, J. (Director). (2012). *The Avengers* [Film]. Marvel Studios.

Wirszyla, C. (2002). State-mandated curriculum change in three high school physical education programs. *Journal of Teaching in Physical Education, 22*(1), 4–19.

Wise, R. E. (Director), & Lehman, E. P. (Writer). (1965). *The sound of music* [Film]. Argyle Enterprises, Inc. & 20th Century-Fox.

Wiseman, R. (2008). Color changing card trick. *Quirkology* [Film]. YouTube: https://www.youtube.com/watch?v=voAntzB7EwE.

Wood, W., & Rünger, D. (2015). Psychology of habit. *Annual Review of Psychology, 67*, 289–314.

Xiang, J., Simon, J., & Elhilali, M. (2010). Competing streams at the cocktail party: Exploring the mechanisms of attention and temporal integration. *Journal of Neuroscience, 30*, 12084–12093.

Yakin, B. (Director). (2000). *Remember the Titans* [Film]. Walt Disney Pictures, Jerry Bruckheimer Films, & Technical Black Films.

Index

About the Authors

Former elite athletes both, the Docs enjoy a special teammate kind of bond that transcends their professional collaboration. Playing ball, talking shop, supporting each other's families, the countless hours the two have spent together at the intersection of their expertise and their passions are the foundation of this book. The curiosity and optimism with which they approach life is its spirit. The Docs love speaking to a wide diversity of audiences. If you are interested in booking them (either independently or together) for an upcoming meeting, event, or training, please contact Katheryne and Aaron Rehberg, founders of Capitol City Speakers Bureau (**info@capcityspeakers.com**).

JOHN ELIOT, PhD

Descendant of Nobel Prize Laureate T. S. Eliot, Harvard president Charles Eliot, and Tufts University School of Education founder Abigail Eliot, Doc E has continued his family's dedication to the pursuit of excellence, having spent the past thirty years as an adviser to professional sports franchises, athletes, and coaches in the areas of management, systems design, evaluation and enhancement of human capital, diversity, and sustainability. During this stretch, 100 percent of his clients have won league, national, or world championships, including five MLB World Series titles, four NBA championships, two NFL Super Bowl Lombardi Trophies, one Indy 500 title, one NHL Stanley Cup, and dozens of Olympic medals as representatives of seven different countries.

When not in a locker room, Doc E consults for Fortune 500 companies; teaches organizational behavior and human performance courses for some of our nation's most prestigious business and medical schools; and serves on charitable boards for children and animals in need, including the Special Olympics and ASPCA.

Doc E is a Phi Beta Kappa graduate of Dartmouth, where he was a Presidential Scholar, Senior Fellow, and two-sport All-American; as well as a high honors, interdisciplinary (business, medicine, and education) doctoral recipient from the University of Virginia. In his free time, when he's not hanging off the side of a mountain for a little R&R or fending off regular Tom Cruise–body double commentary (sorry, Tom, for all the "Do you know you look exactly like Doc E?" inquiries that you have to field), Doc E is a devoted family man and proud cat daddy to two feisty Bengals (named Mayzie and McFuzz in honor of fellow Big Green alumnus Theodor "Dr. Suess" Geisel).

JIM GUINN, EdD

One of the nation's foremost authorities on conflict prediction and prevention, Doc G is the president of the Resolution Resource Group, a training and development company that works with Fortune 500 companies, professional sports franchises, large-scale school districts, hospitals and health care systems, universities, law firms, and governments on effectively handling conflict. As a certified mediator, he has conducted over one thousand successful mediations involving family, organizational, civil, and political disputes. In addition to his firm's corporate work with a large diversity of clients across HR departments, sales staffs, and management, Doc G personally trains CEOs from all walks of life as well as celebrities and sports icons in navigating today's landscape of contentious public opinion.

Doc G serves on numerous corporate and foundation boards, including chairing the Texas Association of Mediators and directing the Dispute Resolution Center, which provides pro bono mediation and arbitration services statewide. He is an award-winning clinical professor serving Texas A&M University and Abilene Christian University, advising doctoral and master's students; providing undergraduates with practical skills for the workplace; and teaching courses in conflict resolution, negotiation, communication, and leadership.

Doc G received his bachelor's in business management, his master's in conflict resolution, and his doctorate in organizational leadership, all from Abilene Christian University, where he was a standout two-sport athlete in football and baseball. When not crushing conflict, Jim is a devoted family man, doting on his wife, Chelsea, and taking his two brilliantly inquisitive daughters, Blair and Caroline, on grand adventures around the globe.

The Conflict Docs

AT A GLANCE

At The Conflict Docs, we offer a range of solutions to help individuals resolve conflicts efficiently and effectively. Our team of experts has been providing top-notch services to clients for over 20 years. We believe in customizing our offerings based on specific needs.

Check out our site!

ADVANTAGES & BENEFITS ⌄

1 **Professional Expertise**

2 **Time + Cost Efficiency**

3 **Customized Solutions**

SOLUTIONS WE PROVIDE ⌄

| Continuing Education Credits | Corporate Retreats | Workforce Assessment and Consulting | In-Person Trainings and Seminars | Customized Online Programs | Corporate Development Tools |

HE CONFLICT DOCS

Follow + Like Our Social Media!
@TheConflictDocs